JEDDAH BRIDE: a memoir of love, betrayal, and reconciliation

by

Patricia Bonis

A Conservatarian Press Publication

ISBN: 978-1-957586-38-0

To my three children, Amanda, Sultana and Karim

Contents

Foreword

By Amanda Turen

Fourteen years! Fourteen years!"
I am nine years old, listening curiously outside the double glass doors as my mother Patricia wails this refrain, over and over, at some unknown stranger on the landline in her office. No one has to convince me that fourteen years without something is practically a lifetime—I'm not even ten. To me, it's unfathomable, more than my lifetime. Concepts like missing older siblings and mysterious, sandy countries in the Middle East, while I understood them intellectually, might as well have been the stuff of legends.

Three months later, my mother popped into my bedroom to tell me she was driving to Boston to meet my long-lost big brother. Years of fables, places and characters I had been told about—your brother Karim, your sister Sultana, kidnapped, my ex-husband before your father, a city called Jeddah—went from passively existing to very real. Everyone says it's hard to imagine their parent living a whole life before they were born. In my case, this was not due to teenage shenanigans. My mother moved to Saudi Arabia before her twenty-second birthday, had two other children, became a Muslim and somehow ended up raising me, her third child, in suburban New Jersey. It's almost as if she lived a whole life before the one she lives today.

Growing up the daughter of a great adventuress was nothing short of spectacular. Her enthusiasm for risky sports like equestrian show jumping, her openness to international travel like my solo homestay as an unaccompanied minor in Japan, and her affinity for the morning wakeup phrase "sleep when you're dead!" are the spoils of a life lived full-throttle. And, her love for us—myself, my brother and my sister—poured forth freely. I, like any only-child-suddenly-turned-youngest sibling, especially one from a vastly different culture, had my personal qualms with my newfound teenage life as somebody's sister, but my mother, steady as a mountain, held us together.

When Mom tore her rotator cuff riding and was relegated to a sling for six month—no riding!—she proposed a risk of the interior kind: I want to write my story. And what could I do but offer my two working arms to type out Draft One as she dictated it?

Weekly, I traveled uptown to my mother's apartment to record her story. There was so much of her jetset life I already knew; I had seen the disco pictures, I had squeezed unsuccessfully into the teeny-tiny gowns, I had met practically every distant second cousin visiting New York for Western medical treatment. The old gossip flowed, and then came those unsavory details about what happened in between, stories I had been spared as a child. I didn't think I would be so surprised, and then, more than surprised, well, I was angry. Furious, in fact. First, at the injustices done to her—how could anyone treat you that way? Then, at my mother herself, not for staying the course at twenty-two in a country and a rela-tionship that was putting her in danger, but at her ability today, decades past, to reflect on this story with forgiveness and love.

My mother's story is one of amazing resilience, the kind of resilience that allowed her to start another new life after her first had crashed, then return, healed, to her missing children and former family with open arms. Her writing of this memoir, every granular misfortune and joy, amazes me. Some say time heals everything, but looking at Mom, I know time alone isn't enough — it's the bravery to live the story again and again, every time she tells it, and to hope that telling the story will some day lead to change.

I see pieces of mother in all three of us siblings—my brother is deci-sive and elegant, my sister is relaxed and welcoming, I am persuasive and artistic. In the delivery of this memoir, I sometimes imagine the beau-tiful, freewheeling, rebellious seventeen-year-old who stepped out onto the Boston club scene and accepted the price of an extraordinary life, entirely without regrets. I don't know if I would have been cool enough to be her friend. I might have admired her from afar. Still, I'm profoundly grateful she's my mother.

Chapter One

That morning, I woke at dawn. Through the tall arched window in the bedroom, the sky beyond shone bright pink. It was cloudless, glowing and beautiful, and for some reason, felt like the good omen I had been waiting for. What was that old sailors' rhyme?

Red sky in morning, Sailors take warning.
Red sky at night, Sailors' delight.

Somehow that pink morning sky offered the greenlight I needed. *Not much to go on but I'll take it.* I threw back the covers and jumped out of bed, deciding today would be that long awaited day. In the bathroom, the carefully planned outfit hanging on a dry-cleaning hook in the closet beckoned to me. *It's time, it's time.* A pair of trim navy slacks, a loose-fitting white blouse, low-heeled sandals and a white Burberry raincoat. It was somewhat plain, but expensive and more conservative than my usual flirty urban uniform of a snug-fitting ensemble, sky-high heels, and a bold outer layer. I was most comfortable with eyes on me, and fashion was a quick way to achieve that. But today I needed to ease in, whisper-soft and motherly.

How many years had I planned "the outfit"? Would it work? I visualized a successful result. *First impressions count. Don't look sexually suggestive, no tight clothes, no mini-skirts, not too young, not too old.* Fourteen years of rehearsing this scenario in therapy came down to one very brief afternoon. It was like preparing for a capstone recital or the Super Bowl. Or Armageddon.

The blush sky slowly gave way to a cool yet still reassuring light blue. Sunny day. A great day for a drive from New Jersey to Boston. Early departure, no one on the road. I tried to imagine myself sailing right through to his apartment, making it there in about three-and-a-half hours, maybe four, again drawing on my faithful therapist's push for positive visualization. But just as I saw myself doing so well in my head, feelings of desperation crept in – *What if I fail? No! Pound those feelings down.* Every positive tool in my arsenal would be needed for today, with no room for doubt. *Imagine the best possible outcome.* I threw a few items into an overnight bag, adding a simple black dress and some pearls, the perfect dinner outfit. If the afternoon did indeed go well, I may be bold enough to even push him a little more.

On my way to the stairs, Amanda's bedroom door stood ajar. My innocent nine-year-old daughter, so safe and snug in her little pink bedroom... she could not know that today might wreck me beyond repair. Masking my panic, I popped in and mustered up a most convincing cheery voice, "Sweetie! Mommy's going to try and find Karim. I'm driving to Boston now. I'll call you later to hear what happened at school today."

"Good luck, Mommy," her little voice rang out as I descended.

Now, it was time to rush. *After 14 years, how can I be so impatient?* In the garage, my well-prepared car awaited. *Full tank of gas, good. No stops needed.* Pulling out onto the street, I switched on my navigation – the latest model. Karim would take note of that. His Boston address popped up immediately. It had been plugged into the system for a week. *75 Peterborough Street.* How hard I worked to obtain that precious address! A year ago, after all but giving up hope, a phone call changed my life. It came in from a long-forgotten acquaintance who, by chance, had seen Karim and his sister in Spain with their father, thirteen years after our separation. The caller overheard talk that Karim was playing polo in boarding school, somewhere in the world, and thought this lead might be of some use to me. Some use? This was the first concrete fact to materialize in ten years!

Boarding schools that offered polo were few and far between and the newly-minted internet provided me with a succinct list. Next steps were tricky. No private school would simply divulge their students' information. I needed a private investigator, and so I hired a good one, offering every meager shred of information that I had: Karim's name, birth date, the list of schools and a 14-year-old photo of a four-year-old in an expired US passport. Weeks went by with only negative results. But just when things were feeling hopeless again, at the end of May we found him. Karim was a senior at Culver Military Boarding Academy in Indiana. *Indiana? Right under my nose in the United States?* After all the meaningless assurances by the State

Department that he was on our country's "Watch List" and that I would be notified if he entered the US? My government failed to notice a missing minor, a U.S. Citizen who had been parked in the Midwest for three entire years! *How many wasted hours had I passed in custody court at my own expense, and completely fruitless!* I was beyond furious but refused to consider the absurdity of the entire last decade and a half. I just couldn't go there in my heart. But I could orchestrate when and how I might see Karim. Graduation was a month away and the window of opportunity would soon close.

I combed the Culver website day and night for any possible clue to where he lived, or what he planned to do after graduation. Naturally, there was a list of graduating students, and it showed Karim attending Boston University School of Management in the fall. East Coast! And ample time for a well-choreographed game plan! Despite my visceral urge to see him as soon as possible, I waited until the beginning of the fall semester to approach him. Those four months of waiting were torture, but I was well prepared. He would be older, perhaps more mature, and (hopefully) fully engaging his new adult independence in Boston. There would be no school security at Boston to deal with. Still, I needed to be stealthy to ensure that Karim did make it to Boston without his father becoming suspicious of any communication with me. I reported back to the private investigator. His next assignment would be to find Karim's new address once school started in September. When fall did come it only took a week to find Karim's new digs. And there I was, making my way up I-95 on a sunny day in September to re-enter a life and a role that was still very much uncharted territory for me and wholly obscure to Karim. It was a small thing in the grand scheme, a mother finding her long-lost son, yet it was also a diplomatic operation of great consequence. I'd been at once wishing for and agonizing over the coming moment since I last saw my firstborn.

I arrived more quickly than I'd imagined, inching down his narrow one-way street, taking in the neighborhood. Pristine rows of uniform, well-appointed brick Colonial facades, reflections of polished brass gas street lamps and geometric webs of copper gutters. Below were showy dense flowers, blooms spilling over painted iron fencing, patches of pampered Kelly green grass, and lush shade trees precisely dotting the neat sidewalk. In my college days, I had parked on this very street for a ball game at Fenway Park. *Was that before I met Karim's father? Did Karim like baseball? Did it factor into his choice of neighborhood?* I could ask…My mind wandered to the millions of conversations we could have, casual insights we could share, all seemingly unattainable until today.

I spotted building number 75 and parked in front of the brand new, high-end brick apartment building—complete with garage parking and a doorman! Quite luxurious for a college freshman, even for the son of a wealthy Saudi. Just the sort of building that would reflect his father's need for the newest and best, a place he himself would reside in. And of course, security, to deflect a potential meddling mother. How could I possibly get to him there?

I felt warm out of nowhere. Perhaps the sun, or more likely anxious perspiration and nerves after spotting all the fancy buzzers, the locks, the doorman. I removed my Burberry raincoat and exited the car, then hesitated and got back in. *What if I look too shabby without it? Ugh.* The raincoat went back on. Sweat pooled in the palms of my hands. Something to drink? I fumbled with a bottle of water. Oh boy, I was starting to panic. Maybe driving up to Boston wasn't such a good idea after all? *No, calm yourself. Remember all your preparation. All that planning counts for something. Breathe, walk over to the entrance slowly. Just take a peek into the lobby of the building.* Past the flower-lined brick pathway–pink and white impatiens–the double-glass front doors stood like two steely gates of a castle, opening to a small locked foyer with a high-tech touchscreen buzzer system. The reception desk beyond was empty. No one was watching.

A shot of hope came from just being inside the modern fortress. Once past the imposing gates, I took a quick look at the screen to find Karim's name. The names on the touch screen rolled past, "A" for his last name, "K" for his first name. Absolutely nothing. He was not listed. I started scrolling through all the tenants' names at that point, thinking that maybe he used someone else's name, one I might recognize. Maybe one of his dad's "people" rented the apartment for him under his own name. Al Arab? Al Attas? Nizaam? Bin Zagr? Khalid? There were so many possibilities. Did I come all this way just to be defeated at the front door?

A uniformed man in his sixties appeared behind the desk in the inner lobby and spotted me punching in names and letters on the touch screen. He smiled and walked over to the set of locked glass doors separating us. My mind was racing. *Oh no…what will I say?* He opened the door and casually tipped his hat. "Can I help you?"

I breathed in and tried to calm myself. *There's nothing suspicious about what you're doing.* Yes, I was foolish to be so paranoid, although the years had taught me otherwise. I looked up, forced a bright smile and sweetened my voice, "I'm sorry, I'm not very techy. I'm looking for Karim Abbar, but I don't see him on the touch screen." To my surprise the doorman answered, "Oh yes, Karim Abbar, he just moved in here last week. We haven't had the time to put his name up yet. Sorry about that! I'll take you up to his apartment. Come in." With that, he swung the door wide open.

Never in my life had sweeter words been spoken. So easy, so simple, so perfect. *He will take me up there! Is this a doorman or an angel?* This doorman with his freckled Irish face and Boston accent—our encounter in the doorway was a moment that I will never forget. *If he only knew.* I tried to act as though this was all normal and casual, and I cleared my throat, chirping, "Great! Thanks!" Nonchalant, I passed through the open door.

We walked to the back of the large, newly-decorated lobby, entered the elevator, and it suddenly became apparent that the doorman was going to accompany me all the way up to the fifth floor. That was not part of the plan. The elevator beeped at each floor, seemingly rising in pitch as the situation spiraled out of control in my head. I stood motionless, paralyzed. Everything was happening so fast. *Too fast! But I wanted this so desperately!* Then, as the elevator door opened, my fears were confirmed: the angel-doorman intended to deliver me all the way to the apartment. Not what I wanted for my first meeting in fourteen years, this stranger, my angel-doorman, standing by to witness what was to follow, but I had no choice. I steadied myself for the next step.

He guided me down the hall to Karim's door and buzzed the doorbell of the apartment. We waited a moment or two. All the thoughts I pushed away on the drive flooded into my head. *What color is his hair? Is he tall? How will he react? Will he slam the door? Will he tell the doorman to escort me out of the building and never let me in again? Will he be scared? Will he recognize me? Will he believe me? Will he hate me?* My stammering heart pounded deep in my chest for only me to hear.

The door opened. There stood my son, lost to me for 14 years, since his kidnapping. *Oh my God, those dimples! He still has them.* He was barefoot, wearing a red tee shirt with a pair of navy-blue gym shorts. He loved walking barefoot as a young boy. In half a moment, I summed up all his physical features. A combination of my father, his father, and various other uncles and aunts. Would I have recognized him if we passed on the street? Maybe not. He had been a four-year-old when I last kissed him goodbye at the airport in Washington DC. Now he was a six-foot-tall man. He looked at the doorman, and then at me, half expecting a pizza delivery, I imagined. His face gave way to an even bigger smile. He liked what he saw? He was friendly? He seemed comfortable with his surroundings. In a gentle, deep voice, jarring the first time I heard it, he asked, "Who are you?"

I glanced at the doorman, who looked as confused as I felt. Fixing my gaze on his face, I stated far more calmly than I felt, "I'm your mother, Karim. May I please come in?" Dead silence, shock. The doorman put his hand to his heart. Karim's smile fell, and he took a step back.

Oh no, no, no. This must work out. My eyes pleaded with my earnest request, "Please let me come in for a few minutes. I would like to visit with you."

Karim relaxed, softened, and pulled himself together. He had decided. He nodded his head quickly and opened the door all the way, "Sure, come in." Trying to maintain composure, I smiled at the doorman, whispered thank you, entered the apartment and shut the door behind me. I was in.

Lingering in the entry area over this emotionally-charged and shocking moment felt risky. With the door right there, he could ask me to leave at any moment. I was witnessing a young man who had not seen his mother since pre-school, while I grappled with my own uncertainty and emotions. I had planned everything this far, but I had not envisioned what would happen when he actually opened the door. The flood of pain, and the realization of my loss–that his entire childhood had come and gone–shook me. In one restricted eyeful of him, I understood that he was all grown up. Radiating from my chest, I felt an ache that only a mother could know: I had lost my son's entire childhood, a bond I would never recreate. This was supposed to be my victory, and yet I felt more desperate than an hour before. It was one thing to imagine what he had been doing all of those years. Now I *knew* what I had lost, and that I would never be a part of it.

Still, I could not allow even one suggestion of those feelings to come through. It would ruin my chances at anything in the future. The endless therapy sessions I had endured prepared me for this most delicate moment, and keeping the situation on an even keel was part of the well thought-out plan. My plan was all I had. My therapist had repeated, *No revelations, no accusations, absolutely no crying.*

Do something! I safely opted for a quick peck on the cheek as is the customary greeting for Saudis, then proceeded into the living room. Another young man lounged on one of the overstuffed sofas, watching sports on a large plasma TV. He was handsome yet relaxed in his t-shirt and jeans, obviously an American. He looked clean cut and preppy, and he eyed me curiously as I walked in. A tennis match was on TV. These two had clearly been sitting together after class, watching the match on TV when the doorbell rang.

Avoiding any awkward pauses, I walked up to the young man and shook his hand, saying "Hello, I'm Patricia, Karim's mom. Nice to meet you." His jaw hit the floor as his face changed from shocked to fully baffled. As he looked at me, I could swear, I noticed his eyes well up with tears.

He answered, "I'm Will. I was Karim's roommate at Culver, our high school." I guess he's a close friend and knows that Karim hasn't seen his mom for many years...*Thank goodness that this kind and sensitive boy is here today and not some brand-new group of college friends from his first days at Boston U.* My unexpected arrival might have turned out to be an embarrassing disaster, but things were looking up. I was still here.

Will jumped up. "I guess I'll be leaving now…"

I instinctively knew that this friend of Karim's should remain in the apartment with us, because somehow, he brought a measure of sanity and safety to this situation. Karim was in shock, but even after all these years, I was still his mother. I took control.

"I won't be here long, and I would like you to stay." Will sat back down, as did Karim, the three of us taking long looks at each other. Will's presence was a big help in normalizing things, and Karim seemed to relax. I knew I had to set a casual, low-stakes tone, and get to know his friend just as I might have if we were a normal parent and child, me dropping in for a visit at his new college just to check on things. Yes, we were pretending everything was fine, but any other course of action would have been too much. I had four years now to get to know Karim; I would have to start in a non-threatening, gentle way. I couldn't risk embarrassing him in front of his friend or freaking him out with my emotions. Small talk was our life raft. I learned Will was attending Northeastern and had played polo with Karim in high school on the very team that helped me narrow down my search.

"That's great that you both ended up in the same city," I offered. "When I went to Wellesley, my best friend from high school attended Boston University. It really helped with making friends and getting comfortable in a new city. In fact, it was through my friends at BU that I met Karim's dad years ago!" I purposefully addressed this to Will, putting safe distance between Karim, his dad and me.

The two boys stiffened as I dared to mention Karim's father. Avoiding further awkwardness, I deftly switched gears and focused on Karim's new apartment.

"What a great place! I'm happy to see you so comfortable. Funny, I lived four years on campus at Wellesley. I had no interest in leaving the comfort of the dorm to get an apartment where I would have to do grocery shopping, cooking, and cleaning! You don't mind having to keep house?"

"No, I don't mind at all."

"Good for you. Can you cook?"

"Actually, yes, I can."

"Really? Did Lallo teach you how to cook?

Again, a surprising look, accompanied by a hesitant grin. "Uh, yes, Lallo did teach me how to cook."

I laughed. "Lallo also taught me how to cook. God bless Lallo. How's he doing?"

"He has a restaurant now, in Jeddah. My dad helped him open it and we eat there almost every night," Karim volunteered. Good, I had drawn him into a conversation. He was cautiously opening up.

"Wow, Lallo has a restaurant? What's it called?

"Lallo!"

We all laughed. Maybe this conversation was seemingly superficial and silly but I wanted to show my son how much I had been a part of his family, even before he was born. And I was succeeding, slowly, inch by inch.

Then came the big plunge. "Karim, speaking about food, I'm planning on staying in Boston tonight. Would you have dinner with me? Do you have plans? Please." I looked at him longingly.

Karim hesitated. "Uh, well, I guess so. I could have dinner with you."

"Great! I am so happy you agreed to that. I'm staying close to here at XV Beacon. Suppose I go there right now, check in, and return here to pick you up at 7pm?"

"Okay, I'll be ready."

"May I have your phone number so I can call you and tell you I'm downstairs waiting in the car?" It felt awkward to be so formal with my own son, but I wasn't sure he would be comfortable giving me his phone number. His father would have disapproved.

Karim hesitated, but his face relaxed and he cautiously disclosed his new American phone number. This was a treasure to me. I still remember it.

With that, I moved toward the door. Karim jumped up to see me out. Good manners. I snuck another kiss on the cheek and felt bold enough for a quick hug as I was leaving. Still, I couldn't quell my fear that even this simple, stilted conversation had been too much for him, and that he might change his mind about me. I felt I had to ask, "You promise that you'll answer the phone when I call, Karim? You won't decide to cancel on me, will you?"

With a striking but quiet confidence, Karim looked me square in the eyes and stated, "No, I will come."

I left the apartment and stumbled down the hallway to the elevator in a state of elation. Our polite exchange was more like a high stakes negotiation. But I was no stranger to Karim's family upbringing and the culture in which he had been immersed for many years. His father, like most Saudi Arabians, was stoic and static, with no tolerance for drama, self-expression, or overt displays of emotion. If I had somehow swept Karim up in my arms and cried into his shoulder, he would probably feel repulsed, and I would lose him once again. Being Italian-American, this emotional restraint was entirely unnatural to me, and I had sparred with my therapist for a year over it. But, now that I had a victory dinner scheduled with Karim that night, I knew the audacious plan had somehow worked.

As I headed to the hotel, memories of Rahman flooded my mind. How his mannerisms, particularly his ability to control himself and everyone in every situation, was present in Karim. And how, behind the niceties and small talk, the form and the function, both men were wounded. Our son, Karim, despite a determined desire to show me otherwise, was in need of healing. How I wished I could introduce him to the free spirited, confident but vulnerable, small but mighty woman who always found the best in everyone, despite their protesting. He would have to know me as his mother first, and perhaps that was enough. I vividly remembered my desire to heal Rahman, reaching into his hidden places only to find a preschool boy, abandoned, afraid, and very much alone, even in a crowd that he had bewitched with ease.

* * *

At seven sharp, pulling up to Karim's apartment building, I felt light years ahead of that very morning. *Wow, how a few hours can change your entire life.* I dialed Karim's number, and sure enough, he answered and said he would be right down.

His hair was soaking wet and slicked back, and he had paired stylish jeans with a tailored white shirt. Simple, chic, mature, preppy. Looks like Culver Academy had made its Midwestern mark, perhaps overshadowing the euro-chic of his dad's world. As Karim got into the car, he eyed the fancy dashboard, complete with navigation system and satellite radio. I knew he would take note of that—Saudis always love the latest luxuries, and they judge others accordingly.

"Wow, you're so handsome! Why is your hair wet?" I blurted.

"I just got out of the shower." Karim blushed.

Compose yourself. "I am so happy that you decided to have dinner with me tonight. Thank you."

"You don't have to thank me," he answered.

"Did you call your father after I left? Tell the truth," I gently teased.

"Yes, I did. After you left."

"And what did he say?"

"Well, I told him that I was going out to dinner with you and he sighed and said, 'So be it, she's a silly woman.'" That was a typical Rahman response–suggesting that I am insignificant. At least Karim feels he can be honest with me. I wonder how much they told him about me and our years together. Would Noura have kept my memory alive?

Still, it left me in the position I needed: the underdog, an unthreatening woman Karim might feel comfortable protecting. "I'm glad that he knows. I wouldn't want you to do anything deceitful that would put you in an awkward position. I'm so happy to be with you, Karim. Thank you so much."

Keeping it light for the duration of the evening was my plan. We entered the restaurant, where our table for two had already been booked. The concierge at my hotel had suggested it. I mentioned to the maître d' that this was my son, and he was starting college this fall. He eyed us and said that I looked too young to have such a grown-up son—how trite! We both giggled. The ice was melting.

During dinner, we discussed his Saudi family members and what they were up to; my American husband and 9-year-old daughter; my work as an interior designer; and various friends and points we had in common. We talked about horses. I told him about my show jumping. He shared that his passion was also show jumping. Ah! Something else we had in common! I thought it best to allow Karim to tell me more about himself in his own time. We could gradually get down to more personal subjects, I hoped. Rather than get impatient, I kept assuring myself, *we have time, we have time.*

For one brief moment at dinner, I dared to mention the "kidnapping" in the course of conversation. This was a definitive mistake. He shut me down in an instant. "How can one kidnap something that belongs to you?" he quoted, echoing his father's exact words. I kept my cool as best I could, wrestling with my shock and anger, that he saw the situation from his father's eyes. But how could I blame him? He was completely misinformed. Struggling to get past this impasse, my answer was that one day, perhaps when Karim was a father, we would revisit this subject, but for now, let's drop it. That quick comeback seemed to do the trick and Karim settled back down in his chair. Whew, a close call.

The rest of the evening went on without a hitch, as we discussed cousins, old friends, and changes made to Jeddah, a typical polite conversation topic in Saudi culture. Looking back, it does seem like the conversation went around and around in superficial circles. But rather than walking carelessly into a minefield, I decided I'd be better off tiptoeing carefully, little by little, until I understood more about this young man who was my son.

Karim gave me two hours of his time, and then, clearing his throat, he declared that he would like to go now; he was planning to meet some friends. That was absolutely fine with me; our first day was a huge success, much better than I had ever hoped for.

"Karim," I ventured before dropping him off at his place, "Do you feel awkward with me? Do you think you will ever be comfortable with me as your mother?"

"With time, I think I will," was his answer. What a perfect answer. He was already sensible, wise and tender—a son to be proud of.

"I'll come up next month to visit you again. Is that okay?"

Karim nodded. Our next meeting was set.

Back in my hotel room, I found myself going over every little detail, every little nuance of the day, trying to extract any clue as to what my son was like, what my son was thinking, what the future for us might look like. Understandably, he held his cards close to his chest, and so did I. I felt optimistic about establishing a parent-child relationship, although the barrier that Rahman had created between us would have to be dismantled slowly and with great caution. But this was America, my home, and I had reclaimed some control. I let my mind wade deeper into what our fractured family might look like years from now. My daughter Sultana was only two years behind Karim and would be attending college, no doubt. I would absolutely find her, too.

My cell phone rang and it was a college friend, Liz, calling from London.

"Liz, you'll never guess who I just had dinner with."

"Who?"

"Karim! Can you believe it?"

"Wow, how on earth did you accomplish that, Trish?"

And so, the details of the day were recounted. Liz congratulated me on my great success. After our call I settled into bed but couldn't sleep. I no longer felt triumphant and couldn't stop thinking about how much more there was to be done in repairing the broken connection with my son. And after that, there would be Sultana. It was daunting.

Liz and I reminisced about our Wellesley days, and how we had first met Rahman at a party in Boston. "We were at the end of our freshman year, Trish, remember?"

"Yes, I remember the moment he first pulled up in that hot car."

Chapter Two

The Beginning

It was a frigid Tuesday night in February, and my date was a snooze whose parents had saddled him with the unfortunate name of Braxton. This was the height of the 70's disco era. We had just left a wild party to pick up soda at the Star Market, and as we walked out into the street, ears still buzzing from the loud music, a souped-up bright blue Trans Am screeched to a halt, nearly plowing us over. In the driver's seat was a bearded young man sporting a wild print shirt and stylishly faded blue jeans. His penetrating almond-shaped eyes framed by dark lashes and even darker brows made me gasp. He looked like a guru. Braxton, now even more boring, leaned into the car and shouted an enthusiastic "hello" to the driver. As I stared wide-eyed into the car, straining to see more, Braxton announced,

"This is my friend, Abdulrahman Abbar. He's from Saudi Arabia."

Saudi Arabia? In the midst of the current gasoline crisis, caused by the ongoing Arab oil embargo, those words got my attention. All winter, we'd been siphoning gasoline out of each other's cars in the student parking lot, pooling our resources to have enough fuel for one round trip to Boston. Gas was expensive and scarce but I couldn't let that get into the way of my need for more nightlife. An opportunity to meet someone from Saudi Arabia was both advantageous and tantalizing.

I bent down as far as I could to get a better look, my eyes darting about to take it all in. The car was immaculate. It must have been brand-new; the seductive smell of fresh leather drew me in further. The guru had long, dark wavy hair and his teal blue, African-patterned shirt was unbuttoned halfway down his chest, revealing a strange gold medallion on a chain. I angled in further to get a better look at his seemingly trim, athletic build, nearly hanging half my body through the window in the process. Expensive-looking zebra stripe sandals, black and white, adorned his feet. *Sandals?* It was a snowy New England winter! I couldn't stop staring. Rude as it might have been, I was fixed on him. My nose caught a whiff of patchouli, or maybe musk oil, and I leaned in a little closer, almost tipping over. Was it patchouli or musk? *It fits him.* Beneath shapely brows, amber eyes blazed like precious stones. It was a sensual assault. He flashed a wide grin my way. At that moment, even before an unaware Braxton introduced me, I had lost myself. *Oh my god—he caught me! What do I say?*

"This is my friend Patricia from Wellesley." The Saudi nodded, somehow smiling even wider and replied, "My auntie graduated Wellesley a few years ago." Auntie, pronounced "ON-tee." That was not how I expected him to sound, with his earthy but trendy appearance. His clipped English accent paradoxically suggested an aristocratic British boarding school education. I was instantly transported back to last summer's London trip with my family, where we enjoyed an extravagant outdoor Elton John concert. This guru would have fit right into that crowd of funked-out peacocks. Still unable to speak, I simply nodded at him. He motioned for me to get into the front seat. Unable to resist, drawn in by his peculiar magnetic pull, I slipped inside. Braxton piled in next, boxing me between the intoxicating man and his stick shift. Teetering on the narrow armrest, I gripped the dashboard to steady myself and hoped we were not driving far.

Braxton babbled on, "We were over at Steven's party but they ran out of soda. We're headed to the Star Market. There's the sign."

My arms were shaking. *Why can't I think of anything to say?* I cleared my throat, "Are you really from Saudi Arabia?"

"I am. Do you know where Saudi Arabia is?"

I struggled for words but was confident in my world geography. "Of course! The huge country across the Red Sea from Egypt and Sudan, right? Mostly desert?"

The guru chuckled, "Yes, you got it right."

I was starting to feel better, now that I had managed to say something that made him laugh. I plunged right in and asked him how it was that he spoke the Queen's English.

"I went to prep school at Forest Grange and public school at East-bourne College." Then, somewhat pompously, he added, "That's in England, you know."

"Oh, I know, I know!" I insisted, having passionately studied everything British after my recent visit. I wanted to say more, now that I had partially recovered my nerve, but I didn't want to sound silly. "My friend Liz also did her prep school in England, although I forget which school she attended. I'll introduce her when we get back to the party."

"That would be nice, but not necessary. You see, I've already met the most attractive and interesting woman of the evening." Rahman gave me a penetrating glance and my head spun. Out of the corner of my eye, I saw Braxton scowl, so I cleared my throat and attempted to lighten up the conversation.

"I hope you don't mind but, uh, your name is long and I'm sorry, I've already forgotten it. Is there a nickname you go by?"

"Yes, people at BU, where I attend, call me Rahman." It sounded like *ROCKmon*. "That's only two syllables. Braxton here is the only one who's been able to master my entire name. And with perfect pronunciation, I might add." He flashed a smile at Braxton, who, as if on cue, beamed with pride. Rahman had us both deifying him in a matter of minutes. I would soon realize he had this effect on everyone.

Back at the party, I halfheartedly tried to socialize with the other coeds. The place had really filled up, the crowd was attractive, young, plastered, and jovial. Barry White hits were blasting on the stereo and dancing bodies were packed so tightly, one could hardly navigate the room. I was thinking of Rahman, playing his hippie aura, his odd but interesting clothing, his hot-rod car, his British accent, and all those intoxicating smells in my mind to an already obsessive degree. I continued to search the party for him... but all I found was Liz.

"Hi Trish, did you just arrive?" she shouted.

"No, I've been here for ages. I met the most amazing man. He's from Saudi Arabia and I was just trying to find him. He's tall, dark and handsome..."

"Aren't they all?" quipped Liz with a laugh.

It was too noisy to say more, so I grabbed her and we turned into the crowd, pushing through, on the hunt. By the time we reached the other end of the expansive room, I realized why I had failed to spot him sooner. There he was, asleep, flat on his back, sprawled across one of the sofas, his zebra-clad feet hanging over the edge. Ha! A sleeping guru! I chuckled before feeling an instant sting of disappointment, maybe even rejection, as he was not so eager to find me again. *Am I not good enough for him?* I was too embarrassed to stay and decided that Liz and I would move on to another gathering. We grabbed our coats and headed out into the night without even a backward glance.

I thought about Rahman more and more over the next week, ruminating on how oddly he had behaved, and becoming increasingly fascinated with him. He was someone quite far removed from the social pressures of Boston college life, someone who seemed much older and worldlier than the rest of us. I wondered if and when we would ever meet again. Secretly, I hoped we would.

That's not to say that I didn't have my own share of adventure during my time at college. Forget the typical 1970s Wellesley pastimes of dating Harvard men and toiling at the library. From the moment my parents dropped me off in my dorm room, I was determined to live it up, finally young and free in the city, far from my overbearing and conservative family.

I grew up on Long Island, in the very comfortable but sheltered village of Sands Point, the kind of beach town where everyone knew their neighbors, and parents looked out for each other's children. My grandparents, first-generation Italians, Sicily and Naples, lived around the corner, and our family's reputation was very important to them. But not to me. I lived for rebelliousness.

I was often in trouble for various escapades such as supplying neighborhood parties with bottles of alcohol from our extensive home bar or robbing my dad's Lucky Strike cartons to have cigarettes at the beach. When I was caught, I was grounded for the rest of the year. But that didn't stop me. I would stuff my bed with a blanket resembling the shape of my body, pop one of my mother's hairpieces on the pillow and crawl out my ground floor bedroom window. No permission meant no curfew, and I met up with friends at wild Led Zeppelin concerts, experimented with ever-present drugs and sex, dated all sorts of unsavory characters, and kept a stash of unacceptable hippie clothing hidden in the bushes behind the house so I could dress the part. Using my car for transportation was out of the question because the sound of the garage door opening would have alerted the family of my exit. So I took up hitchhiking. I got really good at it and was brave enough to hitchhike all over the New York Metropolitan area, often alone. Nothing could stop me from being a city girl. I was living an entire after-hours life of which my family was unaware.

Early into my senior year, I experienced the blunt end of a major parental reckoning after being caught climbing back into my window one morning. That ended the fun for me, at least for the time being, and I was grounded for the rest of the year. No phone calls or friends. Only school, piano, and art lessons were permitted. It was a dismal existence, so

I decided to run away and enlisted a girlfriend at school to help. We would escape to Haight Ashbury, California when the weather got warmer, which gave us a few months to save up some money and make arrangements. When spring arrived, we settled on a warm Saturday morning to escape our captors. Lift off would be at 4 am. My backpack was armed with snug-fitting jeans, concert tee shirts, a hairbrush and some underwear. The $500 I'd saved up from allowance and Christmas gifts would surely get us to the West Coast.

I had recently been moved to a second-floor bedroom, making my exit more precarious as I'd be forced to tiptoe down the stairs while the family slept. To make things worse, I hadn't considered Jacques–a most unfortunate oversight on my part. When my dark silhouette appeared at the top of the stairs, Jacques delivered a sequence of deafening barks, sounding more like an avalanche than a sleepy standard poodle. I was not only caught, I was subject to an interrogation by my mother, the primary disciplinarian, shrieking at me like a bird of prey. When my otherwise mild-mannered father stepped in, I knew for certain that the hammer would drop. If I didn't straighten out, he would not send me to college. That sobered me up quickly and thoroughly, as attending college was the only legitimate way I could ever truly escape the tedium of Long Island suburbia.

Luckily, I was a good student with a good brain and enough common sense to realize that I would need to fall in line if I wanted to be free (and have college paid for). Even that promising plan was not without further resignation on my part. My mother forced me to turn down Radcliffe, my first choice, due to their recent integration with Harvard. One look at their new coed dorms and bathrooms, and she was done. I would either attend an all-girls school or stay home, training to be a full-time concert pianist…a ridiculous fantasy my mother had embraced since my first recital at age six.

So Wellesley it was. Nevertheless, as they waved goodbye to me at my new all-girls school dorm, I felt I had triumphed, determined that they would never again control my life.

I resumed my partying, but without the irksome oversight. At five o'clock every day, I was showering, styling my hair, polishing my nails, and getting dressed up to go out for the evening. It was the Disco Era, and I was not going to miss one moment.

While it wasn't exactly New York City, for a seventeen-year-old in the seventies Boston was a Shangri-la of dance clubs and international students, their pockets overflowing with disposable cash. I remember my first night out. I had used the house phone in the dormitory hallway, available for local calls only, to reconnect with an old summer camp boyfriend,

John. He had started at Northeastern a year before. We agreed to meet up that night. I eagerly dressed in my coolest disco-wear–a black and silver knit halter top over super-tight hip-hugger denim bell bottoms, with silver sparkle 6-inch platform sandals. I had always been a skinny kid, but my figure had finally filled out and I wanted to flaunt it. I looked good and was confident that John would be impressed with how much I had grown up since our canoeing days at summer camp.

He pulled up in a beat-up Saab with his friend in the front seat then jumped from the car to give me a quick hug.

"John! It's so great to see you! Wow, I love your ponytail!" He looked so grown up and downtown.

"Patty, Patty, Patty!' he said, using my childhood nickname. "You look amazing! What a change from your camp tee-shirt." Memories of Camp Hilltop as awkward thirteen-year-olds flooded into my mind and I laughed. At camp I had noticed John, a lanky boy with flowing long hair, admiring me from afar. When my canoe capsized on the lake, he jumped in to "rescue" me. I insisted that I could swim, having grown up at the beach, but John wouldn't let go. We struggled in the water, entangled in each other, then kissed. My first kiss. I realized he had intended to kiss me all along. The "rescuing" act just provided an opportunity.

And here we were, four years later, adults in a big city. John continued to smile, motioning to his friend still in the Saab. "This is Karl." I nodded and John opened the back door for me to get in. "Karl, I think Patty is going to love The Other Side. She'll fit right in."

After a short drive, we parked the car in a dark alley in the downtown district. *Just where have they taken me?*

We arrived at a black door with a tiny peephole. When we knocked, a huge bouncer in an overcoat threw open the door. Music burst out of the small, steamy bar within. John navigated past the crowds, pushing us toward the source of the music. Through another doorway, we landed on a precarious metal platform and peered down at a pulsing dance club scene. *A catwalk in an old theater. I've never seen anything like this.* People crowded everywhere: on the stairs, on the floor below, and on the large, raised stage in the distance. Strobe lights flashed, timed with the music, giving an unreal twist to the scene. Everyone looked like they were in costume with wild capes, hats, and sequined evening gowns. The music was the best I had ever heard. This wasn't dopey bubblegum disco. This was music from the real Manhattan scene, the driving beats of Soul Makossa, with bass so pumped up, your heart pounded to the rhythm. We all started dancing right there on the platform, since there was nowhere else to go. Motioning to John that I wanted to get down to the stage, where I belonged, he waved me on, smiling broadly, "I knew you would like this place!"

Down I crept, still half-dancing, half clinging to the railing, determined to reach the stage. The characters along the way were wild. A mustachioed man in a musketeer hat with clothes to match, two pirates with bandanas around their heads who looked like they might be identical twins, a sexy vampire in a satin cape, and several Marilyn Monroe look-alikes all towered over me.

"Move over, sweetie," barked one of the Marilyns in a baritone voice. I did my best to conceal my surprise: they were all men! Smoking pot at a Led Zeppelin concert seemed tame compared to this club and I wanted more. *I have arrived!*

Finally down on the dance floor, I clambered to get up onto the stage where several dozen partiers were already dancing wildly. I squeezed myself into the crowd, their thrusting movements sweeping me along. I was having so much fun in the heavenly bowels of purgatory, that my sense of time had disappeared and I had forgotten John and Karl. *Where are they?* Feeling a little guilty for losing them, I squeezed my way back up the stairs, searching the metal platform where we had parted. With no sign of either of them, I ventured further into the darkness, a strobe light beam, directing my path. I approached a steep velvet curtain to a private corner and pulled it back to find the biggest surprise of the night – John and Karl passionately kissing. *John's gay!* This made me so profoundly happy. Euphoric, even! There was John doing his thing amidst a small universe of people doing theirs. No rules and no judgment. And I would finally be free to find me, too. Later that night, probably around 3 in the morning, I stumbled back to my dorm room after John dropped me off. Down the dimly-lit hall, a lone girl stood filling her bottle at the water fountain. I needed to share my experience with someone, and it didn't matter who it was, so I rushed over and introduced myself.

"Hi, I'm Patricia, I live in room 214. What are you doing up this late?"

"Hello!" *An unmistakable British accent!* "My name's Elizabeth. I'm in 208 and I just arrived from England. I have jet lag." Eyeing my outfit, she asked, "What are YOU doing up this late?"

"Out in Boston, at a wild club with an old friend. Come sit in my room. I can't sleep yet. I'll tell you all the gory details. Oh, and you need to catch up on Student Orientation Week. You missed the whole thing!"

"Sounds great, I'm all ears."

With that, we tiptoed back to my room and talked until dawn.

This random girl, co-opted from the hallway, was an extraordinary person. Liz was born and raised in Singapore, the daughter of a real Chinese princess and a successful executive. Like Rahman, she had attended only British schools, and oozed sophistication. I was smitten with her; she was my disco soulmate. We became friends instantly and plotted to return together to The Other Side the next evening.

Night after night, we would drop our studies and meet up to coordinate outfits. Both petite, we shared each other's clothes. Liz, with long black hair below her waist, chose a Gothic look while I preferred the 1920's silent film look, and plucked my eyebrows accordingly. Together, we discovered the disco scene in Boston. The Other Side was just one of our haunts. There was Le Jardin, a tacky jungle of hanging potted plants and rich college kids doing all kinds of designer drugs. Being a great dancer really got you noticed there. A club called Arena, a repurposed warehouse near the railroad tracks, was always a good time, until, guaranteed, you found your parked car outside totally ransacked by the local unsavories. But the element of danger made it even more irresistible. We also frequented The Flatiron, an old theater with dozens of unmarked rooms in which one could buy and sell Quaaludes and other prescription party drugs to the beat of a powerful bass. Needless to say, the one thing they all had in common was great music. We danced our way through our freshman year at Wellesley, always on the look-out for the next thrill.

The only major disappointment during those first few months at Wellesley was that I had not figured out where to run into Rahman after that night at Steven's party. But my luck would change. A month later at a dance club, Zelda's, we had our next encounter. Far from the grunge of the other locations, this popular club was decorated in a black and white art deco theme, complete with a huge mirrored disco ball that seemed to float over the circular dance floor. It was glamorous and sophisticated, the perfect setting for my meeting with someone as special as Rahman.

There he was, dressed up in a British-styled suit and shirt with an open collar, his wild, hippie beard now tight to his face. Rahman was at home on the dance floor, and a chameleon. The guru persona had vanished, transformed into a sleek European jetsetter. Catching my eye, he gestured for me to join him. Without a word, I slipped right into position. This was *chemistry*. As we danced, I couldn't stop staring at him, taking in every inch of him, and he too, was following my every move. Once we locked eyes, the pull was too great for me to look away. "Let me twirl you again. You are so stunning in that silky dress."

My whole body broke out in goosebumps. I stumbled a little on my second twirl and he grabbed on to steady me.

"I can't lose you!" he joked with a grin.

"Oh, don't worry," I vowed, "You won't."

Abruptly, he checked his watch and asked me if I would like to meet an Iranian prince.

"Sure, why not?" I answered. I guess it takes one to know one. He grabbed my hand and pulled me out the front door.

Outside the club, a sleek silver Jaguar E type convertible rolled up with a gorgeous young man at the wheel. With his medium brown, short cut hair and his fair skin, he could have passed for the boy next door, but I had a feeling, from the look of the car, that we were witnessing somebody very special—*this must be the Iranian prince!* Shivers went down my spine.

As we approached the car, Rahman quickly explained to me, "This is Kamyar Pahlavi. His uncle is the Shah of Iran. He's a royal prince. Do you know the difference between a prince and a *royal* prince?"

"Aren't they the same thing?"

He laughed, "No. A royal prince was actually born into the immediate family of the ruler. An *ordinary* prince could have been ordained later. Kamyar is a royal prince. He's studying at Harvard."

Spotting us, Kamyar jumped out of his car with his arms outstretched, grabbing Rahman in a warm hug, "My brother!"

Rahman introduced us, and Kamyar kissed my hand with a gleam in his eye. "Enchanté, mademoiselle," he whispered. Well, that did it. I was sold!

"Patricia, you must have some beautiful friends that we could introduce to Kamyar. He studies way too much. Why don't we all go out next Friday night? Better, yet, I'll throw a party. Bring an assortment of beauties, and I'll invite some of my own friends to go along."

And so we agreed. How could I be so lucky?! No sitting around waiting for a date for me!

Over the week, I carefully rounded up "the assortment," making sure everyone was ready for the wild night to come. Wellesley was a Seven Sisters school and most of us were beyond bookish. Still, I managed to convince my closest group of friends to forgo their studies, put together their bravest outfits, and get ready for the night of our lives. Liz, my wing-woman, was experimenting with a Morticia Addams goth vibe, pouring herself into a skintight black gown with black lipstick to match. Harriet, a demure blond Southern belle, floated in, all pastel silk and dimples. Norina, the sexy Moroccan, was sporting an Ali MacGraw flavor, countering our femininity with her tomboy spunk. We assembled like an army battalion of platform shoes and sequined tops, making a spectacular entrance at the party. We were greeted by a dozen young Iranian men, all dressed up in white three-piece suits like an army of Travoltas, though the movie would not come out for years yet. It was a sea of fancy watches and gold neck medallions and as we made our way across the room, we understood that all were impressed with our companions, Kamyar their prince and Rahman the Saudi sheik. Champagne flowed, and everyone seemed to be having the time of their lives. Music blasted, all fabulous European style disco mixes, because the host had hired a private DJ for the party. There I was, a Wellesley College freshman, swept up in an international fantasy. I dreaded the thought of the school year finishing up in a few weeks with everyone leaving Boston to return home to their families. But more, I dreaded being away from Rahman. Our chance encounters had sparked something not only in me, but in him. When a party was going on, we sought each other out. Club hopping from one party to the next, I invariably hoped for him to be waiting at my destination. Sure enough, as if materialized through my willpower alone, there he was, greeting me from across the dance floor with a knowing smile. It was as if we could feel each other, sensed each other's presence, and knew that once we found each other, that was where we were meant to be. Slipping in next to him to dance, feeling him rest a hand gently on my hip or shield me as we exited the dance floor was more intoxicating to me than anything else.

Whenever I mention my relationship with Rahman, people ask me how on earth we met.

"At school," was my simple answer. And indeed, it was that simple. We just met, or rather, collided, and things picked up from there. When I returned to school that fall, Rahman was in Boston, waiting to take me out again, and so I became his steady girlfriend.

Chapter Three

Whirlwind Romance

O ur first official date was a chic dinner at Top of the Hub, a still-op-
erating fine dining room atop of the tallest building in Boston.
Like a bird's nest perched over the river, with floor to ceiling windows,
an unmatched view, and a menu offering five courses of high-end provi-
sions worthy of a jet setter or power broker, or in our case, two students,
one of whom had exceedingly deep pockets. He was only two years older,
but his experiences and travels were vast and otherworldly; yet though he
obviously knew more about the world than I did, our conversations were
always lively and interesting. He played soccer on a European travel team,
took summer courses in Toledo, Spain, cruised down the Nile River on a
yacht, and partied in Beirut clubs. Rahman had endless stories to tell.

My teen memories of summer camp and the local Sands Point Bath
and Tennis Club seemed rather ordinary compared to his travels. I hung on
every word he said. He was impervious to all things traditional or routine
and I longed to escape what I perceived as my American blandness with
him. I would shed the "Patty Bonis" me and become an excursionist in my
own right.

The contrast between his childhood, *sans parents*, and mine, was
striking. He saw little of his parents from kindergarten age, up to adult-
hood and even now. My formative years were quite the opposite. Distance
from home was something I craved and there was never enough distance
or freedom from my parents' thoughts or words. Curious about his familial

relations and how it felt to be at boarding school since age six, I asked him. "Did you miss your family, living at school from such a young age?"

"No, I had my younger brother and my five cousins in England, and our guardian, Mrs. Moxham, looked after us."

"But you toured Europe all summer with the soccer team. So when did you return home to your parents?…"

"I didn't." Boom. Did I detect annoyance? Was I was prying? I hoped I had not said anything wrong. I only wanted to know more. His life fascinated me.

I was so deep in my inner monologue that when Rahman finally suggested we order, I was too preoccupied to eat.

"Let's share a few light things," I proposed, still in a glorious stupor.

"Oh no, not so fast." he playfully scolded. "I want to order some wine first, and then we can tackle the food. Do you prefer white or red?"

"I'm fine with a Coke and lemon."

"I think we must order some wine tonight. Why don't we choose a bottle together?"

We were both over eighteen and completely legal to drink, but I had no experience with wine styles, profiles or vintages. I shamefully admitted wine was a language that I simply did not speak. I was relieved when he admitted the same. He leaned in and whispered, "When in doubt, I order the most expensive thing on the menu!" and that's what he did. *His thinking is brilliant!* Even when he was unsure of himself, Rahman would take charge of any situation. He could step into an awkward moment with his acute charm and abundant flair, manipulating each piece and variable, until he had control of the situation and everyone in it. He had an unrivaled confidence and I, too, was under his spell.

Each date was more magical than the last. Rahman had an infectious personality and somehow made me feel equally gifted and of paramount importance. We met at dawn one morning on the banks of the Charles River to watch our friends in a rowing drill. It was freezing and damp, typical for Boston. An ever-prepared Rahman casually reached into the trunk of his car and produced a warm blanket big enough to hug us both. Once we were wrapped snugly inside, looking like a jumbo burrito, we barely noticed the glassy river or the steam rising from her warmer spring waters. The drill was over before I realized that I'd been fixed on his dark-eyed intent gaze for the entire exercise.

Soon after, on a beautiful Saturday afternoon, he asked me to help him pick out a suit on Newbury Street. As if he needed my help. Perhaps he desired my company but felt the need to produce a proper reason to ask.

We spent an hour at the little outdoor café across the street from the men's boutique, enjoying a glass of wine prior to the new suit acquisition. We were a little tipsy upon entering the upscale tailor parlor, but a tidy bowtied gentleman with an Italian accent immediately took charge, ushering us into what looked like a WWI era smoking room at a gentlemen's club. Once I was cozied into the plush sofa, Rahman took charge of the room, the staff and their helpers doting on him like the wealthy Saudi (read: big spender) that he was. He cracked jokes, tried on outrageous styles, and even asked the store manager to scour the back of the store for any peculiar garments that he might fancy. Rahman was magnetic and most at home at the center, with everyone else feverishly circling around him. And just by being with him, I received the same treatment. I was the lucky one and I knew it. And I didn't miss an opportunity to tell him so. I basked in his presence and reveled in my association with him.

***

Two years passed almost without notice. My mind and time, occupied by a man that was no less intriguing than when he first pulled up in that hot car to say hello to poor Braxton. But when Rahman began planning for graduation that June, I wondered what life would be like when he was gone. And who would I be?

He casually mentioned that his parents might fly in from Saudi for his graduation and I naively hoped that he might introduce me to them as his girlfriend. When I brought it up to Liz, she instantly shot down any possible hope.

"Pat, are you crazy? Arabs are so conservative! The families practice matchmaking, like in my mother's generation in China. But Saudis are still stuck in that time. They wouldn't want to meet the American girl, or *any* girl their son was dating."

"That's exactly what Rahman said. He balked and made excuses. He said it's way too much for them to take in. Apparently, his mother has her heart set on matching him up with his second cousin. How gross! No chance of that happening if I know Rahman." I was convinced that I knew all of him, but meeting his family would somehow make that real for me.

Liz thought for a moment then offered, "Just tell her that you're a good friend. In fact, bring all of us to meet them and they won't know what to think! What fun that will be! I'm sure they will be staying at the Presidential Suite of some fabulous hotel in Boston. Imagine the damage we can do there!"

I had to admit, that was a good suggestion. Keep it light! Make a fabulous party out of it. Show them American hospitality. I told Rahman about our scheme the next time I saw him.

"We'll go in a big group! We'll both bring friends and make a wonderful reception party for your family! I'm dying to meet them."

Rahman looked doubtful, but when I explained that this would make the tedious task of showing his parents around Boston into a festive and easy group adventure, I sensed him budging a bit. We would all help entertain his family! Rahman finally relented, and so, that was the plan. My excitement only continued to mount as Rahman and I made preparations together. It would be our first joint operation!

On our Bonis family vacations, I was used to staying at high-end resorts but sharing a room with my sisters. But for the Abbars, the expectations were beyond lavish, nothing I had ever witnessed in my life. We selected and reserved restaurants for lunches and dinners, lined up different friends for different events, and booked a guided tour of the city by private van, complete with an Arabic speaking tour guide. Not wanting to miss a single thing, we added a private helicopter tour of the entire coastline of Massachusetts, so the family could see Cape Cod and other notable visuals in the region.

The Abbar family's twelve-person entourage landed in Boston a week before graduation, taking up temporary residence at the Ritz Hotel on the park, in the Presidential Suite. They also booked several limousines with drivers to be at their disposal, for them, their staff, and their guests. The plan was to continue on to New York City after the graduation ceremony, with the same cast of characters and accoutrements, then they would head back to Jeddah, their hometown in Saudi.

Rahman's mother, Inja, brought her newborn baby, Imamah, the newest addition to the Abbar family. The baby's Ethiopian nanny, Zainib, was also in tow, as was the ladies' maid Yasmeen. Prior to meeting Yasmeen, I thought ladies' maids had gone extinct after the seventeenth century, but in Saudi Arabia, they were alive and well. Her job was packing and unpacking, drawing a bath, folding and unfolding towels, straightening up the bed linens, making sure the breakfast table was set properly, pouring hot tea, and fluffing and arranging the furniture to suit the family's preferences.

Rahman's father, Abdullah, brought his Egyptian butler for the trip. The butler turned on the TV, set the volume at a comfortable level, sat in the front seat with the limo driver, carried the baby stroller and of course, kept track of the luggage and briefcases for everyone. In addition, there were half a dozen more miscellaneous servants, each with a single job to do. The entire entourage traveled as a group because, as I soon realized, Rahman's parents did not lift a finger, not even to pull a Kleenex out of a box to wipe their noses or pick up a spoon to stir their tea. They lived as if they were an Old Testament king and queen.

Our little plan to flood them with intent hospitality, activities, and people worked perfectly. At first, Inja was wary of me and all my girl-friends. She didn't look very happy when we poured into their suite on the day of their arrival. But on cue, my girls descended on her and gushed over the new baby, asking questions, shaking rattles, tickling, smiling, and picking her up.

Everything was going as planned and I was in heaven. I thought if I overwhelmed the mother with love and attention and won her over, that the father would probably follow suit. In my heart of hearts, I was hoping that impressing his family with well-behaved and well-educated American girls might somehow entice Rahman to proudly present me as his girl-friend. My plan seemed to be working.

That night, Rahman had booked a Turkish restaurant complete with private entertainment. Two belly dancers made their way in, weaving around the room like feathers in the breeze, only louder. Bells jingling and tiny hand cymbals clanging, dancers dipping in and out of the empty spaces, spinning, gyrating, then ending the presentation with a dance duel of taut tummies. I wasn't really a fan of belly dancing but it was amusing and entertaining and quintessentially Middle Eastern. And the show allowed me a few minutes to metabolize the fact that the man I loved and his family were both present and content. These new people, their customs and ways, were strange and exotic, but I liked them. Rahman made his way over to me and we went over every detail of the evening. He fully agreed our efforts were a huge success, assured me that his parents were having a grand time, then pulled me in close and gave me a big kiss. On the lips.

I was shocked because our nonnegotiable, iron-clad agreement (per Rahman's reqs not mine) was no touching, kissing, or signs of affection between us while his parents were in the general vicinity. I instinctively looked up and found his mom, Inja, watching us from across the room. *Not the intro I was hoping for but it's something.* I couldn't tell if Rahman was aware of his mother's gaze or not. But at that moment, as far as I was concerned, it was his problem if she saw. I was just happy that Rahman had felt compelled to break his own ironclad cultural rules, for me.

That night, after our merrymaking, his family had a long and heated discussion about *the kiss.* Inja demanded to know the truth, and Rahman fessed up. He wouldn't tell me exactly what was said, only that we would continue our plan of entertaining the Abbars in Boston and then on to New York City. After much deliberation, they accepted me as his girl-friend, and, as I later learned, a potential wife candidate. Was I considering marriage? I didn't know. I was only nineteen. But any girl would want her boyfriend's parents to like her, especially a girl as desperately, obsessively, and uncontrollably in love as I was. It was that simple.

When the Abbars arrived in New York, they were installed in the pent-house suite of the Waldorf Towers, a sumptuous spread which featured a grand piano in the living room. As their culture dictated, there was an open invitation for all my friends and family to dine out with them every night, and attendance was not optional. My own family had coincidentally moved to New York City the year prior. I had briefly mentioned my new college companion, a top shelf Saudi bachelor, but now, I had to justify their required presence at dinner. Making sense of all of this to my mother in her new Park Avenue apartment was a tall order. I could have been more thoughtful and tread more carefully, but the rebellious streak in me, the oldest and most driven of her three daughters, would not be confined to the ideal future as dictated by my mother, a traditional 1950s housewife. As childish and disrespectful as it seems to me now that I too am a mother, any hint that she was against Rahman and me provided further fuel to push forward with my relationship, whatever it may appear or become.

Once in NYC, I brought in a whole new crew of local friends to join in the festivities with my family. Night after night, we traversed from one hot spot to the next, the older generations dining extravagantly then retiring, and the young ones indulging in NYC nightlife until the wee hours. All at Rahman's expense. My family marveled at how seemingly open-minded and comfortable the Abbars were in New York, but Rahman explained to us that when outside of strict Saudi society, his family had no problem conforming to Western standards within reason. They had grown accus-tomed to it in more liberal Middle Eastern cities like Beirut and Cairo, not to mention substantial time spent in London.

After several days of lavish meals at choice restaurants, my father, flattered but overwhelmed by the Abbars' bottomless pit of generosity, insisted on inviting them to our family's new apartment for cocktails and then out to dinner at Club Ibis, a hotspot that served Middle Eastern food. My mother, starving for a little control over her daughter's situation, rose to the occasion in spite of heavy personal objections and planned the whole affair.

She was the paragon of 50s housewivery, having ice-cold Champagne Bellinis in a luminous crystal pitcher at the home bar when the guests arrived. On her six-foot-wide Karl Springer cocktail table, she composed silver platters of tiny *foie gras* slices on toast, peeled shrimp cocktail and blinis topped with Beluga caviar from Petrossian Caviar NYC. Our apartment was freshly decorated in the latest New York eclectic style, and it truly was as perfect as mom had envisioned, chic and extremely stylish in neutral shades of earthy taupe with black and white accents. The furniture was arranged in three intimate groupings complete with a sleek black Steinway grand piano in the corner. Lacquered walls were further gilded with modern abstract art, including female nudes alongside works of my own. Wide windows clothed with the softest of silk draperies overlooked a radiant twilit Park Avenue view. I was still a little unsure of the degree of opulence the Abbars were accustomed to, but I was confident that by New York standards, our family's home was something to be proud of.

"Look, I think that's them pulling up!" my beloved 16-year-old sister, Cindy, exclaimed from her perch at the window. She had been excused from homework for this special occasion.

"Two limos pulled up! It must be them. Who else would arrive like that?" chimed in my sister Diane, a freshman at Wheaton College who was home for the weekend. Three uniformed doormen rushed out to open their car doors and ushered the Abbars into the building. All smiles, we greeted our guests with hugs and customary kisses as we led them into the living room, where my mother was lighting pillar candles, calm and confident in a flowing yellow Zandra Rhodes silk gown that complemented her dark hair and svelte figure. My mom's elegance echoed early screen sirens and, that night, she was the spitting image of Sophia Loren.

"Well, hello everyone," she cooed with a smile while gliding up to Inja, her arms outstretched. My mother's charms transcended all cultural and language barriers. I started to relax—one could always count on my mother to be a warm and inviting hostess at her own party. The Abbars were in good hands, and I realized that I didn't have to work as hard this evening. My entire family, despite their apprehension, was up for the challenge.

The ladies, including baby Imamah and her nanny, settled on the plush white sofas in the middle of the living room. Even our dog, Jacques, jumped up onto the sofa next to Inja. Her eyes went wide at the poodle sitting next to her on the silky sofa. My father, low-key and relaxed, motioned the men into the adjacent library for drinks and talk of business and politics. I caught Abdullah looking at the brown suede walls and leopard-print carpet with a bemused smile. He obviously liked it.

All socializing was done with limited English on Inja's part and limited Arabic vocabulary on our part. But somehow, we succeeded in filling the entire evening with gaiety and conversation. By the time we were ready to pile into the cars and head to the restaurant, everyone was in good spirits. I heard from Rahman, days later, that Inja decided we were a charming "good" family with three pretty daughters, which was a definite asset in their society. My parents decided that the Abbars were straightforward, hospitable, and decent people. I was exhausted but triumphant.

After time with us in New York, the Abbar family, including Rahman, returned home to Jeddah. As I saw them off at Kennedy Airport, I couldn't help but feel empty. This voice from somewhere inside of me was asking, *What was the purpose of all this commotion? Two entire weeks without taking a break. And not even one minute alone with Rahman. Where is this all leading to? Why am I doing this?* The often ignored sensible me was not convinced but I was young. I was petulant. I was stubborn. I desperately needed to be with Rahman and was confident that I could make it happen.

Even without Rahman's constant presence, my next year at Wellesley was fabulous because of him. Every few months, Rahman would fly in and make a big splash, wilder and more exciting than ever before, because now he was working for the family's import business and had additional reserves of money to spend. He would invite our friend groups to restaurants and clubs and pay the bill for ten or twenty of us, sometimes more. The only requirement for all of us was to dress up and look beautiful. We partied both in Boston and New York, generating a buzz wherever we went. With Rahman, I was always a VIP, in demand and commanding attention. It was my job to ferret out new hotspots for Rahman to drop money at during his visits. We were living the high life, and nothing made me feel better than knowing he needed me as much as I needed him.

It didn't stop in New York. A year later, the unbelievable party life that sucked me in continued even after I graduated college. The summer after my senior year at Wellesley, my family decided to spend a month in Monte Carlo, and, of course, Rahman swooped in from Jeddah for a few weeks and took us all out to every possible venue. We had gone "international!" Rahman's Belgian school friend, Mark Van Laer, joined us, pulling into the harbor of Monte Carlo that summer with his dad, his dad's mistress, and their gigantic yacht, to join us. Although parading your mistress at the yacht club (vs. bringing your actual wife) seemed shockingly avant-garde to my parents, I insisted we accept Mark's gracious invitation for cocktails and dinner. My parents reluctantly attended, but not before giving me a long lecture on the dangers of getting involved with men who flaunt their mistresses. "It's contagious," cautioned Dad, though he seldom offered criticism about my social life. I suppose it was because this was mens' business, he weighed in. Of course, I scoffed at his advice and refused to discuss it further. This was my world now, and they were just along for the ride.

In the fall after graduation, I decided to attend the Sorbonne in Paris to study for my Master's degree in Art History. Studying in Paris seemed to be a better choice than the US, because Rahman was only a six-hour flight away. He visited me often. Rahman routinely carried a little black book double-wrapped with a rubber band, bursting with pages and pages of names and phone numbers. I could never understand how one person knew so many people. We could walk down any street in any city and there was always someone we would bump into who knew him from somewhere. He had spent many years in England, and between school, his soccer team travels, and summer school, he accumulated a vat of friends and contacts. His unforgettable appearance and strong personality only added additional heft to his little black Rolodex. He was a people magnet and I was guilty of worshiping him, too.

Chalk it up to the pleasurable irrationality of a twenty-two-year-old, but I just couldn't help myself. I was in a dangerous place, but I didn't care. I needed him and the way he made me feel.

As the first two semesters in Paris came and went, the idea of a forever with Rahman increasingly occupied my thoughts. And with no warning whatsoever, my greatest hope came true on a blustery but beautiful and quiet Paris winter day. Rahman arrived for a visit, and we headed to the city center. We strolled arm in arm down Avenue Victor Hugo, shopping here and there, chatting about the news on our way to eat oysters at a local bistro. We passed a jewelry shop with a dazzling window displaying Piaget watches. Spotting a striking yellow gold, green malachite, and diamond watch in the window, I gasped. Without hesitation, Rahman walked in, purchased it on the spot, and asked me to marry him. Just like that.

And of course I said yes. Just like that.

Granted, it was not a traditional engagement ring, but I clearly understood that there would be many diamond rings in the future, and this was no time for splitting hairs. What mattered was that Rahman had proposed and I had accepted. I had been his from the moment I peered into that souped-up Trans Am four years ago, and now, he was to be mine for life.

The degree of love that I felt for him at that time was of the deepest kind for a girl of twenty-two. As soon as Rahman and I decided on this momentous next step, we realized that there were many things that we had to do to prepare. At least his family had already met me, and not only did they like me, but they also approved of me for his wife. I had always thought this was the biggest challenge and was relieved that we had already crossed that bridge. The next big hurdle would be learning Saudi Arabia, for myself.

At that time, the government was very strict about allowing its citizens to marry foreigners. In fact, Saudi women were completely forbidden to marry foreign men. Saudi men, much more privileged in that culture, were granted permission on a highly limited basis, provided they received government approval, which at that time meant that King Faisal, himself, determined your matrimonial fate. Rahman took that very seriously, and although I tried to make light of it, he insisted that without permission, no marriage could take place.

"Patricia, this is no laughing matter. And not only is it quite difficult to get the permission, but for a woman like you, from New York, to fit in, to make a life, well I can't think of a more inhospitable place. I was discussing this with my mother's sisters and my cousins, and they all agree that you should come for a visit before we get married, just so you can understand the challenges."

Being the headstrong person that I was, stubborn and in love, I felt insulted when I heard phrases like "difficult to fit in" or "unable to understand," and somehow, it became another challenge for me to prove everyone wrong, just like with my mother when she first raised an eyebrow. A part of me was indignant that anyone would cast a doubt on my judgment or my ability to adapt to whatever I wanted. For this reason, I didn't ask for advice. I didn't want it.

"So, when do you want to schedule your visit to Jeddah?" Rahman queried.

"How about in May when I finish my school semester?" *As soon as possible! What are we waiting for?*

"May is fine with me, but it's hot there in May. It might be better to plan the visit for next winter."

"Why wait? What benefit would that have? I might as well see how hot it actually gets." I dug in and we decided that my scheduled visit would be at the end of May. I had little interest in school by that time although I did complete my coursework. I could only think of my new life with Rahman. Art History, a field that I had once loved, would have no place in my new life in Saudi and certainly no prospects in a Muslim country where art is largely forbidden! I anxiously awaited and prepared for the great adventure which was soon to come.

At my request, the next time Rahman paid me a visit, we went across the English Channel to meet a few of his friends and family who were vacationing in London. His cousin Khalid and his British wife, Valerie, as well as his school friend Nihad and his Spanish wife, Natalie were happy for us and wanted to meet me. I was very excited to meet Khalid, the first member of the Abbar family who had pioneered marrying a foreign woman, and was equally curious to meet Valerie.

Valerie was instantly warm and friendly to me, a platinum blonde raised by a simple English family from Derby, in the English Midlands. She was tall, actually taller than her husband. They met in a club when he was in graduate school, and she was working in a perfume shop. Her accent was strange, more Scottish than English. Before I even had the chance to ask her anything about life in Jeddah, she started to gush.

"So, you're going to come to Jeddah in May?" she squealed with delight..

"You heard? So quickly?" I was surprised.

Valerie took a breath. "Well, almost nothing ever happens in Jeddah and your visit is the most important event of the year. In fact, when Auntie Inja returned from Boston a few years ago, she told everyone about you and your family, and they haven't stopped talking about it since!"

She laughed before taking another breath, "They still haven't gotten over my marriage to Khalid, and now that I'm expecting a baby, well, that was the big news until your news happened. Actually, I'm glad that you'll be taking some of the heat off me!"

"Valerie," Kahlid protested, "the whole family loves you."

"Oh yes, they love me so much, they wanted me to stay in Jeddah for the birth, but no way would I ever do that! You should see the condition of the hospitals there!"

"I would never put you through that…" Khalid assured her.

"Well, I'm relieved to be in London now. The baby is due in two months, and I plan to stay here until she's born. And let me tell you, Patricia, I have my own maid, and I will have a nanny when the baby is born. I won't have to lift a finger except to get dressed and show up at functions. It's a good life. I don't mind the customs, I speak a little Arabic, and as long as I can cook my Shepherd's Pie once a week and bring it to Wednesday lunch with the family, I'm happy."

Whoa. Her bluntness, and the sheer amount of information that had been thrown at me, was overwhelming. I was news in Jeddah? The hospitals were bad? Shepherd's pie? Why was I considering the idea of being there? I felt no more at ease about visiting Jeddah, but Valerie's frankness was so endearing, and her husband seemed like a sweetheart. I had a feeling she would become the trusted friend I would need in such a closed society.

Rahman had his own ideas about what my experience would be and did try to ground me, "Don't take her too seriously. Her side of the family is very laid back and she is living in their house. She has three sisters-in-law there to keep her company. You, on the other hand, will probably be very lonely, and my mother will expect a lot from you. I don't think your life-style in Jeddah will be like hers."

I was beginning to see a pattern here: Rahman was in love with me, but always seemed to poke holes in my optimism when it came to Saudi Arabia. He had challenged me when I first tried to meet his family in Boston, then, after I jumped through hoops, rewarded me with the kiss. He had made me work for that. Even now, in the throes of our love and engagement, he was planting doubts everywhere. Once again, I was working. I was becoming accustomed to this mind play and accepted the challenge with determination. I convinced myself that he was just nervous about his culture or trying to rile me up, and that if I stuck it out, I'd be, as always, rewarded.

The next day, for lunch, we met Nihad Al-Arab and his Spanish wife, Natalie. They had heard we were engaged, and Natalie insisted on a meeting.

"I've heard so much about you, Patricia! Inja told everyone about your lovely mother and sisters! I am so happy that another foreign woman is coming to Jeddah. There are very few of us, you know. I was one of the first. I arrived 15 years ago, when there was literally nothing. Not even paved roads. It was only me and Marianne Ali Reza, but she's gone now. Divorced. Nihad and I are fortunate, we have our own house. It certainly isn't fancy, but at least I have my privacy. You're lucky the Abbars are building you a house, although it's on a dirt road. How's your Arabic? You'll have to take lessons. I'll give you the name of my tutor. You'll need Arabic to communicate with your maids and drivers. And as an Abbar, you will have many of those. Most of the smaller shop owners don't speak English either, so you will need Arabic for that, too."

Natalie, unlike Valerie, had an attitude of superiority and was something of a know-it-all. She was engrossed in her house and her children, things I couldn't yet relate to. I was much too young and romantic to be interested in such things. But I tolerated Natalie for lunch, thinking that she might be a useful person to seek advice from once I arrived in Jeddah. I wondered why Rahman spoke of her in such glowing terms and was actually relieved when we finished lunch and I finally had a break from Natalie's constant words and unremarkable remarks. As Rahman and I walked back, he picked up on my irritation..

"You didn't look so happy with Natalie. Don't you like her?"

"She's a bit annoying. I don't like being lectured. And she's an ass-kisser! All that stuff about your family."

"She was just trying to tell you how lucky you are because you are marrying me," he said with a smile and a wink, "I am a good catch, in case you don't know."

His smile made me melt. "Oh, I know." We wrapped our arms around each other's waists and walked through Hyde Park to our hotel, completely content.

News of our engagement and my impending visit to Jeddah spread far and wide within Saudi society, because for the remainder of the year, whenever Saudis came over to Paris or London for a vacation, Rahman would take me to meet them. They were all curious to see the woman he had decided to marry, and they were all happy to welcome me into the fold.

One weekend in March, we spent time with a very interesting and sophisticated couple, Mahrous Bin Laden and his French wife, Michelle. Out of all the couples I met that year, Mahrous and Michelle made the greatest impression. Rahman told me that the Bin Laden family was, indeed, one of the strongest and most prestigious families in Jeddah at that time. I remarked at the similarity between their last name and Inja's family name, Bin Zagr, and wondered what that meant. Rahman explained that those types of last names, with the "Bin" at the beginning, are a sign that the family comes from the Hadhramaut region in the Southern part of the country. Like Rahman and Inja, Mahrous also had sparkling dark eyes and a strong profile, a trademark of their bloodline. The Hadhrami people were known for being great businessmen, descending from ancient traders. There is a legend about old man Bin Laden, who had arrived in Jeddah as a young man pushing a cart with bricks in it. He became a bricklayer, and then gradually, worked his way to transforming the family business into one of the largest international construction companies of the time. He personally had many wives and concubines, as was the custom in those days, and he supposedly fathered about one hundred children, all bearing the Bin Laden name. Mahrous and his other three brothers were the oldest and most powerful of all the brothers, whether it was because of who their mother was in the order, or just simply because of the fact that they were older. They stuck together and formed Bin Laden Brothers Construction, which was the main branch of the family business.

Mahrous spoke perfect French, which I assumed he had learned when he completed his studies in Beirut, and not only was he a strikingly handsome man, he also had very elegant mannerisms. His wife, Michelle, was an extravagant French personality, oozing sophistication and style, and to me, appeared to be completely in charge of her life. She was very tall and thin, taller than her husband but still rocking high heels with confidence, as was the fashion. She pulled her dark hair back very tightly in a bun, giving her a beautiful but slightly severe look. We went out dancing one evening with them to Regine's in Paris, an unrivaled hotspot. Mahrous smoked a cigarette using a long ivory cigarette holder with carefully manicured hands and such long fingers! It reminded me of a movie I had just seen, Last Emperor of China, and their decadent ways before the Communists took over.

The Bin Ladens' lifestyle seemed outrageous, even compared to the Abbars. They traveled all over the world in the most luxurious style. They were not burdened with any children, and I thought, *well, that's the life for me!* Michelle told me all about their set up in Jeddah during dinner.

"Of course, we have our own house in Jeddah. And I bring my own French servants to work for me. And *bien sûr* we have our cottage at the "Creek" for the weekends. We entertain there most weekends because everyone wants to be at the Creek. We have a fabulous French chef who makes the best barbecues! It's impossible to get even a tiny cabin on the Creek, or even to purchase a small strip of waterfront land these days. Everything is owned by the most powerful princes, and they have no need or desire to sell."

I had no idea of what the "Creek" was, but I didn't care. It all sounded fabulous, and I decided that if it was good enough for this very chic French woman, then it would be good enough for me. I instantly wanted a house at The Creek. Hearing all these tales from Michelle convinced me that I could live an interesting and enjoyable life in Jeddah. She did. Why wouldn't I be able to do the same?

About one month before I was scheduled to visit Jeddah, Rahman called me in Paris and informed me, sadly, that a complicated and somewhat negative answer had come back from the government in reference to our marriage permission. The way that Saudis got "favors" from the government was by forming a friendship or alliance with a particular prince. The higher up your contact prince was, the bigger your favors would be, and the more likely you would be to get a positive outcome. Our contact prince at that time was Prince Ahmad, one of the younger brothers to the King. Amm Abdullah spoke with Prince Ahmad, who, in turn, spoke with the King. The unfortunate answer to our request for marital permission was that I would have to become a Muslim first. It seemed the government was recently making it tougher for Saudi men to marry foreign women. At the time, I didn't really understand why on earth that would make a difference, but now, looking back, I see that it made it infinitely easier for the government to deal with foreign women once they submitted to the Islamic religion. The Islamic religion formed the basis of Saudi law, so becoming a Muslim meant that you were submitting to Saudi law, in its entirety, including marital and social laws.

Rahman sounded upset on the phone. His usual confident, sometimes cocky, tone was subdued and uncertain. "Perhaps we should just skip the marriage. You can stay in Paris or London, your choice, and I will visit you monthly. There won't be any pressure."

What an about-face!! The man who recently proposed to me was now backing away. He seemed very spooked by the idea of seeking royal permission and I could only suppose he saw this as a huge obstacle. Or was he trying to protect me? Or his family? Had one of his friends suggested this arrangement as a way to avoid trouble and less commitment on his part?

"What are you suggesting? That I live here in an apartment like a mistress?"

I already knew two American women in New York City with Arab boyfriends and both were enjoying a grand lifestyle in luxury apartments, all expenses paid for by the rich boyfriend. Maybe they faced the same marital obstacles or perhaps it was fiscally beneficial? Later on, one of those ladies had even received an enormous "settlement," voluntarily paid to her to soften the blow when he married a proper Arab woman and stopped his visits.

"How would that work? Me living here alone, you in Jeddah with your mother looking to match you up with a Saudi girl so you can have children? Not to mention my parents who would permanently disown me for such outrageous behavior!"

I desperately searched for another solution. "Can't you come to America and live there with me? Maybe we can both go to graduate school, and worry about all this marriage stuff in another five years or so."

"Patricia, I must work right now, and that work has to be in Jeddah. The family needs me. The country is booming because of the oil embargo. Business is going crazy; we have formed twenty new companies this year and they all have to be managed."

"Maybe I can convert. I'm open to that. I was never a religious Catholic. I haven't been to a church since high school! Philosophically, I don't mind converting. All religions seem pretty much the same to me, as long as there's one God. But how is it done? Where would I even do that?"

"Wait a minute." Rahman was shocked. "You mean you would actually convert for me? For us? You don't mind?"

I would have done anything for him. The idea of learning Islam wasn't so foreign to me. In an attempt to better understand Rahman and his family, I had already taken a seminar on Islam in my senior year at Wellesley. So, yes! I would absolutely do it. I was dead set on defying, defeating, and defecting.

In a frenzy to get this permission behind me, I would find a way to achieve the conversion in Paris, with haste. I headed to the largest Mosque in Paris, conveniently located down the street from my school in the *4th arrondissement*. Its imposing architecture, looming over the Latin Quarter. Imagine! Now I would be entering that grand mosque on a mission.

Looking back, it all appears somewhat comical, but at that time, I was dead serious. On my way home from class one afternoon, I marched through the iron gates, straight into the mosque, wearing my fashionable tight black jeans, high heeled boots, and an oversized turtleneck sweater in bright turquoise blue. I asked, in hesitant French, whom to speak with in order to convert to Islam.

I reasoned that by speaking in French, my second language, to people who also spoke French as their second language, this would give me cover in case any difficult questions were asked. I could feign linguistic misunderstanding and give myself time to figure out the answer. If I admitted my only reason for conversion was to get marital permission, I feared there was a good chance I'd be refused. I wasn't sure what the rules of conversion were, but I didn't want to take any risks.

The curious men at the entrance of the Mosque directed me to the main office of the Mullah, where I entered his majestic quarters, covered with patterned mosaics and marble. The Mullah, a gray-haired older man with a long beard, all clad in white, was surrounded by half a dozen other identically clad lesser men. With heart beating loudly in my chest, I stated that I wanted to become a Muslim. They all sat up, suddenly very attentive, eyes wide, looking at each other as if asking, "Is this a joke? Is she serious?"

They started firing questions at me: Where was I from? What was I doing in Paris? Why did I want to convert? I answered it all in French, feigning linguistic limitations. When I didn't feel like giving any further information, I would proclaim that I didn't really understand, saving myself from any deep questioning. In a nutshell, I declared that I was a Christian but came to love Islam, and wished to convert. Then I asked if they could they please help me. After speaking to each other in what I surmised was a Moroccan dialect of Arabic, the mullah handed me some papers with Arabic prayers written out phonetically. He explained to me that I must learn these prayers and return when I had mastered them. Next, I would demonstrate my ability in front of a panel of mullahs, who would award me a certificate to prove that I had been converted to Islam. I thanked them and left quickly, clutching the prayer papers.

It all seemed simple enough, and I eagerly started memorizing and practicing. I realized that I would be bending over and kneeling on the ground in my prayer demonstration, so I scoured my wardrobe for something loose and long to cover my body. I giggled when I imagined myself in front of these religious old men, bending over in a pair of skintight jeans. Nope! I would wear a long Tibetan tunic that I used as a house robe to perform my prayers. Relieved that I had it all figured out, I memorized the prayers within a few days.

I returned to the Mosque the following week and requested an interview to demonstrate the prayers to the panel of Mullahs. They all gathered around me and watched, probably wondering if I would get it right. My execution of all prayers was absolutely perfect, complete with the Saudi accent I had acquired from Rahman's coaching over the phone. Triumphantly, I left the Grand Mosque of Paris with my Certificate of Conversion, and proudly called Rahman to tell him of my accomplishment. He was delighted and amazed that I worked so fast. I sent him a copy of the certificate, and anxiously waited for the results of his second request to King Faisal for marital permission. Imagine, a modern day king deciding my marriage decision! It felt like something out of the Middle Ages, like Braveheart or something. And at the same time, deliciously significant. I could only suppose the purpose for this stepped up precaution about allowing foreigners into the fold was to stem the recent flood of Westerners brought on by Saudi's new found wealth.

A week later, all my efforts were rewarded when the phone rang in the middle of the night, waking me from my slumber. Rahman's voice sounded excited and I instantly knew we had succeeded!

"Patricia? Guess what!"

"We got it? Tell me we got it!"

"Yes we did. I hope you're happy."

"I am. And I hope you are happy."

"I am. But I hope you realize that this won't be as easy as you think. There will be more hurdles…"

"And I will jump them," I retorted with finality. I would not entertain doubt. I was convinced that this was my destiny and nothing would stop me.

Now that the trip was a reality, I was giddy, imagining what I would wear to impress my future relatives in Saudi Arabia upon my arrival. My decision took days and many shopping trips throughout Paris. This would be my first appearance, and it mattered immensely to me.

I decided on a beautiful cream suit with brown trim from my favorite designer at the time, Ted Lapidus, which I had saved up for. While his fashion house today is all but defunct, in the seventies his designs were all the rage. The suit had a slender skirt with a single back pleat and a soft silk blouse with a matching flowing scarf. Complete with off-white sling-back shoes and a matching handbag from Charles Jourdan, another extinct designer, I was ready to go. Looking back, I cringe at how superficially I handled the situation. I believed that I could handle any situation as long as I was dressed well. My designer suit and bag were my armor, and I would conquer the world. I didn't think to purchase a return ticket or even speak to Rahman about the length of my visit. I had no intention of failing. No Plan B.

I left my apartment in Paris that morning for the airport, like Alice in Wonderland, going "Through the Looking Glass" into an amazing new world, one I could not even imagine.

Chapter Four

Arrival

Gaining entry to Saudi Arabia in 1979 was near impossible. The only ways to obtain a visa was through being "invited" by a Saudi family or business entity, or through going on a *Hajj*, or pilgrimage to Mecca. Both had to be approved by the immigration authorities, and that took a few weeks and many questions. To avoid gossip, the Abbars decided that the best way to introduce me to the country would be if the Bin Zagrs, Inja's distinguished family, invited me. I would gain entry as a "guest" of the Bin Zagrs. In their culture this gave me more respectability as an unmarried Western woman arriving alone.

I followed their instructions to the letter, submitting to whatever creative solution they provided. I was to speak with no one on the airplane. But if asked, I was traveling to Jeddah to visit friends, Inja Bin Zagr and her sister Olfat, whom I knew from Wellesley. I used this "cover story" frequently. . On the flight, curious passengers did ask me what on earth I was doing on that airplane, alone, traveling to Jeddah. It was irresistible to be the center of such fascination. My enthusiasm must have suggested there was more to the story, and I did sometimes offer more information than I should have. I deviated from the Abbars' script, but only a little bit. I felt like an insider and the attention was intoxicating. Our first-class section was primarily European expats, returning from holiday to their Saudi jobs. A few good souls, who had no idea how carefully the Abbars would be looking after me, seemed quite concerned for my safety and offered me advice about not getting into cars with anyone, and never walking on the street. A German woman, very perturbed, even gave me her phone number to call in case of an emergency. At the time, I couldn't understand why they were so concerned about me, a woman who fearlessly hitchhiked all over Long Island as a teen, but the flood of unbridled warnings should have made me think a little more deeply about my decision.

Although the food was elegant and tasty on Saudi Airlines, it didn't quite make up for the fact that no alcohol was served. No matter, I was more concerned about my hair and make up than my stomach. As the end of the flight approached, I peered out the window often for the view, but there was only a vast amount of rippling emptiness. No color, no angles, and seemingly nothing living below. The desert indeed looked deserted. But after a six-hour flight and my intended again within reach, I could hardly contain myself.

We touched down. As I gathered my carry-ons and prepared to exit, two stiff looking men wearing white robes and carrying walkie-talkies burst into the plane, spoke quietly to the stewardess, then headed towards me without introduction or Western niceties. I barely had a chance to calculate who they were and why they were coming for me. Before I could protest, they lifted me up from my seat and out the door of the plane. But somehow I knew these were Rahman's men. My new acquaintances in first class all gaped in horror. The kind German woman gasped. It appeared like I was being arrested and I felt guilty I'd been so misleading to all these nice people who only wanted me to be safe.

Balancing on sky-high heels, I slowly eased down the staircase with my escorts front and back. Instead of being terrified, like any normal woman would, I buzzed with joyful anticipation, eagerly awaiting my first look at Jeddah. Only the blinding brilliance of the blazing Saudi afternoon sun met my eyes and face. Then came a burst of hot air, which I first thought was exhaust coming from the airplane engines. It was the heat of Saudi Arabia, in the month of May, on a typical sunny afternoon at 100+ degrees. To say the heat was shocking is a gross understatement. *How can anything survive here?* I rethought my crisp Ted Lapidus suit, which was rapidly starting to wilt. My lovely silky scarf, which was meant to float in the breeze, clung to my neck, instantly wet in the thick, dense humidity.

As I stepped onto the tarmac, unsure about where to go next, two limousines approached, flanked by four additional security vehicles, complete with sirens and flashing lights. A small army of white robed men circled me. Then from the midst of these men emerged my Rahman, also dressed in white robes with an ethereal white head gear on, looking like some kind of a vision, my guru angel.

He made his way towards me, wearing a cold, hard, and very serious expression that chilled me to the bone. I attempted to greet him but was instantly rebuked. "Stop!" he hissed. I don't remember ever feeling so afraid of him. Rahman wordlessly gestured for me to get into one of the limousines, and within seconds, I dove out of the heat and into the cool backseat of a limo, alone. The driver up front greeted me in broken English, welcoming me to Jeddah and telling me to sit back and relax. *As if that's possible.* Nothing was as I had expected. Disappointment and confusion welled up inside of me but all I could do at this point was obey orders. The car sped on to the airport terminal where I was told to get out and give Rahman my passport. He exited the other limo and walked towards me, without so much as a warm smile or hello. He stood there, three feet away, although it felt like ten miles. No embrace, no "I missed you," and no "Welcome to my country." I stretched my petite arm as far as possible to bridge the enormous gap separating us, passport booklet in hand. I remained stiff as a broomstick, now silent, much too afraid to move or look up at him. I felt him snatch my passport and walk away. I later learned that these robed men at the airport were, in fact, Rahman's cousins, friends, employees and partners, all security for me, a nobody young American, soon to be the wife of a wealthy Saudi. Not only were they in place to dissuade wandering eyes by other Saudi men, they were also there to avoid possible arrest or detention of me by local police or guards at the airport.

Moving through security, my passport was carefully looked over, the customs officer scrolling through the different visas, before stamping the book and handing it back to Rahman. As if I were property. The officer cracked a few jokes in Arabic with the crowd of men standing around me, none of which I could understand. But I suppose the jokes weren't for me anyhow.

We proceeded slowly to the tiny, primitive outdoor airport terminal of Jeddah. I cannot imagine how that looked to bystanders: a young Western woman dressed for a Paris runway, surrounded by a dozen men in immaculate white robes, passing through a crowded scene, complete with beggars lying on the ground, peddlers in rags shouting in Arabic, and turbaned men milling about using wrapped cotton fabric to hold their scant belongings together. Invalids hobbled along on broken pieces of wood for makeshift crutches, while homeless bleating goats surveyed trash piles for anything edible. As I took in this unimaginable poverty, I had flashbacks to scenes from the movie *Ben Hur*, when the hero is looking for his mother and sister in the leper colony. I finally sobered up and realized that I was in a very distant place, where nothing could be assumed or taken for granted. I was speechless. *I had asked for this.*

Once through the terminal, I was pushed into yet another limousine. I was wholly relieved when my limo door opened and Rahman finally joined me.

"Where are we going now?" I gasped, hardly able to get out the words. I was so happy to see him, but clearly shaken.

"To my parents' house." Rahman was very short with me and would not entertain a conversation. Instead he turned away and stared at the window. As we sat there in silence, I desperately wondered what was going on in his mind. Had I done something wrong? Was he angry at me? Did he regret my visit? In hindsight, I suspect he was confronted for the first time with the reality of marrying an American and bringing her to this country. And here I was, trapped in this limo, not able to see anything outside through the darkly tinted windows, painfully alone with someone who felt like a stranger. *Oh my god, what have I gotten myself into? This is insane.*

When we arrived at the tall gates of the Abbar residence, the limo honked, and yet another white robed man wearing a skullcap came running out of the gatehouse to manually open up so we could pass through. I wondered if the cost of electricity to open the gates manually was more than a gatekeeper's manpower. In the distance, I saw another large group of men, whom I later learned were the gardeners, cooks, drivers, and additional gatekeepers, sitting to the right side of the driveway. They were arranged in a semi-circle on a large oriental rug spread out on the bare ground, all watching a small television which was propped up on a metal folding chair and plugged into a wire hanging from an electrical pole in the road. I wondered if anyone was ever electrocuted by these homemade connections. *Do they even have electricians here? Doesn't look like it.* Our car made its way up the long driveway, lit by strings of small bulbs draped from tree to tree, toward an exceedingly imposing marble house. The car stopped to let us out in front, and two more men appeared, quickly opening both back doors for us to exit the car, both avoiding eye contact with us and our entourage.

Moving away from the limo, I looked over the dimly lit grounds. Those little flickering bulbs revealed a strange world where the absence of any green—trees, grass or otherwise—was filled by everpresent dust, both in the air and on the ground. We were indeed in a desert country.

More men materialized around us, all wearing the same white robes, some with flowing headgear, some with skullcaps, and I had no way of understanding who was who. I guessed that the ones with immaculately white, starched robes might be the family, and the ones with slightly wrinkled, dusty robes were the servants. And for the most part, I was correct. In this unfamiliar place, I had absolutely nothing else to go by. I asked Rahman to tell me whom to greet and whom to nod to. He tersely instructed me to simply nod to everyone, keeping my eyes down. No speaking. Just follow him into the house.

The tall double doors to the main salon were swiftly opened by two more men, like medieval times, and I was greeted by a burst of cold air, which I gratefully acknowledged. Inside was a very spacious, ornate room decorated with pastel colors and gold leaf, French styled furniture and plush Chinese rugs. A few dozen family members lounged on fancy Louis XV upholstered settees lining the perimeter of the room. All were awaiting my arrival. Rahman took me around the room and introduced me. One after the next, I hesitantly greeted each person, struggling to remember the rule that I was not supposed to touch or kiss anyone unless it was a woman and she had to make the first move.

Of course, I kissed and hugged Inja, relieved that I absolutely knew how to behave with her, and then, to my surprise, I was grabbed and kissed heartily by Rahman's paternal, wheelchair-bound grandmother, Sitti, or Grandma, Fardoz. She uttered something very bold and comical to the crowd as she embraced me. When they all finished laughing, I was relieved to hear that she said I was very beautiful and seemed perfect for her grandson. *Well, that's good. Someone likes me…* I was slowly learning that although they all blended in like a sea of long garments and dark hair, each member of this unique family had a very distinct personality. This was my first "on the job" lesson. Sitti Fardoz, born in Afghanistan, was known to be an outspoken joker, blunt and quick with her comments. She was the oldest in the family and had to please no one. This was in stark contrast to the rest of the family, who conversed in little more than whispers. I later learned that "Sitti" didn't need the wheelchair but insisted on being pushed around by her many servants. It indicated her superior position in their culture, showing that she didn't have to touch the ground with her feet or exert herself in any way. Nothing fazed her, she had seen more of the world than any of us, and was always ready to offer an opinion. Inja was known to be the quiet brooding type, with little to say, but she stared at everyone with those big dark eyes, all seeing and all knowing. When she was angry or disapproving, those eyes would merely narrow, and you knew you were in trouble. Sitti Shafiga, a tiny doll-like auntie who wasn't a grandmother at all, but was called that out of respect for her advanced age, sweetly questioned me in Arabic.

"Shufti Jiddah hilwa?"

A smiling teenager by her side translated, "Do you find Jeddah beautiful?"

I nodded my head several times, praying that, over here, the gesture meant "yes." By her joyful expression, I knew my answer was understood. *Success!*

Rahman had many "aunties," I realized, each taking their turn to handle and inspect me as I made my way down the greeting line, some smiling and accepting, others closed and suspicious.

After being passed around the large salon, I was placed into a chair next to a young woman who appeared about my same age—somewhere in her twenties. This was Rahman's cousin, Noura. Not having heard about her before this meeting, I was quite relieved to learn that Noura was part of the Bin Zagr family, and would be my confidante and guide during my visit to Saudi. She, like Rahman, had attended boarding schools in England, and spoke the same Queen's English as my beloved–a welcome surprise!

"Patricia, how are you holding up? Shocked?" Noura asked me quietly when I had settled down next to her.

"I'm not sure. The airport was crazy. Rahman is behaving so oddly. I don't know what to think."

"Don't worry, just sit there and look pretty. You don't have to say a word. They don't expect a blushing bride to speak. You're supposed to be modest." She laughed, "Your suit is gorgeous, by the way."

"Thank you! Whew! It certainly is hot here in Jeddah." I started to untie my scarf, glad to get it off my neck. "You won't mind if I remove the scarf, will you? At least I was able to make my grand entrance with my outfit intact!"

We both broke into laughter and I felt better. *A Western sense of humor.*

Noura explained to me that this is what the family does almost every afternoon after lunch—sit together, talking and joking, drinking tea and smoking some sort of hookah water pipe, until it is time for the men to go back to work in the evening.

"Smile, Patricia. Nod your head. You're doing great." Shyness and reluctance to speak was expected with a bride-to-be, so there was no pressure on me to make small talk. I just sat there in comfort while Noura, one by one, explained to me who each person was, their name, and relation to Rahman. I was so thankful for her presence because, nervous as I was, I had already forgotten everyone and everything.

I noticed that Rahman had disappeared, and mentioned that to Noura. "Why did he just leave me here?"

"He's probably outside having a mini breakdown, Patricia! Seeing you here juxtaposed with his family, in this setting, is a lot to take in." I felt both puzzled and disappointed. Months later, he would sheepishly confess that my arrival was such an unusual social situation that he didn't quite know how to act or what to say. So I was left there to fend for myself, with Noura by my side. I would never have expected that from him, knowing Western-style, life-of-the-party Rahman, but then again, nothing was as I had hoped.

Thoroughly bewildered, the best I could do was sink deeper into my ample armchair and watch the family interact. Noura informed me that my arrival was the event of the month in Jeddah, and that some friends and family had delayed their summer departures just to meet me.

"Patricia, by next month, you and I and a few of the older members of the family will be the only ones left in town," she announced with a laugh.

"Why aren't you leaving?" The thought of Noura leaving town jolted me to attention.

"It's a long story – for another time. In the meantime, I am so glad that you'll be staying with me at the Bin Zagr's house. *Beit Bin Zagr*, as it's called. You must, to avoid gossip. We would never want the community to think that you were here for Rahman's, um…amusement!"

"I understand. And obviously, I am not! Where is *Beit Bin Zagr*? Far from here?"

"Just down the Medina Road." Not much help. I wondered how often I would even see Rahman, and who was living in this house with his parents. Would we be able to go somewhere in a car together? It dawned on me that I had been sadly mistaken, imagining my trip to Jeddah from a Western perspective. A big part of why I had come to Jeddah was to be with Rahman, and being with him might not be possible! I wondered if and when I would be able to give him a real kiss, not one of those sexless pecks that everyone gives. *When would I ever get to be alone with him?* I feared the answer was a resounding "never," as long as I remained in Jeddah as a single woman.

Noura continued to speak, but, as comforting as it was, I remained completely lost in my thoughts. She didn't look at all like Rahman. In fact, she didn't look at all like what I expected an Arab to look like. Noura had chin length, medium brown wavy hair, a flat face, and in no way resembled that dark haired, doe-eyed Arabic ideal. She, like the other women in the room, wore a prairie-style dress, long to the floor. She could have been a Pennsylvania Dutch farmer's wife, or an 1800's Mormon school teacher.

How does it feel for her to be living there in Jeddah after having spent her formative years in England?

I was sure there would be enough time to ask her questions, especially now that I started realizing the limits on outings and the fact that I'd be parked in the house most of the time. All this new information was overwhelming, but at least I had a friend. I turned my attention back to what she was saying and to the room at large.

"…and maybe we can have a nice Friday outing at the beach with the entire family. Your arrival is a good excuse for everyone to spend a day on the Red Sea. I will ask Mama Inja if we can plan that for next week."

"Where is Rahman? He still hasn't returned," I asked abruptly as I looked around. I wasn't listening to her. I just couldn't. "… and where is Amm Abdullah?" I was surprised to notice that while we were talking, in fact, all the men had left the room.

"Oh, they probably went back to the office or maybe they are sitting in the *bashka*."

"What's a bashka?"

"It's the large gazebo in the garden where the men gather and talk politics at night."

Rahman went out to socialize without coming back here to speak to me? He just whisked me off the airplane and dumped me here in this room with Noura to babysit me?

I was too embarrassed to let Noura know what I was thinking. *What a fool I am!* I felt humiliated but tried to keep my cool. "When will he return from the office?"

"Who knows? He goes out every evening after work, to different functions, receptions, or friends' houses. All the men do."

My heart sank. I'd been sitting here, wishfully imagining Rahman close by, freaking out because I was in Jeddah. Instead, he had callously picked up and gone to the office, without a single word to me. To make matters even worse, he was planning on going out to some function with his friends, completely indifferent to the fact that I had just arrived from halfway around the world. *He left me to figure this all out by myself!* That thought was truly alarming, and for a moment, I felt tears well up. But I regained control, reminding myself that I was in the midst of strangers who might think I was a mental case if I started to cry. The more I thought about it, the angrier I became. And anger felt better than sadness, so I resolved to put all thoughts of Rahman out of my mind for the rest of the evening. I had to, for my own sanity.

Our inspection of the group was cut short again by what seemed to be a servant appearing at the doorway and announcing that dinner was served. How exciting! My first meal in Saudi Arabia. I had heard many stories, from Rahman and others, about how the Arabs are such great hosts and fill the table with goodies, more than could ever be consumed by the guests.

As everyone filtered out of the salon, they lined up to enter the powder room adjoining the dining room. When I finally got closer, I found that instead of the usual small bathroom with one toilet and a sink, this was more like a huge public lavatory, with four sinks lined up in a row. Four by four, all members of the family took their turn, washing their hands, arms, faces and heads before eating. There was almost a kind of ceremony to the act.

A very long table, draped in damask cloth, extended the length of the large dining room. It was flanked by two dozen silk upholstered chairs and fully laid out with bone china, sterling silver, crystal glasses and matching napkins. It looked like a big holiday spread, with overflowing platters lining the center of the table. There were lamb, chicken, vegetable, and fish dishes, and platters brimming with rice. A handful of maids moved up and down the room, silently filling up crystal glasses with water. Noura motioned for me to sit next to her.

I couldn't help but wonder where Rahman was at that point, and whether he would reappear that evening. So much for my plan to expunge him from my thoughts. Sure enough, he showed up minutes later, emerging from behind a few of the guests, smiling broadly. I was shocked at how guiltless he appeared, grinning like everything was just fine. He knew this evening was strange for me–did he just not care? Did he want me to hate it here? Or did he enjoy seeing me out of my element? When he approached, he simply nodded to me and asked if I was getting along with everyone, and whether Noura was doing a good job as my guide. He had her jumping through hoops, too.

I curtly replied, "Yes, everything is great, and everyone has been friendly and nice to me!" I had little else to say. I was furious and certainly not going to give him the satisfaction of knowing that I was, as he probably had hoped, completely overwhelmed. I felt betrayed, and oddly competitive. What could I say? *"I have been sitting in a corner with your cousin, a perfect stranger, all evening, staring at a group of more strangers speaking a foreign language? How dare you leave me like this?"* I instead said nothing.

He took the empty seat next to me, and served himself from the platter in front of him. He was careful not to brush against me, or even glance in my direction. He might as well have been sitting all the way across the room. I stared in wonder as everyone around me, as if on command, started grabbing the platters to serve themselves dinner. I supposed they had been waiting for Rahman. Swiftly and smoothly, every person filled their plate. Within minutes, the whole table was deeply involved in eating their meal. There were some humorous comments, a few words exchanged here or there, but mainly, the long table of people was eating with lightning speed and very little conversation.

I quietly portioned my plate with what looked like a chopped tomato salad and a small slice of lamb, then began to eat slowly.

An eruption of laughter came next following a quick but playful jab from one of the old ladies. Noura translated, "No wonder you're so thin, you eat like a bird!" They were all observing me carefully. Surprising, given they were all chin-deep in towering plates of food. Raised to be a good guest, I feigned hunger. This was no time to sulk. I dug into the food on my plate with a newfound enthusiasm, pushing aside my tumultuous emotions, but within minutes of my starting to eat, the guests were already leaving the table.

"Where are they going?" I whispered to Noura.

"They've finished eating and are going home now. It's over."

The abruptness of their departure was fairly shocking to me, in fact, truth be told, that is one thing that I never did get used to in Jeddah - the speed with which food was consumed before the crowd would move on to another activity. This was in stark contrast to the way my Italian relatives behaved at dinner. We would sit at the table for hours, making small talk, telling stories and nibbling at the meal. Lingering was part of the fun and almost required.

I had barely been able to digest the dinner party, and suddenly it was over. Rahman, too, got up, went over to the sinks in the other room and washed his hands and face again, signaling that he had completed his meal. He and the others left Noura and me sitting at the table, and just as quickly as I had been ushered in, my time was up. We had to get up and go.

The servants appeared from the kitchen, presumably to clear the dishes. However, instead, they sat down in the seats, picked up the used silverware, and started to fill the plates for themselves. *Oh my goodness. They're eating the leftovers just like that! No fuss. No bother, using the same plates and grabbing any cutlery on the table, or simply using their fingers.* It was a free for all. I had never seen anything like this. All I could do was stare before Noura whisked me out of the dining room for the night.

It seemed that most of the guests had already left by the time we arrived in the hallway, so we said our goodbyes and to my chagrin, I realized that Rahman, as well, had left. I guessed he didn't know how to relate to me in that situation, late at night, or how to say goodbye. So he bolted. Nice. *What a coward!* Remaining were Rahman's mother, who kissed me and told Noura to take good care of me at *Beit Bin Zagr*, and a few miscellaneous aunts and cousins, all female. Noura, a bunch of spinsters, and I were shoved into the silver Cadillac waiting by the front door. Before I knew it, the driver was taking us down that driveway again, and out to the open road. It must have been at least one o'clock in the morning by that time yet I was wide awake. I realized that Noura, too, was awake.

"Do you usually stay up this late?" I asked.

"Yes, this isn't considered late for Jeddah. Dinner is always at about midnight, and often, parties will keep going until dawn. As you might have noticed, it's very hot here in the daytime, so nighttime is much more pleasant. We do as much as we can during the darkness hours."

As our car moved silently down the street, I observed house after house with those same never-ending high walls and closed gates. Beyond were the same twinkling lights strung up, gatekeepers sitting by watching TV, and it appeared that everyone was indeed up and awake. The only thing missing was sunlight. I noticed that the main road we traveled on was paved, but all the perpendicular smaller roads which crisscrossed to the right and left were generally gravel or dirt.

There were walls and more walls, gates, and not much else. "I wish I could see more!" I complained.

"When you own a piece of land, you must construct walls around it and close it off for privacy. We Saudis seldom appear out in the open. As you can see, we are a very private society. We keep to ourselves, and even marry within a limited group of interrelated relationships. It's been like that for centuries."

"Why are there walls around empty plots?" I pointed to the large section of land we were passing. " What are they hiding in there?"

Noura chuckled. "Patricia, it's a mindset. Your walls around your land are the only thing that confirms ownership, and you protect it. Most of this land has been owned by families for generations, without land deeds or other official papers. This country has nomadic roots, never forget. Empty, open land could easily be settled by others, and good luck getting them off. Then, of course, there's the King. This is a kingdom and the King owns all unclaimed land. And to be honest, the King can claim anything he wants to, even if it's owned. Knowing that, now, don't the high walls make more sense?"

I thought about it for a moment, but before I could really grasp the implications of a kingdom in which the king is a sovereign ruler with no bounds, the car stopped in front of yet another closed gate and honked. We had arrived at *Beit Bin Zagr*!

My heart beat faster as the commanding storybook gates, impossibly thick slabs of solid mahogany, lashed together with iron straps and rivets, swung open, pushed and pulled by two more white-robed men wearing skull caps. Inside the car ambled past the groups of still-awake men sitting watching TV in the dust, then between rows of palm trees and desert plants before stopping at another marble building with wide steps leading to a huge arched front door.

"Noura, why do these homes all look alike?"

Noura seemed exasperated with my questions. She sighed, "As a trained architect, I hate that everything looks the same, but there's not much I can do to change things? Most large family homes were built years ago by Mohammad Bin Laden. He had his own style of building, and hence, all houses were built on that same plan. No one ever objected because it works for our society, with its extended families and limited resources. Clay, marble, bricks, wood? They're hard to come by here. We barely have water, let alone the infrastructure to import all of those materials fast enough. At least the water situation is improved with the new plant, and hopefully the ports we need will be developed soon. One learns to turn a blind eye to flaws in Saudi. I advise you to do the same."

My mind wandered to the stories I had heard in Paris about old man Bin Laden. It all made sense.

As Noura and I turned to approach the front door, invisible hands from the inside threw the door open for us to enter. *Wow, I don't even have to open a door for myself.* I contemplated what else I wouldn't have to do for myself when, all of a sudden, I remembered my suitcases! I had forgotten to claim them at the airport! I told Noura, and she laughed.

"Oh Patricia, you don't have to worry about things like that. I am sure the servants took your claim tickets from you at the airport when you arrived and retrieved all your baggage. Every suitcase had to be completely searched by customs. Since it takes hours, someone waited for that to be accomplished. I am sure they delivered them to the house. The servants know what everyone is doing and what their responsibilities are. You'll see, the suitcases will be sitting in your bedroom safe and sound."

"Searched?" was all I could muster up, feeling a little faint.

"Yes, searched. Every single item in your suitcase will be lifted out, handled, inspected, opened, shaken, unfolded and read."

"Even my underwear?" I joked, but secretly horrified at the idea.

"Especially that. That's probably what keeps the inspector's morale up! They are looking for anything unholy, forbidden - any drugs, porn, or liquor. They sometimes take something like a bikini or really sexy underwear, I suspect, to bring it home and give to their wives or mistresses." She winked at me, "They remove magazines, paperback books, anything that you might have in your suitcase, because all that is strictly forbidden in Saudi Arabia."

And, indeed, Noura was right again. When I was shown to my room, there on the luggage stands were all my suitcases, and when I opened them up, everything was in complete disarray. My carefully folded clothing looked like a hurricane had ripped it apart. A few of my bras were missing, a box containing body cream was gone, presumably because there was an illustration of naked legs on the front of the box, and the music cassettes with great disco club music were missing entirely, leaving behind their plastic cocoons.

Noura popped her head in the door of my bedroom and told me the maid would come up in a minute to take my wrinkled clothing to be ironed. This was so normal to them—they already knew the clothes would be wrinkled. They would return everything early in the morning so I could get dressed.

I slipped into my pajamas, crawled into bed, and fell asleep while recounting my first few hours in Jeddah with Rahman's vast family, and imagining those white-robed inspectors at the airport, returning home this evening with NYC club cassettes, La Perla bras, and French perfumed body lotion.

***

A knock on the door awoke me the next morning.

Barely awake, I shouted, "Come in," without even asking who it was.

I had been sleeping in a huge carved walnut bed. A bed fit for a king! Curious to take a look at everything in the daylight, I glanced around the large room, furnished, as expected, in a heavy Louis XV style. Taking it all in as fast as I could, I noticed the drapes blacked out most of the sunlight, so I had no idea of how early or late it might be. The large wooden door swung open, and there stood Noura, framed by beams of fluorescent light streaming in from the hallway.

"Good morning, Patricia!" she chirped with a smile, "You have a full schedule today, so it's best that you get up now and get dressed. Mama Inja would like to take you for a car tour of Jeddah."

Anxious to see Jeddah, I jumped up and made a beeline for the ensuite bathroom. I turned on the faucet, and noticed that the water pressure was practically nil. Worse, the water, itself, had a peculiar odor. I guess I didn't notice last night.

"Noura, is it okay for me to brush my teeth with this water?" I asked, wondering if Jeddah was like Mexico, where even brushing your teeth with the tap water could be deadly.

"No problem, you can brush, but don't drink because it tastes terrible. It's clean desalinated water from the new desalination plant. Don't forget, this is a desert!"

"How could I forget? I can barely get the smell out of my nose."

Noura chuckled, "Before the desalination plant, water was very scarce and even more expensive than it is now."

Noura sat in my bedroom, on the pastel silk-upholstered loveseat against the opposite wall, while I washed up. The bathroom was quite sumptuous, more American than European style. I stepped into the large stall shower, and stood there while the water trickled gently out of the showerhead. It was barely enough to wet my hair down, but I patiently waited until I was able to apply shampoo. I stared at the soft pink tiles, which went all the way up to the ceiling. The walls must have been 11 feet high, useful to keep the rooms cool, I guessed.

Less than satisfactory shower complete, I stepped out of the bathroom, wrapped in a thick plush towel, again, American style, and onto the soft pink and green Chinese rug in the bedroom. Old World opulence seemed to be the order of the day in this house. Another knock at the door proved that I was absolutely correct.

"She's coming to ask you what you want for breakfast," Noura explained, as she opened the door to reveal a young woman dressed all in white. Presumably, she was a housemaid. I shrugged. Noura smiled and said something to the young girl, who skittered off.

In came another house servant dressed modestly in a long loose tunic, her arms covered with dozens of thin stacked gold bangle bracelets and her earlobes adorned with four gold hoop earrings each. On her feet were leather house slippers, which she removed as she entered the room. The bottoms of her feet were dyed rust-red with what I assumed was henna. Balanced on her head was a tray with a glass of freshly squeezed orange juice, and a small bowl filled with fruits. Amazed, I nodded. I was fine with the fruit and juice. She swiftly placed it on the table in the corner and bowed as she backed out of the room, slipping into her footwear as she exited.

"Patricia, don't be shy. No one cares what you eat or drink. There's plenty, and they just want to make you happy. So speak up if you want something in particular."

"Ok, I will. But this'll do for me. I usually don't eat breakfast anyway." I sipped the orange juice, which was heavenly. "How many servants do you have in this house?"

Noura laughed. "That's a good question. Who knows? There are so many servants that I lost count. We each have a personal servant, but since many of the family members who live here in the house are currently abroad, their servants stay waiting for their return. So that adds up to about twenty."

"Twenty?"

"And then," she continued, "there are the old slaves, who were freed by royal decree in 1964 when slavery was abolished. They choose to remain here because they've lived their entire lives at this house and don't really have any place else to go. They all pitch in with the work. Some do less than others, some hardly get paid at all, but they can sleep in a bed and eat food, and they're welcomed."

1964. Slaves, less than twenty years ago.

I pointed to the door. "Where did she come from?"

"Ethiopia."

While I nibbled away at breakfast, still too shell-shocked to work up a full appetite, Noura explained that the nationalities of the servants were actually a complicated cultural matter in Jeddah. Ethiopian women were most popular to hire as housemaids because they spoke Arabic, were Muslims, and understood and obeyed the strict customs. For butlers and gardeners, Egyptian and Sudanese men were the pick. Filipino men and women were becoming more common as houseworkers because of their meticulous attention to detail and cleanliness as well as their willingness to work on Friday, the Muslim sabbath. The language barrier was, at first, a problem, but the Filipinos were quick to learn basic Arabic. Drivers were the exception to all the rules, and several were a necessity in any large household. Because women were absolutely forbidden to drive, every woman of means had her own driver. There was always a need for a "house" driver, one who could pick up groceries at the market or drop off the children at school. Men of means also had their personal driver, not so much for their collection of Ferraris, but to chauffeur them around on official business in the limo. All traffic signage was in Arabic, so speaking and reading the language became a safety issue. Yemeni men were the preferred nationality for drivers. They had proven themselves to be particularly skilled behind the wheel, so much so that the Saudi government also hired them as pilots. In those days, as crazy as it seems, no Saudi national would ever take a position of menial labor; even the poorest of families could afford at least one servant.

"Mama Inja wants to take you around in her car this morning for a tour of Jeddah. I'll join you. This should be lots of fun."

As I grabbed for my purse, Noura stifled a laugh and said, "You won't be needing that. No need for ID, no need for driver's license, no need for money. Why bother bringing a purse when you're completely taken care of?"

"Habit," I answered. I reluctantly left my purse on the table in my bedroom.

The silver Cadillac was out front with the engine idling. Mama Inja sat in the back seat, wearing a black silk robe with a black chiffon scarf tied around her head and neck. She motioned to us to get in next to her. I had never seen her like this—all wrapped up in black. As I crawled over to my place in the back of the car, I caught a whiff of strange perfume. It had a musky odor, and I made a mental note to inquire about it later. I was reminded of that mysterious fragrance that Rahman was wearing the night we met. For now, I asked about the black robes which Mama Inja was wearing, so different from the pastel prairie dresses all the women had donned the night before.

"What is this called?" I said, motioning to Mama Inja's headscarf. "Do all women have to wear it? Is it because we're going out?" Again, Noura translated.

"Yes. The headgear is called *tarha* and women in Jeddah wear this whenever we leave the house. The religion demands that females over the age of ten cover their head in public, particularly their hair. The *tarha* is wrapped over the head and around the neck, where everything is tucked in and secured tightly to ensure it won't slip off. Ultra-religious women wear this at all times, even at home in front of the servants, and only remove it when they go to bed. You will see some of the older women at Beit Bin Zagr wearing the *tarha* at lunch with the family. This is common practice in the Hejaz region of Saudi, but other provinces and of course, other Muslim countries, behave very differently."

"What does Hejaz mean?" I was very curious.

"Hejaz is the western part of Saudi Arabia, on the Red Sea. We have our own customs, and in fact our own dialect and accent. We are influenced here by Egyptian culture due to its close proximity. Have you seen those women who look like they are actually wearing black armor over their faces, with a slit for their eyes? That's how the women from the Gulf Coast, or Eastern region of the peninsula, dress."

"Yes, I saw some of those types standing outside Harrods in London. I wondered where they were from! It looked strange to me."

"Well, Patricia, every Muslim country has its own particular gear, both for men and for women. I find it very interesting." With that, Noura whipped her *tarha* out of a large satchel and wound it around her head and neck to demonstrate. Then she pulled out a cloak-like black silk garment and placed it over her shoulders.

"This is the *abaya*," she said. "We use this to cover our clothing, so we can wear whatever styles we want underneath. If it's at all...immodest, that's okay, because it's covered by the *abaya*. Most women remove the abaya the moment they step inside the front door. They can't wait to show off their beautiful outfits."

"Do I need to wear one?" I asked.

Both hesitated, clearly stumped, then Noura offered, "No, Patricia, for now you can walk around with your Western clothing and your head uncovered. You're a visiting American. Different rules apply. But please, no mini-skirts." Her answer was a relief to all of us. Mama Inja probably never imagined having this conversation with her son's fiancée. I had a hunch I would be uncomfortable with my head wrapped in a black scarf and my body covered with a black silk cloak. *Maybe I can negotiate my way out of ever having to wear one. It's over 100 degrees out! Who wants to be wrapped in black?*

The car started down the driveway, daylight revealing the ubiquitous layer of fine dust I had noticed last evening. It gave the entire world a grayish cast. I gazed out the window at the date palms and shrubs, all dusty, and had the urge to take a strong hose to it all. I wondered when it had last rained. I asked the question.

"Rain? Not for a long time. Maybe once last year, and only for a few minutes."

The car passed wall after wall, driveway after driveway, gate after gate, all metal, stucco, and brick. Every so often I would peer down the dirt side streets and catch sight of a wandering herd of grazing goats, tended by what appeared to be a female, all wrapped up in a light colored cotton. *Shepherdess? In the streets of Jeddah? Was it possible?* There were no sidewalks and few pedestrians. The monotony was broken occasionally by a small pack of wild dogs or a ragged man pulling a primitive cart full of junk. There was definitely more activity last night when I arrived. I was glad to be passing by inside the cool, luxurious car; I remembered the unbearable heat of the day.

The residential neighborhood morphed into a more commercial area, with telltale Arabic signs appearing across the fronts of small white buildings. I had no clue what any of it meant. The shops themselves were little more than a wide doorway, a sign, and one room; some resembled single car garages with metal doors, the kind that you roll up by hand. There wasn't much merchandise to be seen.

"What is the name of this road?" I wanted to know.

"Medina Road. It's an ancient road that goes to the city of Medina. The other main road is called Mecca Road, and that is the ancient road to Mecca. As long as you know these two roads, you can't get lost in Jeddah." I wasn't sure about that, so I made a mental note to look at a map later and see exactly where Medina and Mecca began and ended.

"Seems simple enough," I lied. As I peered out the window, we approached another huge set of gates opening to a large house with a red tile roof set back off the road. "What's this?"

"That house belongs to Abdulaziz Suleiman. He is a very important Saudi. His house sits right next to the King's palace, which is coming up next. Look over to the left!"

We drove past the largest set of gates I have ever seen. Set even further back from the road was a gigantic white house with a distinctive green tile roof. *The King of Saudi Arabia's palace. Wow. Amazing.* "Does King Faisal really live here?" I asked.

"When he's in Jeddah, yes, but he has palaces all over the Kingdom. If you look toward the back of the property, you'll see several other smaller houses. Those are the homes of all his wives. You know that Saudi royalty have many wives and marry their second cousins."

"Tell me about this multiple wife custom," I was dying to know.

"Saudis practice the Islamic religion in its most fundamental sense. The Koran clearly states that a man is allowed four wives. He must treat them all equally, spending equal amounts of time and money on each one. In Saudi, most members of the Royal family do practice this custom, mainly to gain power for their branch of the family. And it ensures that all women will, indeed, have a husband, a chance to have their own children and be provided for, as well as protected. Not a bad deal, if you subscribe to their way of thinking."

"Aren't those women jealous of each other?" I was incredulous. "I always knew that Muslims could marry several women, but I never imagined them living next door to each other…Do they see each other? Do they talk about him when he's not there? Do they treat each other like friends?"

Noura shrugged and blandly responded, "I never really thought about that. I'm so used to the idea. I can only imagine they're content to be married and have their own children, servants, house and luxuries. They get several nights "off" each week. Some of them might have cousins who are married to the same man, but how can you be jealous of a cousin who you grew up with? Your childhood friend? The husbands usually adhere to strict schedules for when to visit each one of his wives. Princesses can be quite social with their free time. Mama Inja has several princess friends who all seem happy. All in all, it isn't a bad life, especially because that's what they are used to." Seeing my eyes growing wider and wider, Noura protested, "Wait a minute! Don't you have that same custom in the States? I believe your Mormons practice polygamy."

"Yeah. But I've never seen a Mormon in New York. Is anyone in the Abbar family married to multiple women?"

Noura looked mildly offended at my suggestion, "No! We don't do that. In fact, most merchant families are like us. We don't feel comfortable with multiple marriages. It's more of a royal family thing, or something that the really traditional families practice. Bedouins, the tribal nomads out in the desert, always take multiple wives."

We were now coming into what looked more like the city and Mama Inja, who had been silent so far, motioned for me to look out the window. The buildings, still white, were more closely spaced and there were even a few high-rise office buildings. The street widened, and although it was paved, thick dust accumulated on both sides. I peered into the small shop windows, searching for their wares. Anything. A dress? Some shoes? What were they selling? Because all the signage was only in Arabic, I had no clue. Everything looks the same. Noura told me how scarce building materials are. I should have expected this. I suppose I'm spoiled…

I'm not sure what I had hoped for, maybe something more picturesque or charming or exotic. Some flowers in pots, flanking the doorways? A marble paved sidewalk? An Italian sign advertising imported clothing? An ornate Arabic lantern hanging over the doorway? Everywhere I looked was bare and uninspiring. Completely utilitarian. Surely there must be something more…

The streets were getting more crowded with pedestrians, all Arab men. Outside the car, an unending sea of long white robes and head-dresses streamed by. It became quite obvious that women did not walk in the streets downtown. Mama Inja indicated a gap on the left, where the modern buildings seemed to stop abruptly, as if they suddenly ran out of steam. As we passed that opening, I stole a glance and saw a completely different world: a dusty, winding dirt road lined with ancient, two-story buildings, all hand made of rough stucco. Dark brown filigreed window boxes protruded from the second floors, and at street level were merchant stands, their abundant and colorful wares spilling out onto the pavement. Here, Arab men, African men, and even the occasional group of colorfully dressed Ethiopian women wandered in and out searching for merchandise. This was the scene that I had expected to see in the first place.

"Through that passageway is the old souk, the ancient marketplace. That's what Jeddah looked like for centuries, before the oil boom," Noura confirmed. "You won't find anything to buy there, Patricia. It's mostly gold, food, spices and television sets. I doubt you have any need for that!"

"No fabulous old rugs or mother-of-pearl inlaid furniture?" I queried.

"Patricia, you've been watching too many Moroccan movies!" she said with a laugh. "Nothing like that exists here in Jeddah. We have no artisans."

And, indeed, as I struggled to take one last glance at the only indication of "real" Saudi culture and history, I realized that Noura was correct in her assessments. I would have no need to ever shop in that old souk, and my Western idea of "Arabia" was completely distorted.

Just as it was starting to dawn on me that there was nowhere to go in this town, we passed an interesting shop, this one back in the newer, boring section of town. It stood out from everything around it and it did, indeed, have the beautifully laid out window display, the potted plants flanking the carved front door and an ornate lantern hanging over the doorway, just as I had yearned for. There was even a golden sign in French (Beirut influence?) advertising jewelry next to the Arabic sign.

"Wow! What's that place over there?" I perked up and pointed.

Both Mama Inja and Noura giggled in delight that something pleased me on our tour. Actually, they looked relieved.

"Well, you have good taste, Patricia. You spotted the one highlight of Jeddah, Mouawad. They are reputed, these days, to sell the most beautiful jewelry in the world, and the most expensive. You'll probably make many visits to Mouawad when you live here. We all do. Perhaps we can pay a visit next week when we shop for an engagement gift for Mama Inja's niece."

The driver made a turn and it appeared we were heading in the direction of home. I was encouraged that the town offered something for me to do. I would gladly accompany the ladies to Mouawad next week. Not much to go on, but better than nothing. I convinced myself that I would soon find other amusing activities, and I settled back into my seat as the car made its way home to our compound.

Once back in my bedroom at Beit Bin Zagr, I sank into the thickly upholstered settee, kicked off my shoes, and thought about the last few hours, searching for some kind of high note to end the day on. Inja had certainly gone out of her way to give me a tour of Jeddah, and it wasn't her fault that there was nothing much to see or do. Without Noura to spice things up, it would have been pretty dismal, that's for sure.

My eyes wandered slowly everywhere in the room, comparing its cool, lush comforts to the barren, dusty desert I had encountered today. *This place is a land of contrasts. One minute you feel like a posh princess and the next, you feel like you've been dropped into a primitive outpost.* I pushed away the negative thoughts about what I had seen, and what it would mean for my future life.

A strange, repetitive sound interrupted my musings. Is that a…goat bleating? Or a lamb? I ran to the window and pulled back the layers of heavy curtains in an attempt to see what was out there. On the side of the house four small lambs were in hysterics, tied to stakes in the ground. *Why are they inside the walls and why are they tied up and making such a racket? How odd…*A knock at the door startled me. I jumped up and quickly opened the door. It was Noura. So overjoyed to see her, I gave her a big hug. Thank God for Noura.

"What's with the lambs tied up in the garden? I thought I was going crazy when I heard them bleating."

Noura took a quick peek out the window and responded, "Those are the lambs we'll slaughter in your honor. We're having a welcome party here tonight to celebrate your arrival. It's customary to slaughter lambs and roast them fresh. A delicacy, and a symbol of how happy we are to have you here as our guest. Mama Inja is sparing no expense this evening."

I had heard her correctly, but it seemed almost too Biblical to be real. Rather than press further, I was determined to accept Jeddah's unique customs as they were. At least for tonight. I took a breath and put it out of my mind – who was I to judge? And how would judging help me settle in? Noura had advised me only yesterday to 'turn a blind eye,' and it dawned on me that her strategy was a good survival technique. I made the decision to ignore how foreign everything felt, and focus on what any 'normal' girl would do before her engagement party: Open the closet door and pick out the perfect outfit with her newfound best friend, of course!

We spent a good hour talking, laughing, and trying on several of my favorite Parisian ensembles until we found the best one–a red silk jersey Givenchy evening gown designed in a Grecian style, complete with a thick, golden rope belt to cinch in my waist, golden Charles Jordan sandals, and a tiny but apparently useless golden shoulder bag to match. I felt like Diana, the Roman goddess of the hunt, complete with a little bag of gold quills.

"You'll be perfect, Patricia. Why don't I call one of the maids to come up here and help you to get ready? Do you need a manicure and a pedicure? How about a leg wax? Thahab, the new maid, arrived at the house last week, and I hear she used to work in the beauty salon at the Sheraton Hotel in Addis Ababa. Mama Inja brought her over to interview as your personal maid. Should we try her out for tonight? We can have a spa party!"

Noura disappeared to find Thahab. I quickly jumped into the shower to clean off the dust of the day. Somehow, the bad water pressure didn't bother me this time. And, as I shampooed my hair, I realized that the entire day, I hadn't given Rahman a thought. Not even one. Maybe that's why I was feeling so relaxed and happy—a red flag I chose to ignore. I wondered how he would behave that night, but even entertaining the thought made my head hurt. I put it out of my mind.

That evening I made a dramatic entry after most of the guests had arrived. The large salon provided sufficient space to entertain the crowd of sixty or so guests, mostly women. Everyone was dressed in their absolute finest, all showering me with warm smiles and kisses as they greeted me, one by one. Noura led me from group to group. The gracious women offered endless compliments, questions, and invitations. The degree of hospitality that I received that evening was hard to register until it occurred to me that this grand gathering was in fact, also a party for Inja. My soon-to-be mother-in-law had been a VIP in Jeddah her entire life, her oldest son was getting married, and the community was invited to meet me and honor her. A preamble to our wedding.

Later, I was introduced to a fabulous young woman my age, Tasnim, Natalie's sister-in-law. Tasnim's natural beauty was unrivaled in Jeddah. Long thick shiny black hair that was highly covetable, a slender figure, and the silkiest of olive complexions, complete with perfect features. Bright almond-shaped eyes, framed with impossibly long eyelashes, and a perfect nose, sat atop a full pout. And her perfectly white smile! Tasnim had a set of teeth that would make even a Manhattan dentist blush. The rumor was that her husband, Samir, had asked her to marry him after only one week–no wonder! After seeing her, I don't know how he waited that long! Tasnim's level of charm was off the charts, her voice confident yet subdued and humble. I wasn't often intimidated by other women but she was otherworldly and I felt a bit less refined in her presence. She was of Indian descent, raised in South Africa, and educated in London. Tasnim was affectionate and disarming, hugging me immediately, and not leaving my side for the remainder of the evening. Noura, too, was instantly smitten.

Tasnim gushed as if we were already kindred spirits, "I am so happy you arrived here before I left for London! I'll return in a month, and for the first time ever, I'm looking forward to coming back!" We became acquainted without effort, laughing and wandering around the party together. Tasnim helped Noura with the excessive amounts of introductions, sneaking me footnotes (gossip) about each person there. Tasnim, Noura, and myself were instantly a threesome of consummate confidants.

Valerie had not returned to Jeddah, but her three sisters-in-law were present, circling me with delight. They sprinkled me with flattery and even invited me to a women's party, a baby shower, the following evening. Jawaher, another notable beauty, was the oldest of the three. The other two followed her around like little ducklings. Age was a kind of currency in Saudi, and I made note of that.

Tasnim moved quickly across the room, introducing me to a woman who could have easily been her older sister. She had the same face, skin, and hair, but wore what looked like an Indian *sari*. "Patricia, this is my second cousin, Niggi. She postponed her flight to London just to meet you tonight."

I nodded to Niggi, who nodded back and winked.

"So happy to meet you, Patricia. I have heard all about you from Natalie".

"Have a seat, both of you, I think we deserve a drink!" I waved down a maid holding a tray full of colorful drinks in tall crystal. Each girl grabbed a glass. "What exactly are all these drinks?" I playfully asked, before committing to one.

Tasnim looked around before answering sarcastically, "Fresh-squeezed juices are all we get at family parties…" After seeing my furrowed brow and confused face, she elaborated. "Fresh carrot juice, orange juice, pomegranate juice, spinach juice, pear juice, apple juice, grapefruit juice, mango juice…"

"Fine. I'll take the pear juice." *No alcohol for the Abbars? This isn't how they behaved in New York.* As I lifted my glass from the tray, I noticed the juice tender, among the lowest servants here, had gold bangles up and down her arms. Catching my drift, Tasnim commented, "Even the maids are decked out this evening in your honor!"

Niggi interjected enthusiastically, "Thank you for having me this evening. I love Saudi events! So different from my life in the Mercedes Benz compound. I seldom get to wear my Sari here in Saudi."

"Well, it's beautiful! So colorful and intricate! But, what's the Mercedes Benz compound?"

Niggi laughed, "Oh sorry, I forgot you're a newcomer. Welcome to Saudi! My husband, Taher, is the General Manager of the Mercedes plant. We've been living here for eight years. As foreigners in Saudi Arabia, we can't purchase land or a house, so we're forced to live in the company compound with all the other executives and their families."

"Really? You can't live wherever you want? Do you like it in that compound?"

"Well, at least we have a brand new, furnished house, although it's prefabricated and a bit plastic and squeaky. Oh, and most of my neighbors are German. Ugh. So boring! Our only evening diversion is playing bridge. But, there's a huge swimming pool and tennis court for the complex, which is nice for the children. And a few of the top executive wives share a car and driver, so we can get around if we need to do shopping."

"Yes, Niggi picked me up tonight with her driver." Tasnim batted her eyes appreciatively at Niggi.

"I fly back to London tomorrow morning, and then on to Karachi for a month with my family. When Tasnim offered to introduce us, I immediately postponed my flight. I wouldn't miss this occasion for the world!"

"Well, thank you! I'm happy you came. I hope we can get together again when you return."

"Just say the word and I will come!"

From the corner of my eye, I caught sight of Rahman, sauntering in with a few men. I froze, realizing I had no idea what to do. Just when I needed her, Noura had gone to entertain the old ladies across the room. I looked to Tasnim to guide me, "Would it be scandalous if I jumped up and ran over to greet Rahman? He just walked in and I haven't seen or heard from him in a whole day."

"I think you just answered your own question. It would be scandalous! Stay put. Stay cool. Don't move. He will come to you after he greets his family."

I watched Rahman make his way through the crowd. He certainly looked handsome, with his immaculately clean and freshly ironed white garb. My heart beat faster and faster, and in spite of all the confusion and misunderstandings since my arrival in Jeddah, I was so happy to see him, and that he was mine.

Rahman, flanked by three men his own age, drifted around the room, shaking hands, hugging, giving kisses and making introductions. It seemed endless. Although I was impatient to see what he would do when he finally got to me, I watched him work the room, observing his serial elusiveness, gathering the eyes and hearts of everyone there, on cue, just like in Boston. Just when you'd expected Rahman to kiss someone, he offers a handshake. And when you think he might offer a nod, he dives in with a warm hug. I was witnessing a highly developed and intricate social structure that he had mastered and it was intriguing. *When will he come over here? He knows I'm here, he must…!*

Finally, when he had probably said hello to every *other* person in the room, he turned and let out a wide grin as he approached me. Niggi tugged at my dress, helping me up from my chair. All three of us were standing when he finally closed in. First came Tasnim. She got a kiss on both cheeks, "Samir is on his way." Then came Niggi. She got a handshake, "Taher is finishing up at the *bashka*, discussing business with my father's friends." And then he finally addressed me.

Gently pulling me towards him, I was on the receiving end of a kiss for each cheek and a friendly, although not satisfying or passionate, hug. "Well, my dear, you look ravishing this evening. Red is your color! How was your day?"

Seeing me speechless, Niggi came to my rescue, "Patricia does look fabulous this evening, I agree! She has been very patient with my endless complaining about the compound. So nice of you to invite us. I canceled my flight to be here. You know how we cherish our Saudi friends."

Tasnum chimed in, "Yes, Rahman, what a lovely event! Sheer delight! So many people whom I have not seen for months."

"Well, I saved the best for last," he said with a wink. With that, he offered me his hand. "Come this way. I will introduce you to a few of my friends." We floated through the crowd like two social gods, my anxiety finally melting away with his still reserved, latent attentions.

***

Bright and early the next morning, Noura was again at my door with an announcement. The two of us would be heading to the Bin Zagr's beach house today, on the Red Sea. Thahab followed Noura into my room with breakfast, having memorized my consumption habits from the day before. She placed the tray then began to back out the door "Anything more, *amati?*" Thahab softly queried. *Amati? Was that some form of 'mistress'?*

"Thahab. This is perfect. Thank you." Pleased with her command of English, I spoke slowly and smiled. No reason to leave any doubt in her mind that her service to me was absolutely to my satisfaction.

"You like her?" Noura asked, "She has been talking non-stop about how excited she is to be working for an American."

"They like Americans?"

"Yes, especially the young ones. They perceive Americans as being more fair, more modern, less likely to impose strict rules, and more likely to allow them time off. But her salary is dictated by the house customs, and here, at Beit Bin Zagr, all Ethiopian housemaids get the same salary. When you take her to your new home, you can do as you wish. For the moment, Mama Inja is paying her salary."

"And how much is that?"

"800 Riyals per month, so about US $225."

"Wow, no wonder they keep so many maids! They cost practically nothing!"

"That's the way it is here, and it's unlikely to change anytime soon. And they're happy to have the income. It's much better than being back in their country. Here they get food, shelter, medical treatment, simple jobs to do, and a lifetime of security. This is not England or America, Patricia."

"I see that. I'm starting to get it, Noura. I've come to the conclusion that in order to comprehend Saudi Arabia, I cannot start with Western customs in mind. I must instead ignore the dirt roads, unsafe electricity, underpaid servants not making eye contact, lack of employment laws…all the things that are new to me."

Fed up, Noura cut me off. "Well, what we DO have is a plan to go to the beach in thirty minutes! Get ready and meet me downstairs in the entrance. Bring a bathing suit, cover up, a hat, and lots of sunscreen! See you in a few!" She whisked herself out the door.

Half an hour later I was standing in the entry of Beit Bin Zagr with my own personal maid, Thahab, and my newfound friend, Noura, waiting for our car to pull around. Today would be an adventure! As the Cadillac pulled up, I was imagining us girls, swimming, playing, laughing and running free on an expansive beach of fine sand on the fabled Red Sea. Thahab grabbed my beach bag, along with Noura's and hers, and quickly loaded them into the trunk of the car. The driver jumped out, opened our doors, and then packed three coolers full of what I assumed was lunch and beverages, as well as beach chairs and towels… *Just like going to Jones Beach on Long Island, when I was a kid!* Visions of those summer trips to the beaches of Long Island swirled around my mind and for a moment, I missed home. Mom, my two sisters, and sometimes friends or cousins would join us for long days of Atlantic coastal beaches, tall grasses, and fishing boats, all dotting the endless shoreline. Rough waves to ride, the sun and wind highlighting my face and hair, the rich scent of coconut sunscreen, and fresh fried chicken on beach blankets. I was hoping somehow that my new desert home would provide memories to match those of home on the water.

Our car slowed a bit and turned off the (sort of) paved road to flat desert sand. But this sand wasn't like beach sand that was difficult to drive on, this sand was tightly packed and increasingly dusty, if that were possible. "Noura, why have we left the main road?"

"We're on the outskirts of Jeddah. No more roads. We'll need to cross the desert to get to the beach."

"What? Does the driver know where he is going?" I imagined being lost in the desert with no landmarks to guide us. No street signs!

"Don't worry, he does this all the time. He pulls off the road at a certain point and then heads due west until he hits the coastline. You can't miss the Red Sea! Just sit back and enjoy the view."

The view? There is nothing to see out here except sand and the occasional palm tree and I suppose bacon wrapped dates are out of the question here...

I did manage to settle down and stare out the window for about twenty minutes, anxiously awaiting what promised to be a great view. Aside from a flock of goats and another robed shepherdess, the drive continued to be uneventful until I caught a faint glimmer in the distance, like a mirage at first, then growing into a larger body of water that stretched across the horizon. I was surprised at the color. Unlike the brackish Atlantic, the Red Sea was as bright blue-green as peacock plumes.

The sand stopped abruptly and we turned right, following the shoreline until arriving at our destination, a compound of about ten acres surrounded on three sides by a towering stucco wall. Around the corner at the entrance was a hefty set of metal gates. Like magic, a frail gatekeeper popped out of his hut, fighting the wind to push the gates open for us. I looked around and noticed that there were no electrical poles, and no random wires hanging to indicate lights or modern power.

"Let me guess - there's no electricity or plumbing, right, Noura?"

"Nope, there isn't out here, but inside, at the beach house, we have a generator and clean sea water is pumped in for our visit."

The driver stopped and let us out next to a stone house very close to the waterline. This was truly an off-the-grid compound. The lack of basic amenities was as if we were parked in the remote wilderness, but without lush forests and hairy creatures roaming about. The magnificence of the sea pulled me right up to the shoreline, where I stood transfixed, taking a long panoramic look. *So this is the Red Sea.*

Surprisingly, there were no boats in sight. Just the sun, the wind, the water and the jumping fishes. No beach cabanas, no people at the shoreline, no fishermen, no lifeguards, no beach chairs, no restaurants with decks, no marinas, no swimmers, no umbrellas, no debris, no kids building sandcastles. It's easier to list what does exist and forget the rest.

I didn't bother to mention this to Noura, because she had been curt with me earlier that day when I started to explain my thoughts. *I can't blame her. She is trying to make the best of everything, just like everyone else here.*

"Patricia, look! Thahab is waving to us from the patio. Lunch is ready!"

And so it was. Thahab, with the help of the driver, had dragged out the patio furniture, and set up a nice little table and chairs for us, complete with a tablecloth, platters of salads, sandwiches, fruits and drinks. We sat facing the sea and enjoyed our picnic. In the distance, the driver took his lunch and walked over to the caretaker's hut to eat. Thahab stood to the side and watched us with a contented smile.

"Thahab, please pull up a chair and sit with us," I pleaded. "Don't stand there alone watching. Eat something." Thahab looked surprised, gave an inquiring look to Noura, who nodded to her with a smile, so she shyly pulled another chair to the table and sat down hesitantly across from us.

"You're such an American, Patricia. We don't usually allow the servants to eat with us, she would have gladly waited until we were finished, but since it's only the three of us here, we might as well dine American style. I like it! Americans are so refreshing!"

Everything tasted delicious, and we thoroughly enjoyed our meal just like three regular girls having a beachside lunch. We talked about all sorts of things, but the most interesting was hearing from Thahab about her family in Ethiopia. Apparently, she and her brother were university educated in the capital, Addis Ababa. But with the current political unrest in her homeland, she and her brother left to find work elsewhere. Thahab specifically came here to be my personal maid, and she was grateful for the employment. Her brother was in Sweden, working as a waiter.

"Sweden? From Ethiopia to Sweden? How random!"

"No, not really. Many Ethiopians have gone to Sweden since our war started. Swedish immigration policies welcome us. We have many friends and family members who have settled there over the past few years. I was

waiting for my visa to join my brother there, but instead, I took this opportunity to come to Jeddah."

"Well, it's awfully cold in Sweden, and the sun hides all winter, Thahab.
I'm glad you came here. Look! Here we all are at the Red Sea enjoying this
glorious day."

Noura was ready to hit the water. "Come on, Patricia, get your beach
bag and let's head to the dock for a swim!"

The water was truly refreshing. Clean, cold water with no undertow or
large waves. I accidentally took in a mouthful while swimming around, and
it was very salty. Small fish nibbled at my feet and jellyfish floated by as I
remained within a few strokes of the ladder just in case something large
(and hungry) appeared. Noura demonstrated her well executed backstroke
to me. She was on the swim team at college in England and recounted tales
of the many international swim meets she enjoyed.

"Noura, please tell me why you're living here permanently, instead of
in England, practicing architecture?" It was a question that I'd been dying
to ask, still amazed at how safe I felt with her after only three days in Saudi
Arabia.

Noura hesitated for a second, "Okay, fine, let's sit on the dock and I'll
tell all, Patricia. But I'd like to dry off."

As we sat and looked out to sea, Noura shared her story with me, a
story so infuriating and unjust that I wished I hadn't known.

"I was finishing up my architecture degree in London, and I fell in love
with another student, a man from Sierra Leone."

"Wait, that's another nation in Africa?"

"Yes. It's not that far away from England or Saudi. Before you ask, yes,
he was black," Noura paused to gather her thoughts. "Our common archi-
tectural studies made it easy to spend hours upon hours together during
internships. We dated for a while, then moved in together before deciding
to marry. He wasn't Muslim. He was a Christian, and marriage to a Christian man is strictly forbidden to Muslim women. Here in Saudi, it's punish-
able by death. Do you understand?"

"Yes. Death."

"Well, I didn't care. I did it anyway, and never told my parents or
extended family. My sisters and brothers were aware but sworn to secrecy.
We all lived in England, and felt far away and safe from Saudi expectations and religious laws. The rest of the family, particularly my mother,
were unaware of the details of our lives overseas. All they knew was that
we attended good schools and came home once a year to visit. We were

pursuing admirable careers. This went on for about two years without a hitch, until I discovered that I was pregnant."

"Wait, but you don't..."

She cut me off, her face stiff and determined. "I decided that I absolutely had to tell mother and the family back in Jeddah. Enough was enough. I was so happy with my life in England. I couldn't imagine my mother not sharing that happiness with me. It felt so normal being married to my husband there in England and expecting our child like so many other couples. I had completely lost touch with the Saudi perspective and was tired of hiding."

"Noura, please don't tell me that you came here to tell them," I started.

"Funny you should say that because that's exactly what I did. The phone system here in Jeddah is so rudimentary, and this simply wasn't something that I could put into a letter. So I told my mother that I wanted to come home and visit her and they sent me a plane ticket. I arrived home in Jeddah, five months pregnant but not really showing, and explained to my mother that I had fallen in love with and married a man from Sierra Leone. I had been living with him for two years, and we were expecting a child in the fall. Patricia, you cannot imagine what her reaction was. She got up immediately, turned her back to me and started reciting verses from the Koran. She walked out of the room and never spoke to me again, not even to this day."

"But that wasn't the end of it. By evening I discovered that she had told her brothers, my uncles, and they shouted and cursed at me for hours. They called me every name under the sun. Then they locked me in my room for two days, giving me barely enough to eat or drink. I was terrified for the baby. Just when I thought it couldn't get any worse, on the third day of my visit, they took me in a car to the airport, forced me onto a private plane, and flew me over to Cairo. There, they dragged me to a doctor. He sedated me against my will, cut open my stomach, took out the baby, and killed it."

Noura stopped speaking, overcome with tears. Her humorous and easy-going façade had vanished. She was so thoroughly broken, even years later. What she described was the worst kind of family violence any friend of mine had ever experienced or shared. I wanted to comfort her, but I was at such a loss and still in shock that a family I would be related to and have to see, could commit such a vile act against Noura and her child. We sat there, crying together.

"They took me back to Jeddah and collectively decided that I would never be allowed to leave the Bin Zagr premises again. My uncles said what I had done by marrying that man had caused an irreparable disgrace to the family name forever. My passport was revoked. I was not allowed to go anywhere except my rooms and the dining room. I was not allowed to socialize with anyone. No phone calls. No gatherings. No letters, not even to my siblings in England. All the servants in the complex were told to report any suspicious action on my part. I was forbidden to ever speak of it again to anybody. All I have to prove that this actually happened to me is this big, ugly scar left on my stomach." She laughed bitterly. "No more bikinis for me."

"Noura! My head is spinning. How can you stand to be in that house? How can you even look at your mother? Did you ever inform your sisters and brothers about what happened?"

"Well, I couldn't call or write, so I had to wait for months.When one of the Bin Zagr aunties was traveling to London with her maids, I slipped a letter to one of the old servants whom I knew for my whole life, and whom I trusted. She was instructed to quietly give that letter to one of my sisters, whichever one came first to visit my auntie in London. The letter outlined what had happened to me, warned never to let on that they knew the story and be very wary about coming back to Jeddah. I never received a response, not one, and I haven't seen any of my siblings in three years. I hope they understand that their lives might be in danger too and I'm glad they know to stay away. Can you believe it?"

"Noura, this is too painful to even think about."

"Yes it is, even now…But one comes to accept things when they feel they somehow deserved the punishment."

"But now they allow you to come and go from the house. We're here right now on the Red Sea. What happened?"

"Believe it or not, before you arrived here, Patricia, there was a big debate about whether I would be allowed to meet with you. I think they were afraid that you might act as my connection to England, since you were a foreigner. It was Rahman, whom I suspect felt sorry for me after having lived in the West, who argued on my behalf that I should be allowed to come to the Abbar house to greet his new fiancée and take part in the celebration. He fought hard for that, and finally, the family reluctantly agreed to my visit, on a trial basis. One misstep and I am back in isolation, they said. Patricia, you have changed my life. You have been my salvation."

"No way! Three years alone until last week? You haven't been able to leave? What about your husband in England?"

"I've not been able to contact him. Handing off a note to my sister is one thing, but no one will post anything or put my calls through. They won't even tell me if any calls had come in and were ordered to destroy any letters to me from anyone overseas. I have no idea where my husband is or what he thinks happened. Maybe he divorced me and got married to someone else. Maybe he returned to his country. Maybe he's still in London, waiting for me. Maybe he thinks I died. He's probably better off that way."

"What's his name? Maybe I can find something out..."

She held a hand out to stop me, "Patricia, please. I'd rather not say. I can never utter those words again as long as I live."

I searched for the right words to say to her but our intimate conversation was cut short by urgent commotion on the shore. Thahab waved frantically to us. She seemed extremely agitated.

"*Amati, amati!*" She shouted something in Arabic that I could not understand. Noura went white and froze. Beyond Thahab, in the distance, the gatekeeper stood defiantly on the front porch of his hut, with his robe hiked up to his waist. Noura gasped and said quickly, "Patricia, don't look at him."

Stubbornly, I squinted, but, fortunately (or unfortunately) my sunglasses were an old prescription, not strong enough for me to see clearly at that distance.

"He's exposing himself," she whispered, "He's holding his robe up with one hand and privates with the other hand."

I didn't fully understand what was happening or why the ragged little man at the gate would be doing something as crazy as that, in a country as strict as this. But given Thahab's distress, I instinctively grabbed my beach bag and started to put on my cover-up. Thahab may as well have yelled "shark!" as this was quite a serious situation and apparently, I wasn't supposed to witness it.

We watched in disbelief as our driver rushed the gatekeeper like a linebacker, knocking him solidly on the ground, balls still in hand. If it had been the 90s, this could have been a movie, with a Full Monty Borat character jumping from behind a bush to chase them down and end the sequence, wrestling in the nude. We watched in horror as the still half-naked gatekeeper got a second wind, popped right up and engaged the driver in a genuine fist fight. The pervert was winning! Our driver had a bloody nose—bright red blood staining the front of his now less crisp, white robe. *What on earth?*

Noura screamed, "Run to the car, Patricia. Quick! Don't look, don't stop, just get into the car. Come on!" We made a dash for the Caddy on the side of the house and once inside, Noura locked the doors. I felt simultaneously helpless, confused, and outraged. *What's going on? What will happen to us?* I'd never feared for my life, and I'd never seen someone fight to the death. I begged Noura to explain how this happened and why we were in danger, but she was too busy watching the fight. She too was both frightened and terrified of what might happen if the gatekeeper somehow prevailed. "The gate keeper must be insane! I don't recognize him, but who even looks at them? Mohammad, the driver, has been with the family his whole life. He will gladly die defending and protecting us." *But who would get us home?*

"I don't want anyone dying today, Noura. Don't go there. This is absurd! How could something like this happen? And on your family's private property?"

The driver threw one more punch, knocking the gatekeeper down again. TKO. And in a flash, Mohammad and Thahab made it to the front seat of the Cadillac. He revved the engine and pulled the car up to the closed gates. By that time, the gatekeeper had made it to his feet again, and retreated into his hut for safety. Thahab hesitantly got out of the car to open the gates herself, while Mohammad sat at the wheel, ready to step on the gas at a moment's notice. Thahab's face fell as she reported back, "The gate is locked with a padlock." We were stuck inside the compound with a lunatic pervert on the loose and no one but an exhausted Mohammad to protect the three of us! So, we did what any practicing Saudi Muslim would do in the back of that hot car in Middle Eastern Deliverance country: We prayed hard.

Thahab was throwing her hands up and shouting prayers to God, while the driver muttered quieter sentiments, praying under his breath. It was apparent that we had no plan and Mohammad was attempting to devise one. "Maybe we should crash through the gates," he blurted out in a still winded voice.

"Oh my God. Mama Inja will kill us if we wreck her Cadillac!" snapped Noura. "Isn't there some other way?"

Still confused about why this employee would dare lock us in the compound, I piped up, "Mohammad, lay on the horn! There's four of us and one of him. We're safe in the car! He can't harm us here. Just keep honking until he comes out and opens the gate." *A very NYC suggestion! Honk until the other guy relents!*

Mohammad agreed. And to everyone's relief, after a few loud honks, the gatekeeper emerged begrudgingly and stood in front of his hut, glaring at us. At first he stood his ground, belligerent and not willing to budge. Mohammad continued to honk the horn, not knowing what else to do.

All of a sudden, Noura gasped anew and said, "Don't look, Patricia. Don't look at this devil. Oh my God, he's insane!"

Thahab took a break from screaming and began reciting verses from the Koran, all the time averting her eyes from the sight of the gatekeeper exposing his private parts for the second time to all of us in the car. *He's flashing us again? Is this guy for real?* Noura ordered Mohammad to back up, pick up speed, and ram through the fortified metal gates. Cadillac or not, there was no other choice at this point. We were not going to wait patiently while this freak played with his penis. We backed up, held our breath, and braced ourselves for take-off and impact.

Moments before impact, the pervert hurried over to unlock the padlock, and pushed the gates halfway open, just barely enough space to get through. Mohammad inched forward slowly, not wanting to scratch the sides of the car, but anxious to escape as soon as possible.

"Oh no, he is approaching your window, Patricia!" Noura screeched.

"Mohammad, drive faster!" The crazed man had the nerve to stare directly into the car at me. As we drove past him, he reached out to touch the ultra-foreign vision (me) through the glass. I stared at his ugly, twisted face–his beady eyes, a toothless mouth gaping at me–then gasped in horror as his hand, covered in milky slime, slowly slid across my window.

Noura grabbed me, trying to shield me. We all knew what it was, though nobody was brave enough to verbalize it with Mohammad in the car.

He stepped on the gas and we finished squeezing through the opening, but with great haste. Once out of the compound, we sped eastward toward civilization, silent and confused. Nobody wanted to talk about what had just happened.

With considerable embarrassment and disbelief himself, the driver attempted to explain the whole situation.

"*Amati,* seeing you two on the dock was just too much for this peasant from Egypt. Please forgive me for having to relay this to you, but he didn't understand–he assumed you were prostitutes, asking to be raped. He suggested we do it together." I was further horrified that I was not only considered a willing rape victim, but also a prostitute. The only thought that made this entire event worse, was that the gatekeeper had asked Mohammad to accompany him in the vile suggestion. I'm relieved that Mohammad is a decent man.

"What do we tell everyone at the house when they see Mohammad arriving covered in blood?" Noura shouted, panicked. "Patricia, we're in big trouble now. You don't understand how things work here. They'll blame us. They always blame the woman when something bad happens. I'll never be let out of that house again." Noura started sobbing uncontrollably.

At that, I begged our driver not to mention this, ever, to the family. I suggested he claim to have tripped and fallen, or that the metal gate smacked him in the face. He could easily sneak away quickly after dropping us off. He didn't even have to get out of the car!

He shook his head, "*Amati*, I cannot lie to my masters. I have to tell them what happened. You were my responsibility." He hung his head in shame and continued driving in complete quiet. *What will happen to him? To the gatekeeper?*

I felt utterly defeated as I went over and over all the details of our ruined beach day. braced myself for the family's anticipated reactive reaction we would soon have to face. In almost total silence, save for Thahab's occasional sobs, we continued through the roadless desert, back to Beit Bin Zagr.

Once inside, Noura and I hurried up to my room, relieved that no one was lingering in the hallways ready to eavesdrop. We had to scheme our way out of this predicament, as Noura's life sentence had been reduced just last week.

"Let's blame everything on me," I insisted. "I'll say it was all my idea but now that I realize how inappropriate it was, I apologize, and promise to never do that again."

I felt like an eight-year-old child, asking forgiveness for running out into the street to catch a bouncing ball. But I wasn't eight years old, I didn't feel like there was any reason for me to beg for forgiveness. I was starting to get fed up with the entire matter. *Some guy, the Abbar's employee, decides to jerk off on their private property, and somehow, we're to blame?* If it hadn't been for Noura, I would have taken a very different approach. But I knew that above all, I needed to protect her.

Word spread like wildfire throughout the Abbar and Bin Zagr households. Thahab came quietly up to my room and reported that the driver returned to the garage all covered with blood, and to make matters worse, the side of Mama Inja's Cadillac had been scratched—probably by the gate as we sped out of the compound. This was a big deal, in fact, nothing like this had ever occurred in anyone's living memory. Thahab reported that the family sent two cars, loaded with servants and house managers, to the beach house to get the gatekeeper and bring him to Jeddah for justice. A posse.

Later that evening, instead of going to the office, Rahman came to Beit Bin Zagr and asked to speak with Noura and me in the salon. We had not left my room since arriving home, and meekly, we both tiptoed down to confront him. The moment I saw his face, all screwed up with anger, his eyes as black and hard as two coals, I realized that the frontal attack I had planned would not work. Instead, I whispered to Noura to let me do all the talking, hung my head in shame, and shuffled into the room like that eight-year-old I never wanted to be. I wiped imaginary tears from under my eyes and sat quietly in the chair beside him.

"What a mess you two have made! Things like this don't happen in our family!"

Silence.

"We had to send men to the beach to catch the caretaker and bring him to justice. It will be the talk of Jeddah, when it gets out. All the servants are talking about nothing else but that, and just wait for their day off on Friday. They will spread it to every other servant in the entire city."

More silence. I stifled a fake sob.

"Why did you have to go to the beach? Why couldn't you just stay home?"

"I wanted to see the beach. Michelle Bin Laden told me so much about it. I was curious. I'm so sorry…" I whispered in my smallest voice.

"If the police get wind of what happened, you could be taken down to the station for questioning. Maybe even arrested. Do you realize that? This is Saudi Arabia. You can't go prancing around half-naked like you're in the South of France."

"Oh no…" I opened my teary eyes wide, arguing in my heart before he even said it:

"I think you have to leave Jeddah tomorrow."

At that, Noura and I exchanged glances, both wondering how everything escalated so suddenly. *Leave the country?*

Seeing our disbelief, Rahman doubled down, "Yes, Patricia. This idea of your visit to Jeddah was not wise."

"It wasn't my idea…I did everything I was told to do," I reminded him. "Your aunts and your mother wanted me here. They told us what to do and we followed their instructions to the letter! How could Noura and I have known?"

"True. But now that we see the result, it's safer for you to leave Jeddah immediately. There is no telling what could happen in the next few days. You don't understand how Saudi law works, Patricia. Our engagement means nothing in the eyes of the law. If the police have even the slightest suspicion of anything irregular happening, the first response is to take everyone involved down to the station, lock them up in jail and question them later. My family will be powerless to protect you. An unattached foreign woman has no chance at safety or freedom or even living..."

I trembled at his words. He was not so much angry as he was afraid for me, and the full weight of what could happen suddenly sunk in. Forget no lifeguards or paved roads, this was a country where I had no rights. I was at a loss for what to say. Rahman, too, seemed to have run out of energy. He was exasperated. I could see that my silence was the right move. This was not the time for argument and blame. I quietly submitted to his will in this matter. The three of us sat together quietly, all fearing for my life.

Rahman turned to me, and with a reluctant sigh, he continued, "Patricia, you have to make a decision. You can return to Europe tomorrow. Decide if you wish to live there or in the States. I can go with you and help you find an apartment and get set up. Maybe London? Paris? Of course I will visit you regularly. We can play it by ear and decide what to do, if anything, in a few years. Or..." he hesitated, "we can fly to Paris tomorrow and get married at the Saudi embassy. My father suggested it. The ambassador is a cousin, and he will gladly oblige. He owes us a few favors. Then we can return to Jeddah as a married couple and relieve the Binzagrs of this embarrassing responsibility. I am leaving the choice up to you."

Leaving it up to me? I like that it's my decision, but what kind of choice is this? Get married immediately or live as his mistress? These ideas had never been on the table before now.

Noura pleaded silently with me to choose quickly as Rahman offered no other suggestions or opinions. He just sat there, limp, waiting for me to decide by myself. Everything from the last four years flashed through my mind in an instant. Noura, Valerie, Tasnim, Natalie, Mama Inja, Niggi, Michelle, Thahab, my family, his family, the endless nightclubs, the mosque in Paris, my conversion, those kind people on the Saudi airplane, the welcome party here in Jeddah...I felt as though I was already too far down this road. So many were invested in me being here. And something inside me believed that there was really no other choice for me than to keep going. I had never failed at anything and I refused to be his sometimes girl in Europe. I had fought for my right to marry him.

Looking back, this was a turning point, perhaps the one opportunity I had to choose a different path knowing at least in part what I would be getting myself into. Did I simply ignore how strangely Rahman had acted since my arrival? He had proposed to me, introduced me to all of his family and friends, and coached me through my conversion to Islam. But here in Jeddah, he seemed oddly removed from the situation, as if the entire courtship had been my idea. Within four days of being here, I was accosted by a pervert, and was now facing potential jail time or possibly even death for his crime. How was this even a choice? But I knew it was. In fact, returning seemed less attractive, in spite of everything.

Was it my addiction to this fantastic high life that fueled my obsession with Rahman? Or that I was no longer ordinary? How could I go back to New York with my tail between my legs, admit that my mother was right, and date regular guys with regular jobs, after all of this living and excitement? I couldn't bear that. It was everything I had escaped from.

And I loved Rahman.

I chose to stay.

Chapter Five

Married Life

Sitting with Rahman, his father, and his business partner at the Moulin Rouge the following evening, I pinched myself to make sure I wasn't dreaming. Unbelievable. We were married! So much had transpired in a mere 24 hours.

Just yesterday, I could have been imprisoned or worse for—what? A crime someone else committed? It was still confusing. Instead, I chose a hastened wedding ceremony in Paris. In his way, Rahman had offered me an "out"—but I didn't take it.

Rahman stood up and reiterated, "Just remember, this is your decision. This is what *you* want. I hope you'll be happy with it. Now I must go make travel arrangements for us. I have a lot to do. I'll see you tomorrow." Noura and I stared at each other.

"Patricia, I didn't think you were going to say what you said. And so quickly. I must admit, I'm happy you will be with us, but are you sure you know what you are getting into?"

"Honestly, I feel like I'm dreaming. I'm not afraid. I just don't care. I want to follow this through to the end, whatever that means. I can't stop now."

Noura frowned. "Rahman was so cold and matter of fact about it. I never realized he was this way and I've known him my entire life," she supposed.

But I was certain I knew him better. "It's just cold feet. He'll relax, once we're married–Back to the old, happy Rahman that we all love. This isn't him. It's just the pressure of reconciling his Western self with his Eastern self. I'm sure of it."

I was feeling overwhelmed, and he was, too. We were in the pressure cooker, and we were both acting out of character. Our engagement was not typical. Prison, mistress, or marriage tomorrow? What a choice! Anyone would feel that way, and I wanted to give Rahman the benefit of the doubt. I knew he loved me, and that would ultimately be enough. We would be a normal happily married couple, once the barriers and formalities were out of our way. And when I realized at that instant that I was leaving immediately for Paris to marry my Rahman, a lighthearted giddiness took hold. The young, rebellious girl inside me squealed with delight. This is what I wanted! This is why I came to Jeddah. It was so deliciously daring, I couldn't wait to tell everyone we had eloped!

All previous reservations concerning Rahman's odd behavior (and the inherent safety issues in Jeddah I was now aware of) were silenced by the joy of being a new bride. And I'd earned that joy.

"Noura, come up and help me choose a wedding day ensemble for tomorrow!"

Hours later, we were off to Paris. Amm Abdullah and his friend and business partner, Amm Ahmad Zainy, accompanied Rahman and me. They were to be our witnesses for the signing of the marriage papers. And Rahman had thought of everything. We were whisked from the airport to the Saudi Embassy and the Ambassador's office, where we were greeted with hugs, a lovely tea service, and beautiful French pastries that I was too excited to eat.

Unsure of what to do or say amongst these four men, I sat quiet and listened as they started with small talk, then business and politics, until finally the paperwork was brought in. The marriage agreement was in Arabic, but it could have said anything and I'd have been happy to sign and toast if that meant spending the rest of my life with Rahman. We were married!

Moulin Rouge hosted the celebratory dinner and a rosy paradox: Old traditional Paris meets new modern couple fusing East with West (at least for today). The food was gorgeous but I couldn't eat a bite; my heart was simply too happy. It didn't matter that our wedding was rushed, it was more sublime than I could have hoped for! The Arab men were all having a gay old time watching the can-can girls and discussing business in between acts; it was like another day at the office for them.

I could finally relax and let joy and relief wash over me. And once married, the tension immediately lifted for us both. It had been much too long since we'd shared ourselves and once we found our room at the hotel, finally alone, we fell back into the physical and emotional passion that healed all the previous weeks of misunderstandings, uncertainty, and fear. Rahman and I were happy, joined, and in love.

Later that night as he slept, I made a long-overdue and much dreaded phone call to my family in New York. I had not called them since touching down in Jeddah because the phone lines hadn't been updated since 1926 and a connection to the United States could take an hour. A camel ride is faster than a phone call. But here in Paris, I had no excuses.

"Mom, it's Patricia. Rahman and I eloped. We're in Paris," I blurted out. My marriage had ignited a sense of womanhood within me and I was not going to apologize.

"What, Patricia? Eloped? When...when did this happen?" She sounded completely confused.

My younger sisters chattered in the background, prompting my mother to repeat each detail I confessed. I heard Diane mutter something about how irresponsible my actions were. That didn't help matters. My mom's hushed confusion morphed into a quiet fury as I continued, and she grew increasingly distressed. At last, she interrupted my rushed explanations to hurl a savage critique of my recent (irresponsible) behavior.

"Why couldn't you tell us? What happened to waiting and seeing if you like the country? This is insanity—Paris? You weren't even in Jeddah for a week!"

I knew there was no way I could even begin to describe the harrowing scene at the beach house and its potential legal consequences, so I decided it would be easier just to insist that what I was doing was completely normal, blasé even, and that her reaction was overblown.

"His family thought this was the best route. It was Amm Abdullah's idea."

She scolded me in an injured but still stern tone, "What about *your* family? Your dad and I were hoping for a wedding here, in New York. We've been telling everyone we know. Now what are we supposed to say? They'll be devastated." I could hear her heart cracking in her voice.

I kept my cool to diffuse her rage and insult. "Mom, we're having a wedding party in Jeddah in a few weeks. It's a gift from Inja and part of Saudi tradition. I need to do things their way for now, given that their culture is so strict and rigid. Please understand that I need to be flexible to make this work. I'm over the moon happy, Mom! I didn't intend to let all this happen without you. But Rahman and I want to start our life together and we can't do anything there without first getting married. The Ambassador had to marry us because I'm Western. Rahman's uncle here in Paris is the Ambassador. This is the first chance I had to call you. So...Mom, you and Dad and the girls *have* to come to Jeddah in a couple weeks. Don't worry, you'll get the royal treatment! Think you can manage that?"

"Come to Jeddah? Are you kidding?"

"No, I'm not kidding. Please put Cindy on the phone. Maybe she'll get it." My youngest sister was, by far, the most sensitive and understanding of all. I knew she would do anything she could to help.

"Hi Patricia, it's me, Cindy. What's going on? Mom's flipping out."

"Shit. Explain to her that we changed our plans. It wasn't working out with me visiting there. I wasn't allowed to be alone with Rahman because we weren't married yet. I couldn't take it anymore. We decided to fast forward...Now things are better between us. And now you can come and see Jeddah for yourself! It'll be so exciting."

Cindy wasn't convinced either. "What? We have to come to Saudi Arabia? All of us? Patricia, this is nuts. A week ago, we had a hard time imagining *you* going there, and now we have to go? Ugh! All those shots and visas?"

"Yes. You're my family. I need you all there! The party has to be at the groom's family home and it will be fabulous! And very formal! Some shopping may be in order! Just have mommy and daddy give me the date that you all can arrive in Jeddah, make your plane reservations, and we'll do the rest."

"Wait, Patricia," Cindy hesitated, "Congratulations!"

At that, I burst into tears. No idea why—maybe because her voice was so meek, or because no one in my family had thought to congratulate me thus far, or maybe because in my heart, I knew that I'd hurt them. My family was just as left out as they felt. "Thank you, sweet Cindy. I love you." I promptly hung up and attempted to gather myself together but Rahman had heard the entire exchange.

"Patricia, are you ok? You don't sound like yourself." Rahman mumbled, not used to seeing me quite so messy or undone.

"They're confused and hurt and I understand. It's all very confusing for me too. But, I'm fine, I'll be fine," I said, tears streaming down my now-red face. My impulsive actions had hurt them and I felt it deeply despite my natural inclination to dismiss any guidance or direction from my folks. And I hurt my little sisters, steamrolling over any hopes my family may have had for a wedding, a normal wedding.

Upon our return to Jeddah 48 hours later, we learned that the problematic gatekeeper at the beach had been sent packing to Egypt, and the family was free from stain. Luckily for us, the faithful servants who knew everything that happened had stayed mum. What could have turned into a huge incident was snuffed out within a week.

My short stay in Jeddah was a quick education on what not to do and I had to admit to myself that I didn't really enjoy being there. In fact, even after officially joining the family, I still wondered if I was safe anywhere in the country, married or not. Nothing in Jeddah turned out as I imagined it would. Although now we lived together in the same compound, it was rare that Rahman and I could behave comfortably with each other due to the strict codes of conduct. When we were together at home, there were always servants and family members in the room, and he was consequently stiff and self-conscious around them. During the day, I still had very little to do while Rahman was at work or out on business calls. But always the optimist, I convinced myself that it was temporary and soon we'd be traveling ten months out of the year. I was certain we would become the jetsetters we had planned to be.

My family arrived two weeks later. A nervous wreck, I paced back and forth in the sitting room of the Abbar's house, waiting for their car to clear the gate. I wiped my mind clean of heavy thoughts about my marriage and staying in Jeddah. I couldn't have my parents worrying about me–I had to stay positive. They would no doubt be just as shocked by the scene at the airport as I was. I wished I could have guided them through it. But by now, I was well aware that any American woman walking through the airport would cause a stir, and waiting patiently at home is best. I had warned my family beforehand of the mangled mess of broken poor, wild barnyard animals, and large groups of men snickering at the expense of women who do not speak Arabic. I was counting on my young sisters' fortitude to see my parents through that primitive display of poverty and ignorance.

The Abbar family members arrived one by one for the first customary house party of many before my wedding. There would be two dozen relatives arriving to greet my family. I smiled as each one stepped through the doorway of the grand salon, greeting them in the rudimentary Arabic I had learned from my new private tutor. *Amazing how quickly I was accepted here*, I mused. Everyone wanted to meet me, everyone wanted to know me. It was intoxicating. Now everyone was welcoming my family and I was sure Mama Inja had a week's worth of activities planned.

"Patricia, you must be so excited that your family is coming tonight," purred Valerie as she paraded in, wearing a cocktail dress and an excessive amount of gold jewelry. Valerie's baby had just been born in England—a girl, Fareeda—and the family had rewarded her handsomely. She had returned to Jeddah solely for our wedding party. I was touched by the solidarity she displayed to me as another foreign wife in Saudi.

"Valerie, I can hardly contain myself!" I said, so happy to see her and grateful for her friendship.

"My family has not been here yet," she answered. "I've been asking them for the past two years, but they're not ready to leave England for such an adventure. My mum's back in England watching the baby right now. That's about all she can handle. I must admit, your family is quite daring." I loved Valerie's accent. She pronounced it "*daaaaaring.*" And she was correct. My family was daring to drop everything and fly to Jeddah for me. Commotion in the hallway signaled their arrival and I ran to greet them. The elevator door opened and there they all stood, completely aghast but managing smiles, nevertheless.

Cindy jumped right into my arms, Diane following hesitantly.

"Patricia! You look so gorgeous! It's so good to finally see you! We love you so much!" My mom stepped out of the elevator in her usual imperious way, curiously studying the décor. I knew she would find fault in everything, but I was used to her, and didn't care. I happily pulled her into our group hug, "Mom, I'm so glad you're here."

"Who are you? Diamond Lil?" my father teased, his mouth grinning and gaping at the same time. *Great, Dad, right to the point.*

"Daddy, this is the style," I replied with a sassy grin. It was the very same rebuttal I'd used since I was a teen…Ripped jeans? Daddy, it's the style. Braless t-shirts? Daddy, it's the style! Long stringy hair? Daddy, it's the style.

He gestured to my abundance of facets and cabochon. I supposed that my jewelry was a bit much, but over the past month, I'd grown immune to the sparkle of diamonds and gold, and I barely noticed them anymore. "It's the latest from Paris, Daddy! You must admit it's better than my old hippie look!" I said with a wink.

Dad joined our collective family embrace. I had underestimated just how good it felt to have them here and that they had set aside their hurt to support me, even though I had been pushing them away for four years.

My eyes filled with tears as I made the introductions. I even got a few of the names wrong, I was so shaken. My hands were trembling. I was completely overcome with pride and gratitude. My mother shot a curious glance my way.

"Patricia, it's not like you to act so emotional."

"Come on, Mom. I missed you all so much." Everyone in the Saudi family was staring at me. *They probably think I'm a nut.* Such overt displays of emotion were not the norm in Saudi, but I couldn't help myself. I had consciously been without my family for so long. To see their faces, in this salon, was almost too much for me to balance in my head and heart.

Ushering my parents into two large armchairs, I told my sisters to sit down on the Arabic sofa, next to Noura. They would appreciate that she spoke excellent English. My mother silently inspected everything in the room, from the ceiling fans which turned slowly above, to the crystal chandeliers, to the upholstered French style furniture, to the Chinese rugs. Not a drop of sunlight entered the salon because the shutters were tightly closed due to flies, heat, and dust, all of which were considered to be big enemies here in Jeddah.

"How was your flight?" asked one of Rahman's aunts, kindly attempting conversation.

"Very good," my mother politely replied, "They served the most delicious food I've ever had on an airplane and the seats were enormous." My family had taken the non-stop, fourteen-hour flight from Kennedy Airport on Saudi Airlines. I listened as my mother initiated idle chit chat with the aunties. *Thank God, she's being gracious*, I thought. To my right, my sisters gossiped happily with Noura. *Okay, this is going well. Exhale.*

My dad sat next to Amm Abdullah, who had come in early from his *bashka*, just for the occasion. The two of them were a bit stiff, but attempted to recreate the warmth they had shared at our New York apartment. Just as I wondered when Rahman would arrive, he staggered in, sweaty and frazzled.

I rushed over as he briefed me on the latest airport developments, "All the bags have been inspected and delivered to the suite at the Al-Attas Hotel. Hopefully, not too much has been removed from their suitcases."

I motioned to him to speak quietly and whispered not to mention any details to my mom, "She'll melt down if she thinks any of her precious clothing might disappear. Better she thinks that she forgot to pack something and realize that it's missing when she returns to New York!"

A willing conspirator in this operation, Rahman nodded, stifling a laugh, then began his customary circling around the room, greeting each and every one.

Cindy tugged at my arm, "Patricia, come sit with us. You haven't given us more than five minutes on the phone for this whole month! What's up? We miss hearing from you!"

Noura laughed, "Oh, don't blame her, girls. The phone system here is so terrible, you can barely even call it a system." No kidding. Two cups with a string work better.

I chimed in to Noura's defense of me, "It's true! Do you even realize that I can't direct dial to the States? I have to call an operator here and request him to put me through to your number."

"That's not so bad," my mother offered in her usual tempering way, "We used to do that when I was your age."

"Yeah, but did you have to hear the operator breathing on the phone line, listening to every word you say?"

Cindy's mouth dropped open, "What? They listen?"

"Yep," I shrugged. "And they always have comments to make after the phone call is done. Last time I hung up with you, the operator proposed marriage to me," I deepened my voice, "*American girl, you must be very pretty. Will you marry me?*" We all laughed.

Dinner went smoothly and soon it was time to send my family home to the hotel for the night. The quiet and rest was needed and appreciated. The entire Abbar family escorted my little family to their waiting Cadillac. Mama Inja, swelling with proud generosity, announced that tomorrow would be a very exciting day—everyone was going to the Bin Zagr's beach house on the Red Sea.

Is she kidding? After that entire episode, we're all going back to the beach again? At least the gatekeeper has been replaced, but it was only a few weeks ago.

I couldn't help but shoot Noura a glance of disbelief.

"Why would Mama Inja want to return there with my family?"

"Patricia," she said in hushed tones, " Inja doesn't know the gory details about what really happened to us. The men would never tell her such things." Noura shrugged with finality, as if to say that's just how it's done here.

"Will you be returning with us to the hotel?" asked my mother, always the downer.

"No, I think it would probably be better for me to stay here. Coming to the hotel might just create a scandal."

Responding to my mother's look of incredulity, "I'll explain tomorrow." I could never actually explain to her how it would be perceived for a woman alone like me, married or not, to be wandering around the hallways of a hotel. I sent them off into the night, feeling a wave of relief that everything had gone so smoothly their first evening.

Back in the Abbar sitting room, Rahman's aunts raved about how beautiful my sisters were.

"And the mother! What a beauty she is, too!" echoed one of Rahman's cousins.

Now that I knew my family was a big hit, my shoulders and neck finally loosened up the first time that evening. Sinking into a Louis XV chair and listening to Rahman's family's glowing reviews of my parents and sisters, I thought, *this is so much easier.* Amidst all the culture shock of Jeddah, I had gotten used to their passive ways. As long as I was dressed appropriately and following the rules, the Abbars accepted me and expected nothing more than my presence. If I didn't feel like talking, I didn't have to talk. I didn't have to entertain or please anyone. This was the benefit of joining an ancient culture. I almost felt more comfortable with them than with my own family, as strange as it was.

I was up early, dressed and ready, anxiously waiting on the doorstep of the Abbar house for my family to be delivered from the hotel. I ushered them in and sat them down in one of the smaller salons to talk privately and wait until Rahman announced our departure for the beach.

My sisters eagerly described their hotel room, with its attentive servants and somewhat antiquated velvet upholstery and portieres. This was new to me, never having ventured into a Jeddah hotel. "And the doors are all covered with velvet curtains. It feels like a top shelf brothel," Cindy giggled. "The room feels stuffy and we tried to open the windows, but they were locked," complained Diane.

"I assure you, it's the best hotel suite in Jeddah. Rahman is close friends with the owner. In fact, he'll be at our wedding celebration. I'll introduce you. Believe me, this hotel is as good as it gets here," I snapped. *Why are they being so uptight?* I was getting frustrated with their inability to understand that we were in an old-fashioned country. I had told them not to expect a Ritz Carlton.

"This morning, very early, we were all awakened by loud chanting from a nearby mosque. Then I realized there were at least a dozen more mosques within view, all chanting the same thing, every one of them!" stated my dad, baffled. "A heck of a way to wake up."

"Dad, they pray publicly like that five times per day. I've come to ignore the sounds of the prayer. It's like the chimes on our grandfather's clock at home, or church bells in Catholic neighborhoods. You just get used to it and don't notice it anymore."

"Seems like there are many things which you've gotten used to and don't notice anymore! What about the servants standing around and staring all the time? It gives me the creeps!" said Diane, somewhat disdainfully. "Feels like there's no privacy here. Everyone stares!"

"They keep watch in case you need something! The servants are deathly afraid of all of us and only want to be useful. Did you hear how they address me? Either Madame Patricia or 'Amati?' That means 'Master.' Believe me, they just want to do their job properly."

"Will you have servants in your new house when you move?" Cindy eagerly asked.

"Will I have servants? Oh my God, I'll have maybe eight or nine in my new house. The servants don't work the way our housekeeper does at home. They only seem to do one job each and very slowly at that, so you have a different person for every job. And they hardly take any time off! They'll do anything for me. It's frowned upon if I lift a finger! I've definitely had no trouble getting used to that."

"I don't know," Dad said doubtfully. "It feels like some evil is lurking around the corner. I don't trust it."

"Oh, don't be dramatic, Hank!" chided my mother, onboard with the idea of my many servants. "One can see that everyone's perfectly nice and straightforward. Just a little odd, that's all!"

"Well, just wait until you see how hospitable they all are. Everyone has been preparing for your arrival, and they have planned all sorts of dinners and events to entertain you and to introduce you to everyone they know. Please try to relax and enjoy yourselves. It's only a week. Be nice! And smile!"

Thahab appeared at the doorway, "*Amati*, the cars have arrived."

"See? What's so bad about that?" I proudly gestured for everyone to follow me to the cars, setting an example of the Saudi Arabian "good life" for my incredulous family. My sisters and I got into the back of one car and my parents were directed to get into another. I was relieved that I would be able to talk with the two of them privately.

"Tell me, what did Mommy and Daddy really say?" I demanded.

Diane was quick to deliver the cold hard facts, while Cindy uncomfortably avoided my eyes. "Daddy is totally freaked out by everything and doesn't understand why you want to live here. He hates the hotel, he can't stand feeling helpless, and I think he wants to leave earlier than we had planned. As soon as the wedding party is over, actually."

"Wow, that bad?" I asked.

"Yeah, Daddy wants to change our plane reservations. Cindy tried to convince him that it's actually fun, but he doesn't see it that way. I think he wants you to come with us to Monte Carlo when we leave. He mentioned that, too."

"Well, that's tempting. I wouldn't mind coming to the south of France with you all, but I can't possibly leave Rahman this early in our marriage. I wish Daddy were more open to being here. Let's see what happens today. Maybe being on the Red Sea will make him change his mind."

The car pulled off the paved road, bumping through the sand and rubble of the desert. My sisters stared out the window, wide-eyed. *I know that feeling.* The car lurched forward, turning sharply right at the water's edge, and in the distance the gates of the beach property appeared. Scratches on both sides of the gate flashed the silver of Mama Inja's Cadillac, a chilling reminder of what had happened only a few weeks prior.

We congregated on the back patio. Unlike the last visit, the day was peaceful, with a cool and constant wind. Considering the 100-degree heat in Jeddah, this beach house hit the spot. The swimming pool was topped off with sparkling water from the sea.

"Isn't the water inviting? Pumped in fresh." Noura urged my sisters, "Come on, jump in!"

Car after car came and went from the compound, depositing more guests to pay their respects to my family. The younger family members joined us in the swimming pool, but the older people sat happily under umbrellas and poolside awnings.

Take-out food from restaurants and food from the Abbar's city kitchen arrived in cardboard crates, and soon, a mini banquet appeared on tables in the shade of a grove of palm trees. Cindy blinked in disbelief and commented that all this seemed to have magically appeared out of the desert!

"It's always like this. Dozens of servants materialize in minutes, bringing every possible comfort!" Hyper-vigilant, I looked around and clocked that everything seemed to be going well. My parents were comfortably settled into large armchairs, seated at a dining table full of colorful platters of freshly made food. My dad had already figured out his favorite dishes, concentrating on the dips and spreads, tabouleh salad, and grilled chicken. My mom sniffed delicately at every dish in front of her and placed small portions of a few selections on her plate. She had always been a careful eater, watching her weight and avoiding anything unhealthy or caloric.

"Do they ever eat anything other than Arabic food here?" my dad asked me.

"No, not since I've been here. I've eaten Arabic food every day for over a month, and at this point, I've forgotten that other food exists."

"That might be why you seem to have lost weight, Patricia."

"No, I lost weight because I had dysentery two weeks ago. We took a two day trip to Cairo to meet Rahman's grandfather. We think it was from eating several of those *kofta* meatballs."

"Dysentery? Why didn't you tell us about that?"

"I didn't want to alarm you. It wasn't a big deal. The only problem is that I had to alter my gown for tomorrow's party a second time."

Covertly, my mother set down her fork. She had lost her appetite.

"I told you that it was the meatballs, Mom. You can eat chicken," I insisted with a sigh. She turned her nose up then twirled and eyeballed the water in her glass, looking for potential evidence of water-borne illness…

At that moment, Rahman emerged from the sliding glass doors. He sauntered across the patio, at least an hour late. Since my arrival in Jeddah, he had systematically been late to every event, but I was getting used to it. Rahman constantly had something else to do, and I had a sneaking suspicion that he didn't exactly enjoy all the family activities surrounding our new union. And today he has two families to deal with. *Who can blame him? This wedding stuff is stressful. It'll soon be over and we hopefully can resume a normal life.* I hoped that my parents didn't realize that he was a reluctant participant this week. I wanted to get through the wedding and let them go on to Europe in peace. I would work on my problems in due time without them, a strategy I had assumed since my teen years. The last thing I wanted was for my mother to come up with her own solution to my problems, then force it on me.

Guests continued to arrive as the afternoon progressed. Valerie and her husband, Khalid, were among the latecomers.

"Well, hello! Hope you're enjoying sunny Jeddah," Valerie shouted as she came bustling through to the patio. "I am glad there's a breeze out here. I've worked up quite a sweat just getting from the car to the house today." Valerie was a bundle of laughs with her strong, jovial mannerisms and northern British accent. I suspected that she was playing it up for my parents' benefit. Good. She wasn't exactly a taste of home, but better a heavy British accent than a heavy Arabic one.

She was outfitted, comically, in an absurdly huge sun hat and a colorful kaftan, like an out-of-place British tourist. She carried a gigantic straw tote bag on her shoulder full to the brim with other sun accoutrements. I was thankful to see her and certain that she would entertain my parents for the rest of the day with her wild stories about servants, children, relatives, and shopping excursions to the souk.

By the end of the day, every guest was enamored with my family, so much so that Mrs. Zainy, the business partner's wife, had even suggested that her son, Osama, get engaged to my sister Diane.

"She's so beautiful, just his type. And imagine how happy the two sisters will be together, *sawa sawa,* living here in Jeddah!" She intertwined her fingers on *sawa sawa*, symbolizing "togetherness." Valerie nodded eagerly in agreement, while my mother's jaw dropped in distress. Although it was a sweet and complimentary suggestion, I graciously declined, knowing Diane would never consent to such an arrangement...not to mention my dad would murder me for even relaying the marriage suggestion.

Once back in Jeddah, my family stopped briefly at the hotel to freshen up before being picked up again for the pre-wedding reception planned in their honor. Mama Inja shepherded my parents and sisters around the room, introducing everyone. I couldn't help but marvel at the sheer number of people who had shown up out of respect for me and both of my families. I was sincerely moved. So many people, supportive of my presence. And my parents and sisters had come all the way from New York to witness it.

In bed that night, I turned the events of the past two days over in my mind. It was hard work making my family comfortable, and I wasn't sure if they were entirely convinced that this marriage was a good idea. The pressure to appear put-together and blissful had been mounting on me since their arrival, because I could feel their strong distaste. And Rahman had barely shown his face the entire day, save for one short conversation with my parents. He was leaving it all up to me, again. The pressure was mounting and I was actually looking forward to my family's departure as a result. It was too hard trying to please them. This country was not for them, and I understood. Exhausted from defending my choices. I just wanted it to be over. Luckily time was on my side. Three days later, there I was at my delayed wedding reception.

***

The party was nothing like I had imagined it would be. First, Mama Inja brought an Egyptian hairdresser over to the house that afternoon to do all the ladies' hair. I took one look at her old-fashioned hot iron heating up in a crude metal bowl of actual glowing red coals, then smelled burning hair. Imagining my thin and somewhat fragile locks bursting into flames, I politely explained that I would prefer to do my own. With a shrug, Mama Inja relented. She was used to my "exotic" American preferences by now. I slunk away to dress, assuming I would find someone else to help me out with my hairdo. The house was filled with women, after all.

I must have lost track of time, because when I was dressed and ready to work on my unadorned hair, the entire Abbar family, including Rahman, had departed for the wedding reception without me, all very intent on arriving early to greet the guests. I didn't expect this and somehow must have missed the call to the cars. Feeling a little desperate, I phoned the Bin Zagr house to see if Noura could come and assist. She declined, saying that it was her responsibility to take care of the elderly aunties at the party. Had I been a Saudi girl, the entire female half of my family would have dressed me. But I wasn't, so I had to figure this out for myself. Mohammad, the driver, waiting faithfully outside, was all I had. I took a long shot that my sisters might still be lingering at the hotel and sent him there to pick up whomever was available. He thankfully retrieved Cindy, who was eager to help. Together, she and I hastily designed a creative hairstyle, a large bun covered in huge white lilies from a discarded dining room bouquet, before rushing off to the party.

No matter how many times Cindy reassured me, "You look fabulous, Patricia," I wasn't convinced. Where were my servants? How could I have been left alone to completely dress myself for my own wedding? Why hadn't I organized this better? The dress was randomly selected off the rack from Paris and altered a few days ago. The hairdo was one which I never would have chosen! I didn't feel like myself. When we arrived at the hotel lobby, my sister was ushered away and I was taken up into the procession by Mama Inja, who had assumed the role of mother of the bride. *Ugh. Another strike on my family.*

"Hurry, Patricia, get to the front. We're going in. Everyone is seated and waiting to see the bride," she calmly instructed, not even asking me where I had been or why I was late. She didn't seem to care as long as I eventually arrived. I would soon learn that lateness was the norm in Arab society and not to be taken personally.

Rahman and I stood at the front of a long line of about fifty members of the Abbar household and family, men and women, relatives and servants, and together we all proceeded into the banquet hall. Whatever doubts I had about how I looked were quickly extinguished by the gasps, cheers, and ululations, a traditional Arabic trill that I had not heard until that very moment. Rahman was magnificent in white robes with real gold edging, I was adorned in white lilies and organdy, and we floated through the crowd side by side. The servants behind us, dressed in traditional white Ethiopian robes, started to dance, chant and ring hand cymbals. The thousands of gold bangle bracelets lining their arms clicked and clanged against each other, creating music of their own. Here I saw firsthand how nearby Ethiopian culture seeped into the everyday life of Jeddah citizens. The celebration had the joyous feeling of Africa, as opposed to the somber and strict Muslim culture that permeated Saudi Arabia.

It was amazing, although I felt unprepared, and almost as if I were just a puppet filling a slot. The purpose of the entire ceremony was to present me as the bride, yet I was left at home alone? There were about five hundred guests, all standing by now. Walking slowly down the aisle with Rahman, looking for even one familiar face, I saw none. Rahman guided me up to a small dais table in the front of the room, which was shrouded by a trellis of white flowers and silk gauze. I sat down next to him, shaking, facing the crowd of strangers, looking for my family. There they were, sitting in the front row, dumbfounded as I was by all these unfamiliar and overwhelming numbers of guests, sights, and sounds.

I was surprised when I figured out that it was almost over, but without vows, speeches, declarations of love, a father-daughter dance. Rahman and I sat on display, like a cake topper, debuting as a married couple. Just as I was again feeling disillusioned at missing the exact American wedding traditions that I'd so fully dismissed, I met Cindy's bright smile mouthing the word, "beautiful," to me.

I understood that in that moment, I truly was beautiful and it was okay to just enjoy what the day was, and what my life would be instead of what it wouldn't. I'm playing the role of a wealthy Saudi's wife. *It's not as bad as my family thinks. All I have to do is sit and smile.*

***

When my family left Jeddah, things finally settled into a new normal. Without the pressure of pleasing my parents and entertaining all of the Abbars' guests, I could finally just be Rahman's wife. We had our own apartment at the Abbar compound. Waking next to him, greeting him after work, and spending time simply being together felt wonderful. Still, the strict rules of a Muslim household limited our activities and interactions.

It was frowned upon for men and women to be seen in public together in Jeddah, married or not. Rahman insisted we go everywhere in the backseat of a Cadillac with the driver, because a woman and a man alone in a car would always be considered suspect.

At first, I didn't understand what the dangers could be out there in the streets, but little by little, I heard stories. Any woman without a protector, be it a father, driver, brother, or husband, was at risk. Decent families kept all their women under close guard. The worst gossip circulating around Jeddah was about two English women who were being driven by their driver and crashed into another car. Their driver was killed, but the two women survived and were immediately locked up in jail. Apparently, because their Saudi driver was dead and the women were foreigners, no one from their expatriate community realized what had happened to them. They were held for days at the police station without anyone coming to their defense. They allegedly were raped repeatedly by the police officers and prison guards, and when their whereabouts were eventually discovered, the women were senseless and delirious. The British embassy was said to have sent the women back to England immediately for medical treatment. Rumor had it that one of the women never recovered from her delirium and had to be institutionalized permanently. I never knew for sure if this story was true or not, and although it sounded a little far-fetched, it was enough to convince me to be very cautious.

Our life settled into a routine with Rahman leaving for the office at 9 am, unable to see or talk to me until he returned for family lunch. Landlines in Saudi were extremely scarce, so placing calls during the day for anything but an emergency was out of the question and highly discouraged by the family. The reality was that I wasn't making much of a difference in his life, and we would be out of touch most of the time. Life wasn't as exciting as I had hoped, but I consoled myself with the thought that soon our new house would be ready. That would change everything.

While waiting for his return home for lunch, there was almost nothing to do. Many of our friends and wedding guests were on vacation for the summer, but Rahman had to stay and establish his position as Vice President at his father's company. Superficial tasks occupied my days, like finding a pleasantly scented hand cream at the drugstore all morning or shopping for an engagement gift at the jewelry store all afternoon. At night, I attended all sorts of ladies' events, and Rahman separately attended men's business functions. After a few weeks of this, boredom and loneliness set in. Tea parties and baby showers were not my thing. And I missed using my brain. I discovered that Jeddah was devoid of either bookstores or hobby stores, so reading or painting, two of my quiet hobbies, were out of the question. I would have to procure everything on my next trip abroad, but for now, I made do with daily Arabic lessons.

In the west, before my arrival in Jeddah, we heard stories about the heavy hitters of Saudi Arabia, such as Gaith Pharon and Adnan Khashoggi, whose names were splashed all over the gossip columns, and who frequented all the jet-set night spots in Paris, London and New York. Where were these people? Rumor had it that Gaith Pharon had a beach house somewhere and parties were held there nonstop. Maybe it was on the "creek" that Michelle Bin Laden had described? When asked, Rahman promptly insisted that I would not be invited to those parties. They were only for Saudi men and British air hostesses.

Months later at family lunch, I questioned Valerie, finally returned from England, about these mysterious "British air hostesses," thinking that since she was British, she might know.

"Those poor girls are employees of British Airways and are considered to be one short step up from prostitutes. The Jeddah route is a very tough route to work. They take the route to get whatever they can from Saudi men."

"What? What do they get?"

Valerie chuckled, "Oh, you know. Jewelry, trinkets, champagne parties and cash. They're the only single Caucasian girls in this country, and the airline puts them up in shabby hotels for their layovers. Haven't you seen the constant stream of limousines waiting outside those places? You didn't think Saudis stayed there, did you? Saudi men just send their drivers to pick up whomever and whisk them off to the parties every night. I knew one British girl who received a beautiful diamond necklace from her Saudi boyfriend–he was important. But of course," she winked, "He would never consider marriage."

I was desperate for something to do at night, and who could blame me? A newlywed living in her in-laws' house, not allowed to go out with her new husband? Now that everyone had returned from summer vacation, it was my time. I begged Rahman to take me out with him somewhere, anywhere, but he further insisted he had no place to take me. His answer was highly suspect, given he was constantly out after hours.

I continued whining and arguing until finally, he relented and brought me along to the housewarming party of his good friend, Walid Juffali, who had just built a new beach house–modern, all-white facade with a carefully manicured garden. It was perfect! Trees and flowers were planted in colorful groupings, framing the low-slung house. Enormous windows, curbstone lined paths, and dramatic lighting showcased specimen palm. I gasped as we made our way down the path towards the house, amazed at how different this felt! Was I in Saudi Arabia or was I in Malibu?

Halfway down the path, a white robed manservant motioned for us to turn away from the front door and follow him to the back of the house. There, the huge, paved terrace was revealed, full of guests, dramatically lit by lanterns set around the perimeter and accent up-lighting, with disco music playing softly in the background.

I couldn't help but notice that when we walked onto the terrace, every single air hostess, and one could tell who they were by their bottle-blond hair and their suggestive clothing, looked up and nodded a greeting to my husband, as if familiar. My face sank. There must have been twenty of those girls and Rahman had been living here for a few years alone, after graduation from college, with plenty of time to get acquainted with every single one of them. Oh well, he married me. Yet I wondered which one of these girls had slept with my husband. Or was it all of them? I told myself that they were probably jealous of me for being his wife. Flaunting my jewelry and expensive clothing, I tried to distract myself by thinking about the surroundings, as opposed to my husband's lap with a bimbo on it.

There were also other Middle Eastern men, less stiff with tight jeans and shirts unbuttoned halfway to their waists, revealing lots of chest hair– dead giveaways for Moroccan or Lebanese men. Rahman could have passed for one in Boston. Here, not so much with his latent onset of formalities and new penchant for rules.

In the few months I had lived in Jeddah, I observed that Saudi men were as uptight as the women, even though they weren't exactly targets of those restrictive laws. They, too, were bound to Muslim customs of stoicism and propriety. Rounding out the cast of the housewarming party were numerous European couples milling around. *Probably corporate employees.*

As I continued to scan the patio, half a dozen waiters holding silver trays of what looked like pina coladas or margaritas, emerged. I snatched one up, and to my surprise, it was full of alcohol. *Euphoria! A real drink! I feel like a teenager again.* Just as I asked Rahman to introduce me around, Tasnim appeared from nowhere.

"Rahman! Patricia! Welcome! You look as beautiful as ever." Always charming, her hands flitted around as she spoke in a sultry, soft purr. She wore a sleeveless, clingy red dress with sandals to show off her very smooth olive complexion. I was surprised by her voluptuous figure and the fact that her husband allowed her to flaunt it. Rahman wouldn't let me leave the house in a getup like that; in fact, he had made me change my dress two times that evening alone.

"Is that what you think you're wearing tonight?" he barked, arms folded.

"Yes, it's Yves Saint Laurent! Everyone will love it."

"No. No. It's see-through. Take it off or stay home. Your choice." He replied curtly, "I'll be in the car waiting." Of course, choosing my battles wisely, I changed into a flowing, printed (not see-through) ensemble.

Tasnim locked arms with me, playfully dragging me away for some girl talk, "Patricia, how are you liking Jeddah? Can you stand it? You won't believe what my mother-in-law tried to pull this week…she hates me! I'm totally disgusted with my life."

"Why does she hate you?" I asked.

"Because all Saudi mothers hate their daughters-in-laws!" She declared.

"So, who is that cute blond girl standing over there?" I motioned to one girl whom I couldn't quite figure out. She was clearly a cut above the air hostesses, but not dressed as conservatively as one would expect for the wife of a Saudi.

"That's Walid's current girlfriend. He picked her up in London, on a business trip, I heard. They've been together for about six months. Her name is Cathy, and trust me, he's crazy about her."

She certainly was pretty, with her long blond hair and her sweet face. At first glance, I could tell that Walid had been very generous with her. She was wearing a Gucci outfit, complete with matching shoes and diamond jewelry. From the looks of this beach house, this party, and this girlfriend, Walid seemed to be the type of man who wanted only the best and was prepared to pay for it. His girlfriend could have adorned the arm of any monied man on Earth. This place, staged meticulously, resembled something out of a Hollywood movie. The male servants, dressed identically in starched white uniforms, circulated around the terrace with silver trays of hors d'oeuvres and glasses of notable champagnes. I was amazed at the sense of style displayed here, knowing that getting it right in Saudi Arabia wasn't easy.

"Come on, let me introduce you to your host!" Tasnim moved me swiftly across the terrace to the man standing at Cathy's side. "Walid, this is Patricia, Rahman's new wife. She's American."

"Walid, such a pleasure to meet you. What an incredible villa. And this party's great!"

"Thanks," he barely acknowledged what I said, flashed me a tired half-smile and turned away. *Oh well, what could I expect?* Walid was not interested in knowing me or talking with me that evening. He was completely involved with his British girlfriend, Cathy, and busy telling worshippers about the German architects who designed the beach house for him. I listened for a while to him holding court with all those within earshot, but grew bored with what he had to say. Pompous nonsense, I decided.

Tasnim, however, was fawning over our host, "Oh Walid, Walid, where did you ever find these great big shrimps?" she gushed, as she batted her signature long lashes and waved the tail of the shrimp cocktail in his face. Tasnim was clearly drunk already.

"I had them flown in from Malaysia for the party," he yawned.

"Come on, Tasnim, let's get something to eat." I swiftly saved her from making a bigger fool of herself.

I had to admit, even though Tasnim's delivery was borderline ridiculous, I, too, wondered about the incredible quality and variety of the food on the trays and buffet table. Scallops, shrimp, oysters, lobster, steaks, and other items which I had not seen in months were all abundantly available and seemed to be prepared with expert skill. Maneuvering her over to the grill area, we spotted a chef who seemed to be Filipino. He smiled broadly and bowed as Tasnim and I approached.

"Walid hired him away from the best hotel in Manila when he was there on a business trip," Tasnim whispered.

"Seems like he finds everything he has on his business trips," I mused. "No wonder everything looks so perfect!"

After months of the rudimentary presentations of meals by the Abbar cooks, this spread was a welcome spectacle! Every dish had flowers decorating the edges of the platters, with ice sculptures as centerpieces for the shellfish. The perimeters of the platters of seafood were lined with empty lobster shells, propped up, looking like little waiters holding up the trays, their claws dancing cheerily in the air.

"I definitely could get used to this in a hurry. Come on, introduce me to everybody," I prodded, moving deeper into the crowd.

Hani Al-Attas was one of the first to approach us. He was a roly-poly little guy with a permanent smile—a must in the hospitality industry. His family owned the hotel with that red velvet suite my family had so thoroughly critiqued as being like a brothel. Little Hani hugged me mightily, echoing the loose, free feeling in this faux-Malibu environment. He asked if I was enjoying my stay in Jeddah.

"Oh yeah! Just wish I could find more parties like this!" I teased.

"Tell your husband to bring you to my house. I have get-togethers every Wednesday evening. I have a new sound system and the latest disco tapes, all from London."

"Oh look, Patricia, Niggi's here. Come on, let's greet her!" Tasnim grabbed my hand and tugged me across the patio. Niggi looked great, again dressed in one of her stunning saris. She greeted me with a warm smile.

"Patricia, there you are! We were wondering when we would finally get to see you!"

We? What is she referring to?

"Where have you been hiding this past month? Every time we see Rahman at a party, we ask him where he's keeping you. He answers that you don't like going out. Is that true?"

What? He tells everyone that I don't like going out? It was late September, and Rahman had been attending these parties for the last month, purposely excluding me. He kept everything a secret. *But why?*

"Rahman is just teasing about me not liking parties. That's ridiculous. I love parties!" I brushed it off to keep a brave face. "Can you believe this place? Fabulous!"

"We come to all of Walid's events. Walid has been kind enough to befriend us, although technically, he's our boss at Mercedes Benz. It's one of the perks of working for his family company. These glamorous evenings are our only diversions besides playing bridge at the British Embassy."

We wandered the patio then headed towards the house, entering through huge sliding glass doors, whisper-light and twelve feet high. Once fully inside, a second air-conditioned party was in full force yet more intense than the outside. The entire room was encircled with a sumptuous white leather sectional surrounding four separate low cocktail tables full of plated hors d'oeuvres and shallow bowls of white powder. The party seemed evermore chill until someone shouted, "Don't leave the glass doors open! The humidity melts the coke!"

Niggi pushed a white leather ottoman across the pristine alabaster marble floor, settling in front of a shallow bowl. She motioned to me to come and sit down with her, as she quickly sprinkled some white powder on a slab of mirror, cut it with a sharp silver instrument and snorted it before I could take a second glance. Little mirrors and silver knives and utensils were scattered everywhere.

"Here, have some, quick! Before our husbands catch us!" was ordered, shoving the petite silver object up my nose. *Wow, this party is getting strange.* I glanced around the room to see who might be watching me, feeling quite exposed and self-conscious. Not one of the men or women on the couches was looking my way. They were all absorbed in their own activities, mostly watching the large screen TV in the corner, bopping their heads to the loud disco music blasting throughout the house, or engaging in various stages of kissing and touching. One rotund Saudi man sat surrounded by three blondes, all trying to remove his white robe. They lifted up the hem, exposing his thin hairy legs in tall black knee socks, above them, common white boxer shorts.

"Does Harry want to come out and play?" cooed the boldest of girls, with a curious British accent, slipping her hand into his anxious boxers.

Whoa. Not the crowd for me. Rahman would kill me for being in here. But unable to resist seeing more of these surroundings, my eyes moved down a long corridor. Half a dozen doors were open, with scantily dressed girls fluttering in and out. Bedrooms? Was I in Los Angeles at some crazy swinger party? My head started to spin as I thought about Rahman catching me in a house full of half-naked dancing prostitutes, coke buffets, and fat Saudi men with Barbies reaching down their pants.

"My husband will never bring me to another party if he thinks I know what's going on inside this house. We'd better stay out there on the patio. Come on, Niggi, let's go!"

I grabbed Niggi's hand and dragged her up off the ottoman. We slid back through the glass doors, careful to shut them completely, lest we melt the coke, and returned to the crowd at the seafood spread. Unfortunately, we ran straight into Natalie, decked out in a feminine, modest floral silk dress, giving a lecture about Spanish meat vs. French meat. I gave Niggi a glance and pushed her over to the dessert table.

"What's with that housewife rap? Doesn't she ever have anything else to discuss besides cooking tips or child rearing? I am not interested in either subject!" I snapped, judging the only truly sweet person on the patio.

"Well, none of us were, once upon a time. Then you get married, and suddenly, it happens. I don't know how my kids happened. That's Saudi for you." Niggi winked, and we both laughed until we had tears in our eyes. Maybe it was the cocaine, or the drinks, but I felt like I had found someone delightfully honest. I wanted to be her friend. We exchanged phone numbers, promised to get together soon, and meant it.

I glanced around the terrace and spotted Rahman, looking so regal in his white robe, surrounded by Tasnim and a few air hostesses. Tasnim batted her eyelashes at him, while one of the British Air gals reached deep into his breast pocket, obviously searching for something. I fast approached and smiled brilliantly at the group.

"Looking for something?" I queried, grinning as I stared the pocket-searching one down.

"Yes, I need a pen, and I am convinced that Rahman has one in his pocket but I cannot find it." She was clearly very drunk, and I wondered why she wanted a pen. And why was she touching my husband's chest? Was she writing down her phone number for him? I glanced at Rahman and rolled my eyes, resisting my strong urge to say more. I wanted to go to more parties and opening my mouth might get in the way of future late nights out. Rahman glanced at me and asked, "Ready to go?" I nodded and he stepped away from the girl, still too close to him. We exited quietly, off towards the gate without a goodbye to anyone, including our host.

The party at Walid Juffali's beach house was a turning point for me in my new life. Until that evening, I had only suspected that Rahman was leading a kind of double life in Jeddah, keeping me quietly bored and lonely, stashed at his parents place while amusing himself after work. That party confirmed Rahman indeed knew other women and had an after-hours lifestyle that he'd been hiding from me. Niggi and Tasnim strongly hinted that having two lives, chanting in the morning while snorting in the twilight, was an option. I wondered if their husbands were less rigid than Rahman and perhaps less selfish. Even the prudish Natalie was socializing with the group.

Rahman had done nothing to help me feel at home in Jeddah. Nothing more than take me off the airplane and dump me on Noura's lap. He relied on the old-fashioned women of his family to initiate me into their version of Jeddah society, and their way was not going to work for me. He neglected to include me in his life outside the family, where there was fun and potential new friends for me. I desperately wanted to speak to him about this, but I knew that would get me nowhere. Rahman was not interested in my opinion on any number of things. Even when he asked for my help, like when picking out a suit, he was looking for an audience, a cheerleader, not an opinion. And Rahman did not react well to criticism, especially not from me at twenty-two years old. Besides, I simply didn't have the courage to stand up to him.

His ability to command any situation was what initially attracted me to him but being married to a controlling person wasn't so easy. He would say that he had done what I asked for, to be in Jeddah, as his wife. He had warned me that life in Jeddah was boring and difficult. I could practically hear his voice and see his eyes, stone cold with anger: *You asked for this. Suck it up.* So, I decided to work smarter, not harder, for what I needed to survive here without dying of boredom or loneliness. I had to cement my friendships with Niggi, Tasnim, and the other modern women of Jeddah. Having friends outside the family would be a big help in my quest to settle into local nightlife, so I started working on a way to present this possibility to Rahman.

Chapter Six

Strategic Approach

The next day was a Friday, the weekend in a Muslim country. As soon as I woke up, I pestered Rahman to take me to visit another couple, friends that I had not yet seen in Jeddah - Michelle and Mahrous Bin Laden, after Tasmin had reminded me of their fabulous beach house at the party.

"Puzzling, he hasn't taken you there yet…he and Mahrous are close." I had no answer for that but was determined that today I would get to that beach house and meet them.

"Can we go visit the Bin Ladens at their beach house today?"

"Why on earth would you want to go there?" he replied, disinterested. "It isn't even a house, it's a cabin within a shitty compound. We have our own private beach house directly on the Red Sea."

"I don't care if it is a cabin or a house, I just feel like getting together with people other than your family and seeing what's out there in Jeddah. Please take me! Come on! I've never seen the Creek and I'm so bored I could die."

"I warned you that life in Jeddah was going to be boring. You wanted to come live here. I gave you what you asked for…" Hook, line, and sinker, he was doing exactly what I knew he would. I was counting on this response. There was no way he would ever admit that he wasn't doing everything expected of him. I forged on…

"Please, come on. Let's get dressed and go to their cabin. It's a nice sunny day! Come on, please!" I said as I batted my eyelashes and literally crawled over to his side of the bed, "Please!"

Rahman cracked a smile, and I knew that I had won. He loves to feel in charge and apparently also loves it when I act like a needy bimbo. He pulled himself up out of bed, then nodded in agreement that we would go. "It's always a sunny day in Jeddah, Patricia, but…well…okay, get ready to go. We leave in one hour sharp."

I was thrilled! I vowed to make no mistakes, and do nothing to upset Rahman this morning. I would not object to his driver taking us to the beach instead of having privacy and driving ourselves. I would not wear a bikini to keep him from complaining about lack of modesty. And I would make him happy because he had made me happy. I showered and donned a long, loose white sundress, perfect for the beach. Under that, was a nice conservative one-piece Gucci bathing suit, something that no one could criticize.

We packed our gear and took off with the driver. Rahman didn't look particularly happy, but we were on our way. We sat quietly, nibbling on fruit and cheese and listening to the latest smuggled disco cassette as the car sped through the desert to the Creek. From what I had gleaned in many conversations, this beach was located on a kind of inlet which drained into the Red Sea. Unlike in the vast sea, the waves were tiny, one could easily swim or go boating, and there were no large fish to speak of. Because of the milder water conditions, it was the preferred location for beach properties outside the city of Jeddah. As the car approached the walls of "Family Beach," the name given to this property shared by the tenants, our driver honked for the doorman to open the gates. My heart dropped. *This place looks a mess.* The walls of the compound were made of weathered cement block, painted light blue in another lifetime, faded and chipped. The gates were rusty corrugated metal, swinging on sagging, crooked hinges. Someone had taken a large piece of cardboard, probably torn off the side of a discarded delivery box, and scribbled Arabic words on it, which I assumed was the name of the property. In a failed design attempt, the artist had added some wavy lines below the name, which were probably meant to symbolize the sea. I stifled a chuckle at this, *I'm getting good at interpreting Arabic signs.*

This homemade sign was secured with frayed rope to a crooked metal post sticking out of the sand. Always alert to gatekeepers these days, I noticed that this particular gatekeeper looked like he had just emerged from a leper colony. He wore a long, dirty rag wrapped around his head, and his scant clothing was ripped and torn, revealing a body, all skin and bones. I had a sinking feeling that things were not going to be at all glamorous today. As I took in additional eyefuls of the derelict property, I keenly remembered Michelle Bin Laden in Paris, glittering in her Dior gown and blowing smoke from her long, ivory cigarette holder into my face as she *simply insisted* that the Creek was the *only* place to be.

Our car made its way through the sand, down the center alleyway between the cabins. Yes, they were truly cabins. Tiny, one room cabins.

We stopped at the last one. *At least it's in the front row, with a water view.* We slowly emerged from the car, blinking in the already-beating sun. Our driver carefully unloaded our Louis Vuitton totes and refreshments from the trunk, making sure he didn't forget anything. We had brought goodies for lunch and a few changes of outfits, each. A makeshift path led us to the tiny wooden abode, driver trudging behind us hauling bags and two coolers full of drinks and ice.

The entire front of this cabin was an enclosed screened porch and from within, a voice shouted, "Rahman, what a pleasant surprise! Come in, come in!"

It was Mahrous, who apparently had been looking out and spotted our car pulling up the alley between the cabins. He swung open the screen door and grinned at us cheerfully, looking sincerely pleased that we had arrived at his beach cabin, a picture of Saudi hospitality. Since there were no telephones at this place, obviously, it had been impossible for Rahman to call ahead and warn them of our intent to pay a visit, but, true to custom, they made us feel like dropping in was the absolute best thing that could have happened to them today.

Mahrous was dressed in a long, light blue kaftan with a white embroidered design on the front and looked like he was visiting from Marrakesh, a far cry from the three-piece suit he wore in Regine's nightclub in Paris the last time I saw him. He seemed very relaxed and offered us a cold drink. I purposely did not kiss him hello, still trying to act like the model wife to please Rahman. I reached over and shook his hand instead.

I spotted Michelle, snuggled into the corner of a low sectional which filled the entire space.

"Bon jour, Patricia!" She greeted me and got up for a kiss and a hug. She, too, was wearing a long blue kaftan, the female version of the one Mahrous was wearing. *Hmm, his and hers kaftans. Probably souvenirs of their latest trip.*

This would presumably be a very relaxed meeting–precisely why Rahman hadn't really wanted to come. Rahman liked to be entertained yet there was absolutely nothing to do in this cabin but sit in a circle and look out at the sea. I don't even think there was electricity. The place reminded me of the rickety tree house that my sisters and I had built together years ago, where we and the neighborhood kids would sit around, talking for hours.

Once we were cozy in the sectional, Michelle popped the cork on a bottle of champagne, passed around plastic champagne flutes, threw some nuts and chips into a bowl on the cocktail table, and the conversation began. To my surprise, instead of the racy interesting subjects we discussed at our last meeting, which had been in Paris, today, all we talked about was gossip. Jeddah gossip. Who was in the country, who was out of the country, where they were, how long they were staying. Who got married, who moved back, who moved away. Why they left, and why they stayed. Rahman and I were tired of the gossip, but perked up when asked about our home being built. I knew little about this house. For some reason, Rahman was very tight-lipped about giving me details. In retrospect, it was control. He had felt no need for my input on our home and would maintain tight control over me, our home, his lifestyle, and our marriage.

"When will you be moving into your new house?" Michelle asked, pushing aside a long wisp of brown hair which had fallen across her eyes. She secured it tightly in the bun which she always seemed to wear. Michelle resembled a ballet mistress with her severe hair style and long slender neck.

Rahman spouted details that I had never heard about our new home. "In about one week, the houses will be complete. Eight houses in all. The plan is to enclose the two front houses, one for me and one for my brother, Ghazi, creating a small compound surrounding the pool area. Ghazi is still in college and won't be back for a few years, but when he returns, his house will be waiting, lucky guy. We're digging a swimming pool in our shared backyard, and putting finishing touches on the landscaping. The plan is to rent out the other six houses, and there seems to be a waiting list of prospective tenants. We can name our price at this point, with the lack of new housing in the Jeddah market."

"I'm so glad I caught you before they're all rented. We might be interested in renting one of the six. How many bedrooms does each house have?" Michelle queried.

Renting the other six houses? Enclosing two houses with a swimming pool? Ready in one week? I had no idea we were so close to moving in and that they were already digging the pool. When was he going to tell me all this? Was he planning on waking me up the morning of and announcing, *"Pack your bag, we're moving today?"*

I was quiet on the way home, occupied with the growing list of deceptions now mounting in my mind. I was happy to concede to Rahman that the Creek wasn't at all the way the Bin Ladens had advertised it to be. But these first few months of our marriage, he had hidden so much from me, too much. While he sipped cocktails and danced to smuggled disco music with his friends and their wives, I was relegated to baby showers for distant cousins with my mother-in-law by my side, ensuring I behaved myself.

He was a liar, plain and simple. I held back the tears until we entered our apartment at the Abbar compound.

Putting the bags down in the doorway, he sighed, "Patricia, what's the matter now? Didn't I do what you wanted today? Everything you asked for?"

"When were you going to tell me about the house?" I blurted out, "Why did you keep that from me? It's my house, too."

"Patricia, calm down. I wanted to wait for the right time. That special moment." He grabbed my hands, pulled me towards him and gave me a kiss, "You know I love those special moments. They give me great joy."

"Glad someone is getting great joy!" I quipped.

"Maybe I will give you great joy, too. Maybe you deserve it…" he led me over to the chaise and reclined.

"I like that. I need some joy," I said hopefully, slipping into his arms.

"Okay, ready? I'll say it how I wanted to say it. Our house is almost complete and I want us to move in by the end of this month. Next week we can start packing our bags and anything else we want to bring with us. The servants will take everything over to the house and unpack. You realize there are no movers here, don't you? Should only take a few weeks."

"What? Are you kidding?!?" I practically shouted. Can a person be furious and overjoyed at the same moment? I was ready to kill him and I had already heard the news at the Bin Ladens', yet somehow, I was ecstatic! I leapt up and started dancing around the room, stopping occasionally to give Rahman a kiss. In spite of my better judgment, all was forgiven. We were moving into our house.

"I'm gonna be FREE!" I chanted as I danced and hugged and danced some more, "Everything is gonna be great! We can finally start living our lives! Finally!" His six months of deception disappeared in a matter of minutes. My dashing college boyfriend was back. Rahman switched on the music, jacked up the volume to maximum, and we both proceeded to dance around the room like a couple of teenagers in love.

Chapter Seven

Culture Shock

Abdullah, please go knock on the front door and ask for my friend, Tasnim. Tell them Patricia is in the car. I'll wait here."

"At your service," he announced proudly, indicating keen enthusiasm for his new job as my private chauffeur. He had been hand-picked by Mama Inja, who made sure all the ladies of the family had the trustiest of drivers, and I felt safe in his care.

It was Saturday morning, and I had finally made it out of the stifling dreariness of the family compound to see my new friend, Tasnim. As the front door swung open, she appeared on the steps of her in-laws' rather tired-looking Jeddah home. She practically skipped down to the car, her infectious smile beaming with hundred-watt brilliance against the back-drop of a drab, dust-covered exterior.

"Patricia, I'm so happy to see you. You have no idea! You've saved me from yet another ridiculous argument with my mother-in-law. What a bitch!" she muttered while planting a kiss on each of my cheeks. Tasnim squeaked out a plastic smile, then waved at what must have been her nosey mother-in-law, pulling back the ever-present heavy curtains to stare out the sandy front window.

"Well, we're here now. I have an idea—perhaps a little sparkle to make our day more pleasant? Abdullah, take us to Mouawad jewelers, please."

Tasnim's face and mood quickly switched gears. "Oh goody! I love that place."

"I've been sent to purchase a gift for my brother-in-law's new fiancé. There's a party next week and I need to get something nice for the bride-to-be." It was a little strange picking out an engagement gift for a girl I had yet to meet, so I needed Tasnim's seasoned Saudi wife opinion.

"Who's Ghazi marrying?" Tasnim asked, curiously.

"His distant cousin, Najlah...Mama Inja spotted her at a wedding and made the deal. They described Najlah as tall and beautiful...with ample breasts." I teased, a little surprised at the details Mama Inja offered. "Mama Inja claims to be an expert on Ghazi's preferences." And apparently, cup size does matter to him...

"Hmmm. Yes, the piece you choose must be exquisite. And we may need to try on a few things for ourselves...You know, just to be sure..." Tasnim batted her signature eyelashes. We both laughed and settled back for the ride to town.

Within minutes, the car slowed to a crawl, well before reaching our destination. A traffic jam in quiet downtown Jeddah? How was this possible? We heard the noise before seeing a large group gathered in the small square across from the shop—the shouting in excited Arabic, snippets of prayer, the rush of feet kicking up dust. People began to come from behind our car, hastily moving towards the square to join the others. Abdullah honked his horn as our path forward shrank, excited onlookers quickly filling the streets in front and behind us without a care for vehicle traffic. We could see the jewelry shop in the distance, and our car was inching its way towards the door.

Abdullah, just like my former driver Mohammad, was fastidious and would sacrifice his life to protect Abbar women. Despite the extra time it might take, Abdullah was determined that my feet would never touch down even ten feet back on the open street. After what seemed like forever, we arrived at the doorway of the jeweler and Abdullah sprang from the car to open our doors. The sun beat down mercilessly as we stepped out and into the heat.

Standing in the fine marbled entry area, I pounded the intricately carved wooden door. It was clearly fortified, lined with enough locks to keep a castle. The exterior windows showcased diamond jewelry priced out of reach by nearly everyone but our small circle of monied families here. With such pricey baubles, the store owner didn't want "just anyone" walking in off the street.

As we waited by the door, the group in the square behind us started to chant, channeling the chaotic anger of what would be a protesting crowd back home. Tasnim and I turned to see what the commotion was. A solitary black-robed woman, still as death, stood on a crude platform in the middle of the square. The crowd all faced her, their rhythmic cheers increasing in volume. Was she a celebrity? Or the town heroine? No. I knew she was in terrible trouble.

I could feel the tension rise, palpable and foreboding. The woman suddenly recoiled, taking the first hit, then steadying herself as if for another. *They were throwing rocks at her.* The stones began to fly with increasing frequency as the emboldened watchers took turns finding incrementally larger rocks to hurl from conveniently placed piles. Her body jerked forward and back, hands now stationed at her face offering useless but instinctive protection. She cried out in torment, her wailing broken and terrified. I wanted to turn away, disgusted at what I was witnessing, but I could not pry my eyes from her.

A public stoning. Something I had heard of but couldn't quite comprehend. They were murdering her right in front of us. The somehow still-standing brave woman let out one final, horrible, blood-curdling scream before collapsing to the dusty ground beneath her.

But the crowd wanted more of her blood. They roared ever louder, pushing forward for a glimpse of her now limp body. It was savage, like lions on broken prey. Heavy stones continued to pile up, until her still body was fully entombed above ground in the square. Her shape was now nothing more than a hill of sharp earth.

I tried to bring her back, quietly in my head. *Maybe she's alive under the rubble. Is she still breathing? Can I help her?* I could not reconcile in my mind what my eyes had just witnessed, the definitive sound of a brutal murder of a type that civilized societies had abandoned centuries ago. I could feel nothing but hopelessness and the guilt of allowing this woman to die a slow and protracted death. No judge, no jury, yet she was no more. Blotted out. Was she innocent? What was her crime?

The elaborate embossed door of the jewelry store swung open to a burst of fragrant, cool air. A handsome man immaculately dressed in a European suit stepped out with a wide grin, beckoning for us to come in.

"What just happened?" I asked Tasnim, in a jagged whisper.

"A stoning. Probably for adultery." she replied, unaffected.

The handsome salesman reached out and literally herded the two of us into the store, shutting the door tight behind us, and locking the place back up from the inside.

"No need for you two ladies to stand out in the heat watching such a spectacle," he chided in perfect English.

I looked at Tasnim in horror, "A stoning?" I verbalized, still in shock. I searched her face for a reaction, any reaction, but she was indifferent, unfazed, blasé even. She nodded then turned her attention to the attendant.

"Yes, it happens about once a month in the square. Not very pleasant but part of the Saudi culture. I'm Lebanese, myself. We don't do that. Can I get you ladies some tea? Coffee? What is it that you are looking for? Is this a gift for someone? Is it for you?" The salesman continued to prattle on, easily transitioning Tasnim to a more agreeable "purchasing" mood. But I couldn't process a word of that idle chatter. Who could think about coffee and gold trinkets?

"Please bring us some tea and cookies," snapped Tasnim very firmly, "Come on, Patricia, enough. That isn't the only shocking thing you'll be seeing here in Jeddah. Get used to it. And stop sulking. I want to enjoy my Saturday. I don't get into town much, so I've never seen one of these stonings before, but we all know it happens. It's part of the culture. Come on, lighten up."

I eased down into a nearby sofa. It was soft and luxurious, a rich shade of red. I took note of the overt luxury and sumptuous surroundings presented, obviously inspired by fabulous Parisian jewelry shops, with deep jewel-toned walls, carpet, upholstery, and furniture, all enticing a powerful mood for buyers looking to treat themselves. But my legs were unsteady and my head still reeling. Shopping seemed unbearably frivolous now. I have so few friends here and I'm desperately lonesome. *Maybe Tasnim is right…I'm in Jeddah. Either take the entire package, or live somewhere else.*

***

At family lunch with the Abbars that afternoon, I was unable to eat, still shaken by the gruesome events of the morning.

Aziz, Rahman's older cousin, quite the joker, gave me his customary greeting, "Patricia, what have you been up to? Staying out of trouble, I hope?"

Without hesitation, I blurted out the entire episode at the town square, longing for one person to validate my feelings of horror. But no takers. The forks and knives clanged, food platters passed around, and everyone was eating just as quickly as was standard.

"So, nobody's surprised by this?" voicing my incredulity to no one in particular.

"Oh well, welcome to Jeddah," said Valerie, in a motherly tone, "I saw one of those last year. Was it a woman, Patricia?"

"Yes. She actually fell to the ground while I was watching. So many rocks were thrown, even after she fell. She just became this large heap...I think I watched her die." It took every ounce of my energy to keep my composure but I was angry, and even more so given no one else would be angry with me.

"Well, Patricia," Aziz added brightly, "Now you understand why you must stay out of trouble." With that, he winked and burst into a hearty laugh. I could hardly believe I was hearing this, especially Valerie's subdued reaction. A dystopian novel comes to life here in front of me. Or was it that I was living in the seventh century?

After all those light and fun stories about shepherd's pie, jewelry, and maids, Valerie never once thought to warn me that I might casually run into a public stoning? No one had prepared me for this. Perhaps they had become accustomed to it themselves but couldn't bear to admit that. I somehow had to accept, or at least stomach it for now.

***

I stayed home for a full week after the stoning, not fully recovered and terribly lonely. Hunkering down at the Abbar compound was comforting at first but became increasingly frustrating. Hesitant to return to town after what I had seen, I settled on home visits with new friends for a while. Despite my growing bewilderment with Saudi culture, I was still eager for some kind of social enrichment and female company, especially given Rahman's post-matrimonial reluctance to include me in his after-hours exploits.

The stoning event was still fresh in my mind but already forgotten in the minds of all others. I had no one to speak honestly and openly with, and I needed fellowship with women who actually had feelings like mine.

I decided to target Niggi for my next friend. I was determined to spend time with her. I needed a new best friend, a wingman. I missed the kindred spirit I had back in America with Liz. So I asked Abdullah to drive me to the Mercedes Benz compound one morning. As we pulled up to the large set of gates with the Mercedes Benz logo, Abdullah quickly went over who we were and why we were there with the gatekeeper. This was a compound in every sense of the word. Similar to Levittown on Long Island, a place not too far from where I had grown up, there were winding streets with sidewalks and street lights and identical tidy houses complete with children playing outside, housekeepers pushing baby carriages, and groups of ladies talking together on well-manicured front lawns. It was a perfectly executed planned small-town-USA community, albeit a tad "Stepford-esque," somehow dropped into the middle of a vast, expansive desert. I wondered why everyone made a forlorn face when they mentioned this Mercedes Benz compound. For me, it was tidy and sweet, safe and familiar. We pulled up to a house next to what appeared to be a large community center, and Abdullah jumped out to open my door. As I exited the car, he announced that he would wait for me while I paid my visit. Nothing could tempt him to drop me off here and leave. He felt it was his duty to stand guard in the front of the house, so I shrugged, told him that I may be a few hours, and approached the front door.

Niggi greeted me with a warm smile before I even had a chance to ring the doorbell. Behind her stood her six-year-old daughter and an Ethiopian servant, both wide-eyed and open-mouthed. Visits from someone like me, a young, stylish American with a fancy car and chauffeur, must have been rare.

"Put your eyes back in your head, Sara. This is Patricia Abbar, Amm Rahman's new wife. She's American and we are welcoming her to Saudi," she said sharply to her daughter.

Niggi grabbed me with a big hug, pulled me into the house, and shouted to the manservant lingering outside to get my driver some tea, "Invite him into the servant's quarters. He can't wait outside in the hot sun all morning."

Niggi led me into the living room of her prefabricated house, stocked with plush American-style furniture. Aysha, her servant, offered us tiny cups of tea, and as expected, Niggi asked me how I was acclimating myself to Jeddah. I almost brought up having accidentally witnessed a stoning, but decided against it. I didn't want to upset her on our first date. Besides, every concern I had had about Jeddah was met with complacency or defensiveness, or both. As much as I longed for normalcy, my most immediate need was a good friend, and that would mean holding my tongue, at least for now. Niggi would probably feel the same way everybody else did here, and I couldn't bear being scolded for not just accepting atrocities one more time. So I kept our chit-chat light and superficial. Polite, noncontroversial conversation would be easier to bear than no conversation at all. For hours on end we talked about the Abbars' household and my life there, while Niggi interjected her own laments on life in Jeddah as a second-class foreigner.

It seemed that I was not the solitary soul in Jeddah who was miserable. Niggi bemoaned the fact that she and her husband, who was an Oxford graduate from a "long line of Khans," had sacrificed their social standing in Karachi in favor of the uber-generous Mercedes salary. With his contract renewal coming up, Taher wanted to add on an extra five years to their stay, but Niggi had doubts about raising kids in Jeddah. As foreigners in such an insular place, her daughter's education options were quite limited. She'd considered boarding school for her two young ones but couldn't bear to be apart from them.

Aysha was particularly submissive while she carefully topped off our tea, her head dropped down to her chest, murmuring how much of a pleasure it was to serve me. It was strange, almost uncomfortable, even in a place where servants outnumber all other workers. Niggi insisted that Aysha was indeed blessed to serve there.

"Believe me, she's so happy to have this job and we hardly pay her! Before working for us, she was working for a Saudi princess in Riyadh, and from what she tells me, they wouldn't allow her to sleep. She had to work all night serving at their endless parties. When she did anything wrong, they burnt her with a hot iron or hit her on the head with a wooden stick. She said that the other servants would hit her and sometimes even bite her. She was never allowed to leave the palace."

"Are you kidding?"

"No, I'm not kidding, Patricia. You should hear what these servants tell us about the treatment they receive from their Saudi employers."

At the chance to discuss gruesome Saudi habits, Niggi was on a roll, "Saudis are well known for mistreating the servants. They have been known to cut off the hand of a servant who dares to steal. I was raised Muslim, so I know that's what the Koran dictates as punishment for theft. But they actually impose that on thieves here! The servants are often locked up like animals, never receiving a day off, especially when they come from countries like Indonesia. Yes, I believe the Indonesian servants are treated the worst for some reason, and paid that way, too. And forget it if you're a halfway attractive woman. The men of the household keep you a prisoner and use you for sex whenever they please. Many of them get pregnant, and they're lucky if they get shipped back to their countries. The unfortunate ones meet even worse fates."

"Like what?" I asked, dumbfounded.

"Like what? Like what I heard last week around town. This attractive Filipina servant was repeatedly raped by the Saudi boss of the house, and when she informed him about her pregnancy, she suddenly ended up drowned in the water tank on the roof. Found floating in the tank, after a week of being reported missing. Everyone is speculating whether she drowned herself or if she was pushed in. Either way, it's not a pretty picture."

"Wait a minute! Do you mean in the water tank containing the water they bathe in and cook with? I'm not sure which is worse. The drowning or the idea that people were cooking and washing in that same water."

Niggi shrugged and flipped her hand to show that she didn't know or care.

I was deeply disturbed, thinking back to not only the stoning I had witnessed but also, my own experience as a woman in Saudi thus far. My first week in Jeddah had been marred by my ugly encounter with the beach house gate keeper. But by the logic of Niggi's story, had I not been the guest of an influential family, I would have surely ended up dead. Whether her rumor was true or not, it was too gruesome for me. I told Niggi so and she scolded me.

"Oh, Patricia. Wise up! You are in a very dangerous place. Never forget that. The things that actually happen here every day are worse than this. You are still so naïve. I know these things for a fact. I grew up in a very similar place. Think medieval. Think lawless. It's all around you. The sooner you wise up, the better off you'll be."

Even Niggi, a foreigner, dismissed the absurdity of this place and was complacent with every backward behavior and tradition. It's funny how perspectives can change. I couldn't wait to experience freedom, and here I was, the least free that I'd ever been. Had it not been for my husband's money, I could be floating facedown in a water tank right now.

It was almost lunchtime and Niggi suggested we fetch her son from the community pool together. On our brief walk, she introduced me to a few Germans whose husbands worked at the Benz factory. "Our house is next to the pool complex because of Taher's important position in the company. But frankly, I would have preferred a house all the way at the end of the road. I cannot stand these German people, all congregating here with their children! The good news is that we barely have time to get overheated. The pool is right inside."

We entered more imposing gates into a large, shaded outdoor complex. Guards at the door checked Niggi's ID.

"Why the ID?" I queried.

"Beats me, Patricia. Who would ever want to sneak in here? On Friday evenings we have German Beer Garden night, with non-alcoholic beer, where everyone comes to stand around, eat sausages, and gossip. It's horrible."

Some German ladies, curious about seeing a new face, approached us for an introduction. After making the requisite small talk with her nosey neighbors, Niggi pulled out her wallet and walked over to some vending machines. She returned with ice cream for us then called across the pool for her son, Hammad, to join. It was the first ice cream I'd had in weeks, and the most exercise. Just walking to the pool felt so good on my limbs. I stood there smiling, remembering what it felt like to be a kid, frolicking at the pool in the summertime.

A tall bow of a boy made his way over to us, tugging at the tee shirt stuck on his wet skin. He said "hello" to me while brushing wet, matted hair from his face. As he smiled and extended his hand to shake mine, a thunderous explosion echoed from outside the compound. We watched as smoke rose up in the distance. "Come on, Patricia, kids, let's see what this is about."

We made our way out of the complex and into the open road, where spectators were gathering. The cloud of smoke and soot grew larger and darker, heading straight up to the heavens, like a black column. The smell of burnt plastic commandeered the air. Niggi instinctively grabbed her kids.

"Let's get inside. This smoke can't be a good thing to breathe." We hurried back inside the house, gathering at the window, looking out as the spectacle unfolded.

Dozens of people ran towards the smoke. There was shouting, maybe even screaming, coming from outside.

"Niggi, I think it's getting worse. I hear screaming. Don't you hear it? We should try to see what's happened."

Niggi begrudgingly got up and pulled a few tissues from the box. "Here. Hold these over your nose. It stinks of plastic out there."

We emerged from the house, and there were neighbors running in every direction, shouting, "Fire! House burning!" in multiple languages.

"These prefab houses are made of plastic," said Niggi. "Everything is flammable. Do they even have a fire department here in Jeddah? I wonder whose house is on fire?"

Two security guards ran alongside the crowd announcing on a loudspeaker that they were looking for anyone from the Seifringer residence at Villa #212."

"Do you know those people?" I asked, relieved when Niggi shook her head.

"It might be the young family with two toddlers that arrived last year. The kids are still too young to be in school, so I haven't really met them yet."

Abdullah found me and insisted we leave immediately, in broken English. Niggi agreed. "You should probably get out of here before they close the compound gate or something. No telling what the authorities will do when they arrive."

In spite of the emergency situation and related drama, I was disappointed that my visit was cut short. But she was right, so I quickly said goodbye, promised to call later, and rushed to my car. Abdullah cautiously exited the compound, careful to avoid the pedestrians running in the street. As we drove back towards the center of Jeddah, not one fire truck drove past. And there were no fire alarms going off anywhere. It was as if nothing had happened. I asked Abdullah if they had a fire department in Jeddah.

He shook his head sadly, "Maybe, Amati, maybe," which I could tell was a "no." I remained silent for the remainder of the drive. But when I arrived home, I quickly switched on the TV to the one live news station, waiting to hear something about the explosion. Nothing. I just couldn't wait until lunch at 3 pm to tell Rahman about the fire. He may know someone that was there. I dialed the main number and waited as the operator put me through to him.

"What's wrong? Why have you called me? Did something happen?" he demanded.

Sheepishly, I replied, "I was at Niggi's house having tea when there was a big explosion and a fire in the compound. Abdullah brought me home immediately, but I was wondering how to find out what actually happened. Did your friend Walid call you today? His family owns the compound. Or did you happen to see or hear anything on the news? I've been listening to the news on TV, but there's nothing."

"An explosion? What were you doing there anyway? It was probably nothing. A backfired car or something like that."

"No, there was a column of black smoke that kept getting bigger and bigger, people were running and screaming and they were searching for the residents of a house when I left. I'm sure something serious happened."

"And you call me in the office, hold up the entire office phone line and everyone else's calls to tell me this?" he hissed. "We can speak more about this when I get home. See you at lunch." And he hung up.

Terrified that Niggi's home might also burn, I called her next, but there was no answer, not even a ringing sound. The phone lines had been shut down.

I later learned from Niggi that the mother of the family had left her children sleeping in the bedroom while out visiting a neighbor. The house-keeper was picking up mail from the commissary and the children were alone. An electrical fire blazed through the plastic house, melting everything in a matter of minutes and the two preschool children died in their beds. Upon relaying the tragedy, Niggi begged me not to mention it to anyone, for fear that our outrage might be misinterpreted as criticism of Saudi Arabia. I'll never forget the darkness in her tone as she warned me, "Patricia, don't go there. It is never wise for foreigners to complain about this country to its nationals." I took her advice and suffered my heavy heart in silence.

***

A few weeks later at family lunch, Mama Inja addressed us all, "I need some of you to come with me this evening for an azah. We will sit at my cousin's house for her sister's death. Who is available?"

I looked to Valerie and whispered, "a wake?" She nodded, so I volunteered, "Valerie and I can come, Mama Inja. How should we dress?"

"I can come too, Mama Inja," Jawaher chimed in. She looked at me, "I will explain what to wear, Patricia."

"Thank you. Why don't we girls all go in the same car?"

Jawaher nodded and agreed that one car would be best. She explained that the house was in the old souk, the part of town that satisfied most foreigners' fantasies of Arabia, with its shopping stalls and layered carpets. We would have to wear all white, the customary color for deaths, covered fully by a *tarha*, a headscarf, and an *abaya*, the long black cape. Mama Inja's second cousins never left the old part of town, and the old souk was rigidly traditional.

Later that evening, as Valerie, Jawaher and I were on our way, Jawaher gave us the full story. I had assumed the deceased to be an old auntie, but it was a young woman, a mother, and her two children.

"She is Mama Inja's second cousin, and she was married to her second cousin from another branch of the family. They had two young children, a boy and a girl, and I guess the husband, who was reputed to be a bit unstable, discovered her having an affair with another man. They say he came home two evenings ago, took some electrical cable, tied her and the two children up with the cable and plugged it in. They were all electrocuted and died instantly." *But not painlessly.* I was horrified, again but somehow choked out my disbelief.

"He did that? To his children too?"

"Well, they say he wasn't even sure they were his...Anyway, he fled to Medina to seek refuge with the other side of his family."

Valerie chimed in, "I'll bet he gets off the hook, too. I think husbands and fathers have the right to kill any woman in the family who commits adultery."

We both stared hard at Jawaher, waiting for her response. She was a bit uncomfortable with the two of us confronting her, but found the right words, "I'm not defending this at all, but these people are the old-fashioned type. They live by ancient customs. Yes, if there are witnesses to her adultery, he will go free. Look, these people chose to live this way. There are fewer and fewer of them today in Jeddah, but it's their way and they don't want to change. They believe that this is the way the religion dictates these matters to be handled..." Her voice dwindled off as our car came to a halt in front of the square, leading to the old souk. Usually a driver would pull right up to the front door to let his female passengers disembark safely, but the dirt roads of the old souk were ancient, narrow, and inaccessible to cars.

Mama Inja, protected by her ever-present driver, was waiting for us in the square and we got into line behind her. Together we proceeded through the imposing gates of the old city and into the souk like a mother goose and her three goslings. Mama Inja slipped the remainder of her tarha over her head, covering her entire face. She became a black mass of fluttering fabric, completely shapeless. And completely unrecognizable. *I suppose she wants it that way...Maybe she's embarrassed to be related to these people.* It was dark. But above our heads, strand after strand of small white cafe lights dangled, creating a well-lit, almost festive pathway for us to walk along past shops filled with wares that might have predated Islam. The buildings were made of rough white stucco with crude dark wooden doors, roofs, and window grids. No glass, just grills of dark wood, a rudimentary form of ventilation. Some of the second floor window bays jutted out above the street. I caught a quick glimpse of someone, a lady, sitting inside an overhang, her face pressed against the grill, attempting to catch a breeze. As we approached each shop, shopkeepers would hold up their wares—a tee shirt, a glass vase—trying to entice us to come over and browse. I couldn't understand anything they were saying. It must have been some dialect of Arabic I had not yet heard. The street swarmed with men of every age, most dressed in white robes with a few in colorful kaftans dotting the scene. At night, local men congregated in the cooler streets, talking or even sitting at makeshift tables, playing backgammon. But up inside those homes, it must have been hotter than a toaster. Occasionally clutches of women passed, dressed like Mama Inja, invisible in all-black ensembles. I began to feel self-conscious, fearful. My face was exposed and I felt obscene for the first time in my life, though I was otherwise fully covered. All but my Western face. I longed for anonymity. I imagined what it would feel like to glide past all of this without the burden of anyone knowing who or what I was. I understood, for the first time, the veil. I avoided the eyes. I felt insecure and vulnerable and wished Rahman were with me.

Mama Inja turned into a small alleyway and knocked on a nondescript door. Beyond were endless identical white houses. *How did she recognize this house? They all look alike.* An Ethiopian maid answered the door, and we climbed a narrow and steep stairway to the apartment on the second floor. The room was barely lit, full of women all dressed in black or white, all sporting black headgear. About half of them had faces completely veiled. No men were present, and thankfully, there were no dead bodies. Muslims bury their dead on the day of death, if possible. In such a hot climate, that made sense. I was very relieved to not see the bodies of those poor children, killed by their own father.

I watched as Mama Inja lifted her face veil, kissed a few of the mourners, the mother and sisters of the dead woman, I gathered later, then dropped her veil again. I followed her, wordlessly, deeper into the room. As I passed each relative, Mama Inja muttered something, then prompted me to kiss each one on both cheeks, down the line. I tugged further on my veil, almost covering my eyes and cheeks. Mama Inja sat on a low colorful cushion against the wall. I followed suit, staying close to her. These low, thick floor cushions were covered with tightly woven cotton material in every color. Gay patterns were everywhere, contrasting with rough, dingy white plaster on the walls. The room was lit by scant light bulbs in the ceiling. One could see the actual wires nailed to the wall all along the ceiling line. *Electrical wires.* A single ceiling fan slowly turned above in a futile attempt to stir the stagnant air. I looked over to the window and saw that it was, as I had guessed, a sort of daybed surrounded by three sides of wooden grills, projecting out over the street. A few women sat there, surrounded by their young children, presumably to get the freshest, coolest air.

I stared at the floor, sitting quietly next to Mama Inja. I knew none of these people, and had no intention of making conversation. The sadness was too profound for my fumbling beginner's Arabic. Mama Inja spoke to no one. But Valerie couldn't help herself and, as usual, she muddled through small talk with anyone who would engage her. Jawaher had sat down across the room and was quietly conversing with what I assumed to be members of her own family. She had grown up in Jeddah but came from a different lineage.

Desperate for some kind of meaning, I latched onto the few words that I recognized. "Medina." That was where the husband was presumed to be hiding. I heard the Arabic word for electricity, *kahraba*. Someone must be describing the gruesome death. I saw one woman gesturing at the floor and saying the word for blood, *dum*. *Had they been beaten to a pulp before being electrocuted?*

I heard *sitti*, the word for "grandmother," and saw one skinny older lady, all dressed in white but completely veiled. *She must be the grandmother of the dead woman.*

Surrounding her was a bevy of other very old ladies, probably her cousins and sisters. Imagine the horror of having your granddaughter and great grandchildren electrocuted by their husband and father, who was also your third cousin. Imagine living, trapped, in this house. Imagine suffocating in that little enclosed balcony, day in and day out, peeking through the holes of the grill at the dusty world out there, hopeful for a weak breeze. That was almost as hard to imagine as being electrocuted. I could feel the sweat trickling down my back already.

Thankfully, Mama Inja got up to leave after exactly one hour. We all three rose and dutifully followed her out of the building, careful to not slip going down the crooked stairs with our long dresses. Out on the street, which felt like paradise at that point, our drivers were standing at attention,waiting to escort us back to the cars. Mama Inja chose to go home immediately but Valerie stubbornly insisted that we pay a visit to a little shop with American pots and pans.

"You cannot find anything like that in modern Jeddah. It's worth the walk, as long as we're already here in the souk." Feeling kind of limp and indifferent, and actually wishing I could go home as well, I protested weakly that I had not brought any money with me, but Valerie assured me that it didn't matter.

"Don't worry about money. Buy whatever you want and they'll send a bill to Rahman at the office tomorrow. Even in the old souk, they know the Abbar name."

We drifted down the dusty dirt road, deeper and deeper into the souk, the three of us wrapped head to toe. Abdullah took up the rear, keeping careful watch from behind.

I supposed it was a way to keep our minds off things, shopping on a hot night, but I was thoroughly haunted by those people and their tragedy. *Electrocuting your own children is akin to animals eating their young.* I could almost understand Tasnim shrugging her shoulders at the stoning, and even Jawaher's frustrated explanation of the old blood laws, but Valerie? A Westerner? How could she stomach rummaging around for some Teflon pots she would never use, in the wake of these events? She must have become acclimated to this place and its seemingly inhumane customs—would I ever be?

Not unlike the news of the compound fire, nothing more was ever spoken of or discovered about the family from the souk. Life in Jeddah moved on as smoothly as it always seemed to, whether I was ready or not.

Chapter Eight

Patricia, Pilgrim

One afternoon before lunch, Mama Inja pulled me aside. She shared that the old aunties would take me to the blessed city of Mecca for a pilgrimage, or *Umrah*, that evening. In Islam, there are two kinds of pilgrimages—the *Hajj*, a several-day, once-in-a-lifetime journey to Mecca, only performed during specific dates of the lunar calendar, a requirement for all Muslims; and the *Umrah*, which is a lesser pilgrimage and can be done in a few hours, as often as you wish, any day of the year. *Hajj* is a much more intense and overwhelming ritual, with millions of Muslims flying from all over the world into Saudi Arabia specifically to complete their obligation to the religion. The Saudi government takes very seriously their responsibility to oversee and facilitate these large yearly gatherings, providing food, transportation and housing for all pilgrims. *Umrah* is something in which locals can easily participate at any time, especially elders and women, who are more comfortable with the less rigorous requirements. The aunties, excited to initiate me into the religion, felt it was the optimal time to go because the air would be less humid that night. Although deserts are usually dry and dusty, Jeddah boasted the unique (and unforgiving) combination of *humid* and dusty, due to its proximity to the Red Sea.

Although I was a little worn out from weeks of dubious events, I admit I was curious to see Mecca. This might be interesting. "That's wonderful. What do I have to do?" I asked Mama Inja.

"The girls will explain it to you later. We'll bring special pilgrimage garments for you to wear. Put them on and be ready to leave at 9:00 pm. You know your prayers, don't you?"

"Yes, of course."

"You're not menstruating, are you?"

"No. But why does that matter?"

"It's unclean. Ask the girls," and with that, Mama Inja disappeared through the doorway into the dining room.

At lunch, I had a hard time masking my enthusiasm for seeing Mecca that night. Jawaher caught on and decided to join us, even offering to dress me. I didn't realize how complicated it would be until Jawaher began to verbally prep me for the tasks at hand:

"One doesn't simply make do with a long skirt and an *abaya* to worship in Mecca. There are special linen tunics, sandals and even underwear. Stitching, clasps and buttons are not permitted. Pilgrimage rules require specific clothing worn in a specific way. Nothing else is allowed, not even a rubber band to tie back one's hair."

Jawaher also instructed me to shower and wash my hair thoroughly beforehand, as hyper cleanliness is expected and inspected as well. "No cream rinse or lotions, no nail polish, no make-up…"

I was ready, mind and body. I'd never been so pristine and primed for a religious event—even my first communion didn't require such precision. And after weeks of tragedies and the indifference of friends and family here, I longed for respite, something to inspire me. My heart was so heavy. I needed a shot of calm and a better understanding of this culture to remain here, contented.

Jawaher arrived at eight. Always up for a new adventure, I felt more excited than when I was dressing for my own wedding. We started with the underdressing, which was a flat band of undyed linen fabric, wound snuggly around my breasts and back. But it kept slipping down as I moved.

"Jawaher, this doesn't work! How will I bend over to perform my prayers with a loose bra?" So I rewound it up around my neck like a halter and then down and under the breast band, securing it with a little knot. *Perfect! This will hold.* It looked like a bandeau bikini top. It was sure to stay on and I was delighted with my ingenuity, adding a little nugget of style to the otherwise bland bra-like wrapping. The bottoms were easier, like a cloth baby diaper, but knotted firmly on both sides. As for the tunic, which covered everything, my beach days in the South of France came in handy. I had mastered twenty ways to create a fashionable cover-up out of an oversized Hermes scarf. So, putting the tunic together was a small order.

I looked so chic, and felt so secure and confident in my pilgrimage attire, that Jawaher took hers off and we redid it just like mine.

"Wow, Patricia! You should open a shop in Jeddah designing pilgrimage outfits! I'll be your assistant!" she teased.

Our journey was underway. We were traveling in a different direction, not towards Jeddah and not westward towards the Red Sea, but due East, inland, to the historic spiritual home of nearly a billion people. Unlike our other drives, the road was well-paved the entire way to accommodate the great number of pilgrims who landed in the Jeddah airport and continued on to make their pilgrimages—another indication of how the government took it upon itself, as the guardian of Mecca, to ease these journeys. This was serious business.

In less than an hour, we approached the ancient city. One could already hear chanting coming from the Great Mosque. No merchants hawking their wares, no groups of men lingering by the side of the road. Everywhere, people dressed for pilgrimage moved silently toward the center of town. We parked the car and joined the crowds as they walked. But Mecca was different. The strict social customs of Islam in Jeddah seemed to fall away here. No separation of men from the women, no black head scarves or veils, just humans from every corner of the world, in the same simple linen attire, journeying together in the supreme act of obedience to Allah. My eyes jumped from bare face to bare face, the most diverse group of men and women I had ever seen. Every race was represented here, more races than I knew existed. By the hundreds, all quietly continued on toward the center of the Mosque where the *Kaaba* awaited.

I was under a spell. A strange feeling came over me, as if time stood still. I couldn't tell how long we had been walking, or which direction we walked in. But it didn't matter because a quiet peace was settling into my soul accompanied by the ever-present soft chanting that filled the air. So intent was I to follow the pull of people, I wasn't really sure when I entered the mosque. I expected a grand entranceway to a building like the Vatican, a well defined structure. Or the Great Mosque in Paris. After so many years of studying European art history and architecture, I was familiar with enormously high stone cathedrals and fabulously colored glass windows, designed to put worshipers in a state of awe. But these towering churches were built in northern cities and needed walls because of the winter weather. The Great Mosque in Mecca was different. In a matter of minutes, we went from being under a clear night sky to an ornate covered canopy, held up by countless columns that went on, seemingly forever. There were no walls to speak of, just thousands of perfectly white marble pillars supporting the heavenly ceiling high overhead. No beginning and no end. Like an eternal colonnade. In a hushed voice, I asked Jawaher if we were in the mosque. Yes, this was it. Disoriented, but in a euphoric kind of way, I followed blindly, enjoying the start of a cool breeze gliding through the open air expanse. The sun was setting and the temperature followed. Unlike Jeddah, the desert air here was fresh and dry.

We drifted past one column after the next, until finally, I spotted the end of the covered area. We pushed forward into a new space so monumental in its openness that I had nothing to compare it to. It was as if every pilgrim alongside me experienced a tangible promise of eternal Heaven. A sea of people, all humbling themselves to their Maker in the most sincere form of worship I'd ever seen. The aunties nudged us into line. We stood there waiting for the call to prayer. When it came, we prayed together in unison, offering up a prayer as one people.

The service was oddly organized for such a crowd. I could detect no one in particular leading us to prayer. Seasoned pilgrims and newcomers alike, stood obediently, facing the *Kaaba*, a cube-like structure the size of a large house, completely shrouded in heavily adorned black silk. I didn't expect that. I had assumed it would be a large but natural, naked boulder, like Stonehenge. Instead, the holy enshrined black rock, enormous and prehistoric in origin, was covered.

Since ancient times, pagan Arabs journeyed from afar to worship as we would that night. The holiness and mystical qualities of the rock carried over into formalized Islam, with the *Kaaba* representing the central house of our one God. Instead of rows of worshippers facing some faraway point, Mecca was the one place on earth where Muslim worshippers formed in increasingly larger circles around the Kaaba, all bowing to the center. It was remarkable, and somehow, it all made sense to me.

The atmosphere was spiritual, hypnotic and unifying. Unlike any other place of worship I'd ever been to, thousands upon thousands of people were all dressed alike, all praying in the same language. Thousands of voices resounding in the open air, all facing the very same spot on the Earth. And I was part of it. A tiny speck but somehow feeling grafted to our planet and universe through this experience. Nothing to hear or see but a seismic chorus of prayer and the canvas of sky above, stars and heavens smiling down on us with celestial validation. This was the most intense prayer that I had ever experienced. I will never forget it.

When the prayer was over, we instinctively grabbed each other's hands so that we weren't separated. The aunties, Jawaher, and I, along with hordes of other worshippers, next made our way into the center of the mosque.

It was our turn to circle the Kaaba seven times. This was a ritual, perhaps symbolizing the planets revolving around the sun, never stopping, never slowing down, every minute of every day, for untold thousands of years. Slowly, inch by inch, we spiraled in, closer and closer to the *Kaaba*. Finally we were right up against it, still circling, and I saw that the corner of the shroud was raised so people passing in their march could touch or kiss the stone underneath. One by one, everyone had their moment to touch the stone, some reciting words when they touched it, some choosing to kiss it. As I passed, I touched it.

It was shiny, black, hard, and enigmatic, but not like any metal or stone surface I had ever encountered. The black rock was finely polished by centuries of worshippers touching the corner, indented by billions, no, maybe trillions, of hands. I wanted to linger, to take in more of its ancient powers, but the crowd behind me was pushing forward, almost lifting me off the ground in the process. I was sure the rock had dropped from the cosmos above, thousands or even millions of years ago. As I circled back to the outer edges of the open space with the aunties, I longed to know its mystery. I understood that this was more than just evidence of a rare meteorological event, but I couldn't explain, nor could I even begin to articulate, how it deeply affected me.

I wasn't ready to leave just yet. Thankfully, I was told to rest by a low wall with one of the oldest aunties, who was fatigued and short of breath, while the others went to visit a different part of the shrine. I didn't ask or care where they were going. I was content to just stand there meditating and gazing at this holy spectacle that had changed me so thoroughly.

This place was not about Man. It was not even about the Earth. It was about the Universe and our collective response to it, somehow formalized into the religion that lived and breathed in this place. Ancient, alive, humbling and simple, yet highly complex, Mecca was nothing short of otherworldly. Sadly, I never returned.

Chapter Nine

Mrs. Abbar, Mistress of the Home

True to his word, Rahman and I finally moved into our new home. I could think of nothing else but the privacy the new house would offer our still budding (read: confusing) marriage, and the ability to finally make a home of my own. This new place was exactly what we needed to reconnect and shed the iron-clad rules and regs of the Abbar family compound. We would finally be free of the eyes, opinions, and expectations of family.

I was ecstatic, dancing from room to room, jumping on the gigantic square marble cocktail table that would anchor the living room, spinning around and reviving dance moves that had been collecting dust in my now doughy body. I missed feeling the pulse through my previously lean muscles, and I imagined that table was the stage at Studio 54. Rahman had left for work so I pumped up the music, rejoicing in my newfound freedom. Finally, we had our own place.

Hani Al Attas had given me a cassette tape with the newest early 80s disco hits and I wasted no time making copies: one each for my car, Rahman's car, the downstairs stereo, the upstairs stereo, the outdoor stereo and finally one for my beach bag, in case we paid another boring visit to the hapless beach house on the Creek.

Our home had turned out even better than my expectations and word was getting out. Void of all furniture (less my dancefloor table), it was still primed to be the coolest place in Jeddah. As if on cue, Donna Summers' "I Feel Love" started to play. Still spinning, I stretched out my arms, throwing my head back, closing my eyes and meditating on the crescendo as her hypnotic soprano voice filled the room. Between songs, I peeked out the window, awaiting the arrival of the freight truck carrying the bulk of my new furniture. Rahman said it was coming some time today. Life was good.

A knock on the door abruptly awakened me from my disco reverie. I peeked out the window to find a man standing on the front porch in jeans and a tee shirt, laughing hysterically at my party for one. I jumped down, turned down the music and ran to open the door, praying that he was the truck driver and that my furniture was finally within reach. As I approached the entry, I bumped into Asya, one of my new Ethiopian maids, looking awkward and repentant in the entry.

"Asya, why didn't you answer the door?"

"Madame Patricia, I was afraid to open it because you...well...I couldn't get your attention...and I...didn't want a strange man to surprise you...while you were...uhhh...busy. So I waited here." She bowed her head in respect.

So I wasn't *exactly* alone in my living room, but who cares? *It's my house and I'll do what I please.* I savored the thrill of that thought.

"Thank you, Asya. Let's open the door and see what this gentleman wants."

Together we tugged at the tall mahogany front doors to reveal a husky but handsome bearded man, probably in his early twenties, grinning from ear to ear.

"*Sabah al keir,* good morning," I said in both Arabic and English. I had started doing this when I saw a person dressed in Western clothes. I wanted to cover all bases, as there were many Lebanese in the country who looked and dressed Western but spoke only Arabic.

"Good morning!" he replied brightly, with an American accent. Did I detect a bit of a midwestern twang?

"Are you American?"

"Nope, I'm Italian, from Naples, ma'am, but I just graduated from the University of Kansas. Topeka, Kansas. I went there on a football scholarship."

How random! And he called me "ma'am." He's my age. My status in Saudi Arabia never ceased to amaze me.

"Do you have my furniture out there?"

"No, sorry to disappoint you, but I arrived a few weeks ago in Saudi to help my dad. He is working for Abbar and Zainy. Heading up the construction division. Amm Rahman sent me here to see if I could help you with anything around the house. Is there anything you need? Anything heavy you would like me to carry? I worked at the US Naval Base in Naples when

I was a teenager and learned all kinds of handy skills. Electrical, plumbing, carpentry, painting, and best of all, cooking. At your service." He bowed with a huge grin.

"Well, please come in out of the heat. What's your name?"

"Lallo."

"And that's short for?"

"Alessandro."

"I'm Patricia," I said as I happily ushered him into my empty but cooled house. *What a lucky thing to have a nice, clean, handsome, Italian, English-speaking helper who is strong and handy!* I knew there would be much for him to do once everything arrived, and I already liked Lallo. After just five minutes, we were instant allies and it was nice to have more normal-to-me in my world. Asya, still wide-eyed, ran to the kitchen to fetch us some cold water. A strange Italian male visitor in the house was a bit shocking to her, but I wasn't going to allow her to ruin my delight. I showed Lallo around quickly, explaining what each room would be and where the furniture would be placed. He responded enthusiastically, making mental notes of my to-do list for him.

"Wait! Is that a phone over there in the corner?" Lallo had spied our precious telephone, an elegant Italian-style upright black phone that looked more like a Jean Arp sculpture than an appliance. Still waiting for tables, we had placed it on the floor, and there it sat, like a little mouse in the corner.

"Yes, Rahman used every shred of influence he had to get us a private phone line in our house! And to celebrate, he bought these crazy-looking phones. We have extensions all over the place. Even in the dining room and the bathroom. Amazing, right? I mean, who needs that?" I laughed. I was sounding more and more like Natalie or Valerie.

Lallo's tone darkened, "Can I ask you a big favor, Patricia?"

"Sure," I said, puzzled. "What?"

"Can I use the phone to call someone? I haven't had access to a phone since I arrived here. Of course my dad doesn't have one in the apartment, and they won't allow me to use the phone in the office. I guess my business isn't important enough," he supposed.

The moment I nodded, he made a nosedive to the floor, happily punching numbers into the delicate, black, sculptured apparatus. It rang once before someone, a female someone, answered curiously. He whispered gently, nearly cooing into the phone. "Jamila? It's Lallo…"

A woman! And that name—she's Arabic! That was fast! He's only been here a few weeks! I chuckled, heading out of the room, allowing them some privacy. I looked around for Asya, wondering where our cold water went.

When I opened the kitchen door, I nearly knocked down a very guilty eavesdropping Asya, listening from the other side of the door. "Asya! What on earth were you doing standing behind the door? You didn't even bring the water I asked for."

She hung her head, clearly embarrassed and confused, "*Amati*, Madame Patricia, I am sorry, but I was so worried. A man in the house. You are a young woman. This is Jeddah. I wanted to keep watch in case anything bad happens. What would Amm Rahman say?"

"Asya! Don't be ridiculous! Amm Rahman sent him over here to help me and he obviously doesn't mind having him in the house. Pretend you are not in Saudi, please. You are in my home, an American home. I'm a Muslim, and clearly understand the rules here in Saudi. I am not going to do anything stupid, but I am also not going to hide under a veil and pretend that I am an Arab. I'm not. If my husband invites this nice Italian gentleman into our home to help me, to help us, we will welcome him and he will be our friend. Understand?" I repeated the word as she nodded, taking my words to heart. Being a Western woman, I wasn't expected to wear a veil over my face, although I voluntarily covered my hair in the brief walk from the car to the door out of respect. But when it came to the rules of my house, I chose an approach that would reflect the more relaxed place I had in Saudi society.

In the living room, Lallo was stumbling through a half-baked conversation with his Arabic angel named Jamila, who clearly didn't speak English very well. I busied myself with the stereo controls as Lallo said his good-byes and hung up the phone.

"Wow, you don't know how thankful I am for that! Jamila lives in the same apartment building as my parents. She lives with her parents next door. I met her on the stairs when she was on her way to the university. She studies there. Jeddah Girl's University. I'm in love with her."

"What? Are you crazy? You'll get yourself killed, Lallo! I don't know you, but I'm warning you. Didn't anyone explain how it works here? I've seen a woman get stoned to death. A foreign man with a Saudi woman? Oh my God. I have no idea what they would do to you both. After they torture you and stone her, they'll behead you. Yeah, that seems about right." I went for the shock value to put some sense into his naïve head. Jeddah had started to change me—now I was absolutely beginning to sound like Niggi and Tasnim.

"I know, I know, Patricia. She's not Saudi. Her family is Indonesian. Her parents came here a few years ago for work, and I think they're more modern than usual. She is in love with me too. I want to marry her."

"Now I *know* you're crazy. Even crazier than I thought! You just saw her on the stairway and what? You have had a few conversations with her? And you want to marry her? Nuts. Completely nuts. You must have heatstroke."

"Well, no. She climbs out of her window at night and meets me behind the building. We sit there and talk all night. We really are in love. I know it sounds crazy, but I've never felt like this for a girl. I want to marry her."

"Did you tell anyone? Rahman? Your parents?"

"No, just you," he said sheepishly. "If my father found out, he would put me on a plane and send me back to Naples."

"Your dad's plan sounds better. You'd be much safer. Now I'm going to worry about you all the time. Please don't do anything rash. You can come here and talk to her on the phone whenever you want. That's saner than meeting in the night behind a building. I won't tell a soul. Hopefully, you'll get over this infatuation soon."

"Thank you so much! You saved me! I'll do anything you ask. Just give me work. I'll cook for you on the weekends. I'll drive you anywhere." Lallo's dark eyes glowed with gratitude. I had to admit, his sweet face and vulnerability were getting to me. I had to help him.

"This is sounding good! You get unlimited use of the phone and I get a strong Italian handyman and a personal chef. I like it. Who expected this to fall on my lap today?" Maybe it was our shared Italian heritage, or his time in America, but Lallo already felt like a little brother.

That evening when Rahman came home, I quietly thanked him for sending Lallo over, "He's so nice and he works non-stop! He managed the furniture delivery and placement, assembled all that needed putting together, hung some mirrors...And! He cooks Italian food! He wants to go to the fish market on Friday and bring us a fresh catch. He'll barbeque it at the pool for lunch." I was satisfied with the arrangements I had made with Lallo, my new friend. "And I must mention that Asya was a little peeved that you had invited a foreign man into the house. I told her that she had better accept it."

"That's good. The servants will get used to working here," he said dismissively. This didn't seem to bother Rahman at all, so I decided that it wouldn't bother me either. Since we had moved out of his parents' compound, Rahman and I were finally on the same page once again. I knew he would come around.

Always on the lookout for diversion and attention, Rahman was intrigued by the novelty of a private Italian chef for the weekend. His eyes lit up. "Why don't we invite some friends over for a swim and lunch this

Friday? We can have Samir and Tasnim, maybe Hani, Nihad, and Natalie and the kids. They'll love the idea of fresh-cooked fish. I'll give Lallo some money to buy everything we need. Lots of garlic, vegetables, spices...Maybe he can find some decent Italian olive oil? I heard that the Italians in Saudi have their own market somewhere near the port. He can go there. I have a feeling Lallo will prove to be very useful." He grinned.

I failed to disclose the deal I'd made with Lallo, just in case Rahman would object to Lallo using the phone for illegal activity. I didn't want to take any chances. Lallo would work out perfectly here and we were already planning our first party around him.

Anxious for the Friday lunch gathering, I sped through the otherwise mundane activities of the week. Lallo came every day to help set up the house and do any handyman tasks I needed. We began planning and shopping for Friday's poolside barbeque, including new dishes (from Paris!) and beautiful glasses to drink from, complete with little paper straws and umbrellas. We were bringing a tropical vibe to our patio party, complete with alcoholic pina coladas! This was *our* house, and without Mama Inja's watchful eye, we could keep and drink all the smuggled alcohol we wanted.

Rahman and I had invited quite a few people. Tasnim was coming with her husband. Natalie was delighted to be invited and she suggested we call Niggi, too. Valerie and Khalid were going to drop by after tennis. Rahman also invited a few American men from the embassy and a few from the Italian Embassy.

Niggi, in particular, was thrilled to be invited after our last meeting had ended so grimly. "Lunch at your pool? Brilliant! We're coming! What time? What can I bring? This is the best news I have heard all year. What luck! Just when you think nothing is going well, Patricia calls and saves the day! I was going to sit around and read a book today. Thank you, thank you so much." Niggi couldn't say enough nice words to express her excitement and I was happy that I'd been able to cheer her up. As soon as I hung up with Niggi, the phone rang. "Hello?" *Who would be calling me now?*

It was Niggi again. She spoke quietly, if that was even possible for her, "Patricia, I just spoke to Taher. He is delighted that we are coming but told me not to mention the fire to anyone at the party. I just wanted to remind you. Don't say a word."

"Understood. See you soon." I sighed. Just when I had the illusion of flying high, the conversation with Niggi jolted me back into reality. This country was not safe. I was not safe. Those two children were not deemed newsworthy, as their deaths were an insult to Saudi nationals. I hadn't forgotten that horrible event in those plastic prefab buildings with substandard wiring and no building codes.

Lallo was at the dock early Friday morning when the fishing boats arrived. By midmorning, we were prepping in the kitchen, bags and armfuls of beautiful produce and fish from the Italian market. It felt like home, chopping, slicing, gutting, scaling. Lallo showed me how to prepare every dish, using almost offensive amounts of parsley, garlic, sea salt, pepper, onions, basil, and lemon. The housekeepers were amazed to see the two of us doing all the work, but perhaps also feeling a little useless. In Saudi, only the cooks or servants would bother to work in the kitchen.

"In America and Italy, everyone cooks!" I announced to the room in general. "It's considered a hobby, an amusement. Same as gardening," I said with a wink, recalling something I did earlier in the week, namely, trimming a few dead palm branches. The butler was horrified and the gardener practically threw himself at Rahman's feet later that day, completely guilt-ridden about the dead branches. No amount of consoling could calm him down and after dealing with that drama, Rahman asked me to please refrain from touching any plants in the garden.

The party was absolutely perfect, everyone was so happy to be there and the food was the best I had ever tasted. Lallo was an amazing chef, a good friend, and I caught myself hoping that he would stay in Jeddah forever, or, at least as long as I was there. What a breath of fresh air. What a godsend!

The children splashed and swam all day and at one point, even the adults jumped into the water, the guys playing water polo with a large beach ball. It felt like a normal summer day in any backyard in America. Sitting on my lounge chair, I couldn't help but take stock of all the parties I had been to and how differently every household seemed to uphold or not uphold Muslim customs. When the Abbars threw a big engagement party for us, we weren't allowed to drink alcohol, although they had enjoyed champagne cocktails at our party in New York. At Walid Juffali's, cocaine was on the menu, but I was sure that wouldn't be the case had it been a family affair. When it came to private events, the rules changed depending on who was in attendance and who was hosting the party.

Later in the afternoon, I caught Lallo slipping back into the house to call his beloved Jamila. Nervous that Rahman might catch him, I glanced across the pool, but there was my husband, sipping his frozen cocktail on a comfy lounger, under a huge umbrella, chatting with his friends. Rahman was as happy as a lark, and would likely want to do this every weekend. *Fine with me!*

***

Finally feeling optimistic about how my life in Jeddah was shaping up, I decided to plant my flag even deeper by making good on a promise I made to my parents when they visited.

"Patricia, be sure to register your passport with the American Embassy here in Jeddah," my mother pleaded. "Our neighbors, you know, the Al Ghanians, from Iran, well, they said it's important to do that if you're living abroad. It's a precautionary move, in case of an uprising or some other disaster."

"Mom, I'm not expecting an uprising anytime soon. This is Saudi Arabia, not Iran," I hissed.

After realizing she was sounding just north of paranoid, mom suggested a more diplomatic approach and suggestion. "Well, what about meeting other Americans in the country? Is that of any interest to you?" *Hmm. Not a bad idea.*

"Okay, Mom," I sighed, "I'll visit the Embassy when I'm more settled. I promise."

I proposed a trip to the American Embassy at the Abbar family lunch the following afternoon. Valerie picked up mightily on my suggestion, "What a great idea, Patricia! My friends over at the British Embassy wonder what the Yanks have to offer. Americans here mostly keep to themselves. You'll be our ticket in. Maybe you could invite a few of us for a tennis game or some other amusement…That complex is huge. I bet they have a bridge club, too."

"Well I can try. I'll go this evening." I was liking mom's idea more by the minute.

The American Embassy compound was only a mile from my house and very impressive from the outside. Abdullah proudly drove me to the gates where armed military guards kept watch instead of the usual gatekeeper. Because they looked so serious, I decided that Abdullah's scant English would not be sufficient. From the back window, I announced myself and my intent to the severe-looking soldiers. After demanding my passport and searching the car, the heavy gates were raised and we were directed to the parking lot at Consular Services.

Feeling independent and safe to be me for once, I left Abdullah with the car and marched through the doors into a very plain and empty waiting room, painted a dismal shade of green. It resembled the local DMV back in the US—surprisingly underwhelming. There was only one person inside—an Egyptian (?) clerk. *Where are the Americans?* Handing him my passport, I repeated the purpose of my visit. Perplexed, he told me to wait and gestured towards a row of empty and quite plain plastic chairs.

After about five minutes, a disheveled, bottle-blond middle aged woman emerged and gestured me to her barebones office.

"How can I help you?" she inquired, appearing as perplexed as the clerk.

"Well, it was suggested that I come to the Embassy, introduce myself and register my passport. I'm married to a Saudi man and live here in Jeddah now. My house is actually right down the street."

"There's no need to register your passport." She was clearly not interested in my presence or my story and I was confused as to why. After all, wasn't I the most interesting thing to happen in Jeddah all summer?

"Aren't Americans supposed to register with the embassy when they are living in a foreign country?" Something about her flat refusal was patronizing and I was getting irritated, yet increasingly concerned. I found myself suddenly agreeing with my mother that my passport must be registered.

"This Embassy is not a social club."

"Well, I know several British ladies who visit their embassy regularly for different events and to play tennis. I've played there a few times..." Each time I visited the British Embassy with Valerie, they fawned over us, couldn't be nicer, asking where we were from and who we were married to. Why would it be different here? Is my own nation disinterested in its citizens abroad?

She stood firm. "No, there's nothing for you here. If you wish for us to file a photocopy of your passport, I'll do that, but don't expect any services. You're on your own," she stated curtly, nearly spitting the words at me.

"What about if there's an uprising?" I queried, parroting my mother.

Her face softened slightly as she opened my passport, scanned the first page and replied, "Look, uh, Patricia...this is a terrible country. It's dangerous, it's inhospitable to women—There's nothing we can offer you. In my entire career, I've never worked at a more difficult post." Unbelievably, tears welled up in her eyes as she continued, "I cannot imagine why anyone, a woman, would live here voluntarily. I can't wait to leave. What were you thinking? I'm sorry." She led me to the door. "Sit outside. The clerk will return your passport in a few minutes." I felt humiliated and confused. I never returned to the embassy again, nor did I mention my visit to anyone.

***

In the weeks following, Lallo had become a welcome fixture in our house, camping out for a phone call with Jamila once a day, between carpentry and assembly tasks. One morning, Lallo's voice called to me from the office.

"Oh, she's coming in right now. I'll tell her," I heard Lallo whisper into the phone as I walked in. He hung up, "Patricia! I have a favor to ask."

"Another one?" I laughed. Lallo was turning out to be a bit of a hustler, albeit an adorable one. He had certainly helped us throw a great party, so whatever it was, he earned it. Without even hearing the favor, I agreed to grant him his request.

"Patricia, you're like a sister to me," he lowered his voice to a murmur, "I want you to meet Jamila."

"Oh, how sweet," I was flattered but he obviously had more to say. He looked like he was going to pee his pants.

"Yes, she's an amazing girl. I want to have a meeting with her…And, we need a chaperone."

"Oh, chaperone? Here I thought you were just wanting me to meet her," I teased.

"I do, I do! But I really need your help. We can't keep meeting behind the building. It's not safe. We have some important things to talk about, face to face. I'd like you and me to drive to the university right now, pick her up, and bring her here. Today is perfect because she has three hours between classes…"

I was stunned. "Wait a minute. You want me to go in the car with you? Suppose we get pulled over. I'd go to jail!"

"Don't worry, I have an Arab headdress with me. I'll be the chauffeur. You sit in the back. I work for your husband's company!"

"Okay, and how will I get into the university?"

"I told you, any girl can just walk in. But you have to cover your head. You have that, right?"

"Well, yes. But, how will I know who she is? I've never seen her."

"Oh, don't worry. She's seen a picture of you. She's waiting, and she knows who to look for."

He has a headdress with him? She's seen a picture of me? He probably stole one from our library shelf. Clearly, Lallo had been planning this for days. In fact, Friday's fish BBQ lunch was probably the down payment.

But I couldn't possibly refuse him. I understood precisely what Lallo was going through, because I was going through it, too. Two foreigners trying to survive in Saudi Arabia, and it wasn't easy. You did what you had to do. While he went to his car, I snuck upstairs, donned my black silk *abaya* and *tarha* and darted down the outdoor stairway, bypassing all the servants. Once across the garden, I dove into the back of Lallo's car and hid while he pulled through the gates.

"You can get up now!" he sang from the front, as if we were doing nothing illegal.

"Lallo, I'm scared shitless. And I'm not getting up! It's safer if I hide."

Crouched behind the driver's seat, I realized all too vividly that being here in Jeddah had changed me. Four months ago, I would have brazenly sat in the front seat, laughing as we sped off to hijack his girlfriend from school. Now, I felt like a fugitive having a panic attack. Breaking any rules in this country carried grave consequences, especially for a foreigner, and I was no longer interested in making waves. Lallo's borrowed Toyota was very different from my Cadillac Limousine with blacked-out windows. If I were caught in the back seat with a European posing as a Yemeni driver, we would be hauled into the police station immediately. I envied Lallo's naïveté, but I couldn't share his optimism.

When we arrived, I crawled out of the car, still terrified, and approached the gate house, clutching my *abaya* around me. I shyly requested Jamila, turned and walked through a maze of high walls into what appeared to be the campus courtyard. There was no seeing into the girls' university from the outside. But as I cleared these required privacy barriers, I found a square full of young women, all dressed like me. From one of the benches, a girl stood up, walked toward me and called out my name. It was Jamila.

She was a tall girl, with a round face and broad shoulders, sort of like Lallo. She could have been his sister, she resembled him so closely. Nothing about her appearance seemed particularly compelling, and I struggled to imagine what interaction they had in the stairwell that could have possibly ignited such a fierce love. But who was I to judge? I threw my arms out and shouted, "Jamila, so good to see you," acting like the old friends we pretended to be. We embraced, as if our lives depended on it, in front of the whole university, before I smuggled her out to the backseat of Lallo's car.

This time around, Jamila joined me in crouching on the floor of the car. She at least understood Arab culture, and was as scared as I was. We didn't emerge until Lallo had pulled into the gates of my villa and parked safely behind the garage. The three of us fled to the house, successful in our ruse.

Safely back in the privacy of Rahman's office, we had little to say to each other. Jamila hardly spoke English, and Lallo and I hardly spoke Arabic. It was actually comical that I had risked my life for these two fools in love. I left them alone in the room and went back to the kitchen. The servants were growing so used to Lallo's presence in the household that nobody noticed him camped out in Rahman's office with an unescorted young lady.

After about an hour, I knocked on the office door. I must have startled them, because I heard them fumbling around. Lallo shouted, "*Momento*," in Italian, and I waited a few moments, then entered. We all sat down awkwardly. Lallo started the conversation by flattering me once again.

"Patricia, Jamila says you're so beautiful." Jamila nodded with a smile, reinforcing his sentiment with an Arabic, "*Inti hilwa ktiir.*"

"*Shukran*, Jamila. Thank you." Fed up with these pointless pleasantries, I turned to Lallo and said, "Okay, cut to the chase. What do you want from me now?"

"Patricia, Jamila thinks her father saw us behind the house last night. I need to propose marriage to her family, or she won't be allowed to go to school anymore. They may even send her back to Indonesia to live with her cousins."

"So, propose marriage to her family! What does this have to do with me?"

"Well, she says that a woman has to speak to the mother of the girl. That's the only respectable first move."

"Then have your mother go across to the apartment and speak to her," I snapped, feeling more at risk than ever.

"She would never do that. My mother doesn't even know that we're in love. You have to be the one to go to Jamila's mother with the proposal."

"Me?" I laughed until I was doubled over. I laughed until tears rolled down my face. They both stared at me, not knowing what to think.

"At least she's not angry!" Lallo said to Jamila, holding her hand, waiting for me to say yes.

"Are you both insane? You're basically asking an American foreigner your age, whom you've only known a few weeks, to walk into a Muslim household and propose a marriage on your behalf? It won't work!"

"It will work. You're an Abbar. That's how it works here," Lallo blurted out.

This time, Jamila spoke up, confirming Lallo's proposition, "It's normal here. It's the right way. It's good. You can do it."

Their hope and innocence touched my heart. If I helped them achieve their dream, maybe I would be as happy as they were. I suddenly wanted it as much as they did. I needed a beacon in this dismal place. "Okay, fine. Jamila, what exactly do you want me to say, and when do you want me to go?"

We decided I would visit her mother the very next day to broker the marriage. I would state that I was from the renowned Abbar family, introduce Lallo as my distant Neapolitan cousin and an employee of my husband, and endorse the match. Just like that. Keep it simple. Lallo and Jamila's plan actually did make sense given I'd seen Mrs. Zainy attempt to proxy the same stunt with her son and my sister, Diane. On the bright side, at least this Muslim approach to marriage was quick and direct with more predictable outcomes. The couple sat on the sofa holding hands like simpletons, looking at me as if I were their salvation. I was moved to succeed for them. That night I practiced my speech in Arabic with Thahab but kept my plans for Lallo's engagement secret from Rahman. He hated drama so it would be easier to just tell him after the scheme was complete. Thahab, to my surprise, thought it was wonderful that a man wanted to propose to a woman in the respectable way. She was proud to be helpful.

The next day, I awoke and Rahman was nowhere to be found. This was highly unusual. I had fallen asleep before he came home. *He never wakes up before me, especially not after a night out. Something must be wrong.* I got up quickly, searched the dressing room and bathroom, threw on my house robe and flew down the stairs to the ground floor, nearly knocking Asya over in the hall.

"Have you seen Amm Rahman, Asya?"

"*Sabah al kheir,* Madame Patricia. Good morning," was her automatic answer.

"Yes, yes, *sabah al kheir,* have you seen Amm Rahman anywhere?" *These people never tire of their polite formalities, do they?* I was increasingly impatient, pushing past her without even waiting for an answer as it was taking too long. I went to his office first, and there he was, deeply engrossed in a call with Domenic, a friend from BU and now a law student at Georgetown. It was one in the morning in DC, so the call must have been important. Rahman jotted down a few names and numbers on a piece of paper, thanked his friend, and hung up.

"What are you looking for so early in the morning?" Rahman asked, clearly amused that I had come down, searching for him.

"I didn't see you last night and woke up alone in bed. Going to sleep alone...waking up alone...spending my entire day alone...no one to talk to. I was scared," I opened my eyes wide and gave him a little pout. Oh yes, I had learned how to play him.

Rahman broke into a playful smile, beckoning for me to come and sit on his lap. I curled up in his arms, my hands draped across his shoulders. He teasingly dismissed my complaint, "Aren't you going to ask me why I was on the phone with Domenic at this hour?"

"Okay, why were you on the phone with Domenic at this hour?"

"I think I've decided to go to law school next year. I want to apply to Georgetown. Domenic is there and he knows the Dean."

I blinked in disbelief. *Law school? Returning to the US? Hadn't we just moved into this house? What's a Saudi Arabian going to do with an American JD degree?* He had never mentioned anything like this before. But after it sank in, I realized these impetuous decisions were classic Rahman…and I liked the idea of going home.

In my cutest, tiniest voice I prodded him, "Why law school?"

"Well," Rahman started, fully relishing the opportunity to be all-knowing, "With the country growing as it is, there's bound to be an ambassadorship or business emissary position available. An International Law Degree from one of the world's most renown institutions can only help me achieve that goal. One never knows, Patricia."

An ambassadorship? Maybe somewhere interesting like France or England? Now that would be a ridiculously exciting opportunity!

"Wow, that sounds like a great idea. Libras make the best lawyers. And you deserve the best," I gushed, basting his prickly ego even more.

"Yes, I do," he kissed me, as if to say *and the best is you.* "To be honest, Patricia, I don't know if working in my father's company is right for me. They run everything the old way and never listen to my ideas. I'm wasting my potential."

I lived for rare moments like this, when Rahman would confide in me. And I loved it when that man smiled. He'd been so stingy with his thoughts and words since we got here. I wanted him to fully understand that I would do anything for him, again and again. Despite his aloof (read: bizarre, selfish, erratic, rude!) behaviors in the previous months, all I wanted was for him to share himself with me, mind and body, the way that he had before, when it was the two of us against all odds.

"Then what are my orders, sir?" I asked, trying to keep a straight face and sound serious like a soldier prepping for a major operation.

"I want you to get me one of those study guides for the LSAT. Ask your sister to send it to the Abbar and Zainy office. DHL would be the fastest way to do that, and I'll book a trip for us to visit the school in a few months. I'll take the test while we're there, meet with the dean, and we'll see what happens. What do you think about living in Washington, DC?"

Rahman was all business again, but in a kinda playful way and I was ready to get moving on our next stop, DC! He slapped his hand down on the desk, signaling that he was done, not even waiting for a reaction as he picked me up, placed me on his desk then walked out of the room. Just like that, it was decided. Then, he popped his head back into the door, "Oh, and don't breathe a word about this to anyone. I don't want to encounter any resistance or have to answer any questions. We'll break the news to everyone when I'm accepted."

This plan hinged on his acceptance to Georgetown, which was not an easy task, but with his background, brains, and connections, he had a good chance. Suddenly, nothing in Jeddah seemed to matter anymore. If we were leaving soon, maybe for good, I could dig deeper into my reserves and find the tolerance I needed to face daily life here. *It will only be for a few more months...* My old optimism returned. Everything would turn out fine. And with a morning like that, getting through the rest of the day was a breeze.

That evening, just before six o'clock, I called down to Abdullah and had him bring the car around. I was dressed up and ready for this marriage proposal meeting. I had chosen a lovely silk St. Laurent dress, accessorized smartly with matching sandals, gold and diamond jewelry, and a small gold clutch. This would impress and even intimidate Jamila's family, which was my plan. They'd be too stunned to ask questions. Abdullah looked confused when I ordered him to take me to Lallo's apartment building. Fully expecting this reaction, I came clean with the explanation that I was visiting a girl in the complex to speak with her mother about marrying Lallo. Abdullah thought it was a wonderful idea and told me that I would be blessed by God for my good deeds.

Once we arrived, I knew exactly what to expect, and I felt pleasure and power confirming that I was indeed in control of this evening. The door to the apartment seemed to magically open for me to enter. This place rated somewhere between the Arabic sitting room at the souk, and the Bin Zagr's informal daytime lounge, with its low Arabic seating, stained Oriental rugs, and small crystal chandeliers. Traditional, modest. They would probably be thrilled to marry off their eldest daughter.

I smiled broadly as Jamila's mother approached me, her two daughters trailing behind. Startled, I realized that she was greeting me enthusiastically in Arabic. *Oh, that's right! I forgot. She only speaks Arabic!* I mumbled a few words and in the absence of anything better to do, reached out to kiss her and the girls. A good set of kisses was always a safe move. I was supposed to call her Mama Layla, as per Lallo's instructions. I nodded my head and spoke her name clearly as I embraced her. She clapped her hands, acting as if I had recited a long and complicated speech. *That's right. Doing fine. She's eating out of my hand. I wonder if she already knows what's going to happen?* I glanced quickly at Jamila. *This young woman is a sly one.*

Jamila rushed to my side on cue, pulling me toward the seating area. She motioned for me to sit down between her and her mother, which I gladly did. The servant materialized carrying a tray with little, steaming cups of tea. I thanked them for the refreshments and made my attempts at rudimentary polite conversation in Arabic with Jamila translating when-ever words failed me.

I gathered up my courage, cleared my throat, and asked Mama Layla if she knew why I had come. She motioned with her hand in a vague way, neither confirming nor denying, so I proceeded to tell her that her daughter, Jamila, was a lovely and intelligent girl. *Pause.* I explained how fond of her I was, and for that reason, I wanted to keep her as my friend forever. The use of hyperbole in situations such as this was customary, I had already learned from my many ladies' functions. *Pause.* I asked her if she happened to have made the acquaintance of the Italian family down the hall. Again, she made that same non-committal wave of the hand. *So this one isn't going to admit to anything.* I forged on with my beautiful lie about Lallo being my family, mentioned our shared Neapolitan heritage, and went in for the kill, "Because I love Jamila so much and I love my cousin, Lallo, so much, I would like to propose that they get married to each other." There. I dropped the bomb!

After presenting my logical explanation, I pointed out how this marriage would make everyone so happy, on all sides, bringing together two wonderful young people, bringing two families together. *Sawa sawa.* I told her that Lallo was now working for my husband's company, implying that somehow, he was hired because of his relation to me, and that he would be earning a fabulous living at his new job. I mentioned how educated he was, a graduate from an esteemed university in America, and what a bright future he had here in Jeddah. I also mentioned, because these things were important, that both Lallo and Jamila were very tall. "A perfect match," is how I concluded my speech, and Jamila translated these last words to her mother.

I waited for a reaction, some words from Mama Layla, and when she finally responded, I was certain that she had been forewarned about the purpose of my visit and had already given this some thought. I stifled a smile and tried to remain serious. She agreed that everything I said was wonderful, and she was sure that Lallo would make a good husband, but unless he became a Muslim, there was no question of marriage between the two young people.

I didn't skip a beat. I quickly replied that I had become a Muslim to marry my husband. In fact, I had even visited Mecca recently. She seemed surprised and impressed. I carried on. I told her that I was absolutely sure that Lallo would convert, and quickly. I promised that within a month, he would come, himself, to speak directly to her and Jamila's father, as a proper Muslim man, to ask for Jamila's hand in marriage. Mama Layla said that she would be happy for that day to arrive, that it would be a blessed day, and I understood that to mean she had accepted my proposal.

From the smile and tears on Jamila's face, I knew I had succeeded in my mission and that Lallo would be ecstatic. Our crazy plan had worked. But in the end, Jamila was getting a good deal, and so was this family. They were getting to marry off their plain daughter to a hard-working Italian man from Abbar and Zainy, someone who would give her a better life than she could have hoped for, and as a bonus, he was going to convert to Islam! Well, as far as I could see, they had hit the jackpot.

As my car rolled through the gates and up my driveway, I caught sight of Lallo, pacing the front yard, anxiously awaiting the answer. He dropped everything and came running. "What happened?" he shouted excitedly. Abdullah and I, joyously and simultaneously, gave him the thumbs up signal. As I jumped out of the car, the housekeepers emerged from the house, all crowding around Lallo to congratulate him on his upcoming marriage. We gathered in the driveway, enjoying Lallo's good fortune, delighted that in this land of hardship and suffering, something wonderful had happened today. The Ethiopians maids, true to custom, started dancing and trilling their tongues in that celebratory sound they make for weddings. As they twirled around Lallo, clapping their hands and shaking the gold bangle bracelets on their arms, I announced to everyone the condition of the marriage deal.

"You will be allowed to marry Jamila, on two conditions."

Everyone stopped, listening intently as I made my proclamation. I savored the moment.

"Number one. You will become a Muslim. Mama Layla said that is the only way she would consider our proposal. I agreed to her terms on your behalf."

Lallo's eyes popped open, "How will I do that, Patricia?"

"I will teach you. I did it in one week. You have one month. That should be enough time. Condition number two. You will return to their home in one month's time, as a Muslim man, and propose marriage to Jamila's father and mother. They are ready to accept your proposal, as long as you fulfill the first condition. So let's get to work teaching you the prayers."

Upon hearing this, all the servants let out a huge cheer in unison. They restarted their trilling, chanting and dancing, so much happier were they to hear that Lallo would become a Muslim. Abdullah continued blessing me and the Ethiopians agreed that God would reward me with a long and happy life. All of the staff agreed to help Lallo practice his prayers and together, we would share in the job of delivering Lallo to God's path. The path of righteousness.

Lallo and I were both taken aback at the effect my deeds had had on the household servants, never expecting so much support, and we remained there a while longer, enjoying the moment together. I felt so pleased with myself and hopeful to have made a difference, and Lallo was too grateful for words. Then I announced, "Okay, it's time to get down to work." I pulled Lallo back into the house and we sat together, mapping out our plan of how he would convert.

Lallo was slow at first, but after much practice, he finally got the hang of the language and the rhythm of the prayers. We would work on his prayers every day as furniture arrived, with Asya and Thahab looking on, smiling happily in approval. A few evenings later, Noura even dropped by, wanting to see with her own eyes what exactly we were doing. Everyone had heard about the marriage and conversion I had brokered for Lallo. The servants had spread that news. It was the most interesting thing happening in Jeddah that month for sure. Everyone rejoiced and helped Lallo with pronunciation and diction; the house was almost complete, as were his prayers, both dazzling and living testaments to our ingenuity.

Even Rahman had to admit that what I had accomplished with Lallo was extraordinary. He laughed and shook his head when he heard about my meeting with Mama Layla. Lallo was a trusted friend, part of our family, and together, we had turned nothing into something with hard work, friendship, and a little imagination.

We were all getting something good out of this. I was getting a fabulous home, a place that would dazzle all future visitors. I couldn't wait to invite more people over. Lallo was getting his bride. And the servants were getting the pleasure of participating in the holy conversion of an infidel into a Muslim. Between these enjoyable evenings of camaraderie and my secret knowledge that Rahman and I might be leaving Jeddah, I would have to say that it was a happy time for me. I carved out a life for myself. It wasn't the Jeddah that I had expected, but it was still good. In fact, I found myself almost wishing that I would not have to leave one day.

While Lallo was working on his proposal, Valerie came to me with an exciting proposal of her own at family lunch a few weeks later.

"We foreign wives are having a little get-together tomorrow at Ann Hariri's beach house. Come along with me, Patricia. She wants to meet you."

"Who is Ann?" I asked.

"She's American, from one of your western states, North Dakota, I believe, married to Muhammad Hariri. She has four daughters and has been living here for about ten years. I told her that you were American too, and she insisted I bring you with me. Her house is incredible—her husband spared no expense. I'll come 'round for you at eleven. Bring a swimsuit. She has a lovely pool."

From the moment we caught sight of the undulating stone walls, decorated by groupings of colorful flowers creeping over rugged mined Red Sea coral and mature palm trees, I knew I was somewhere special. The house abounded with visual delights. I surmised that the couple had visited a five-star desert oasis in Arizona or Palm Springs and had been inspired by the landscapes there which make liberal use of boulders and creeping flower ground cover. Valerie and I followed the winding pathway to the house like two little girls in a secret garden. There was no need to knock on the door because a colorfully dressed servant awaited our arrival. "Madame Ann is on the patio. Please follow me."

As we rounded the corner, I caught sight of a group of a dozen beauties, all reclining comfortably on low, oversized teak lounges stuffed with embroidered pillows. At the center of the group was most definitely Ann. I could tell by the adoring way everyone seemed to gaze upon her that she was our "hostess with the mostest."

"Ann, this is a new addition to the Abbar family, our sister-in-law, Patricia. She comes from New York City!" gushed Valerie, seemingly proud to mention my hometown.

Ann, all decked out in an Hermes kaftan and exquisite pearl jewelry, flashed me a big smile and reached out to embrace me. "Welcome to our home, Patricia. I am so happy to meet you, a fellow American. I hope we will be close friends!" *And she really meant it.* What an extraordinary feeling I had. Ann's joy at meeting a countryman sent chills down my back, and we stood there for a moment in the entry, both overcome with emotion.

Homesickness, patriotism, loneliness, kinship, whatever we felt—it was mutual and surprising for both of us.

"You are already a sister. Thank you for inviting me," I answered as she led us to the two remaining lounges.

I quickly pulled off my coverup and doused myself with suntan lotion. The sun was getting hot and I wanted to work on my tan while it was still bearable. I chose the lounge that seemed to be getting the most sun and lowered myself eagerly into the mass of fluffy pillows. "Mmmmm. Heavenly," I uttered.

Looking around, I realized that I didn't know any of these other women, none of whom had any intention of getting up to greet us, so strong was the pull of the luxurious chaises.

Ann announced, "Ladies, you all know Valerie, but Patricia is new to Jeddah. She comes from New York City."

All eyes were on me as I nodded and proceeded to tell each lady my name and listen for their own intros. They were all foreigners, as Valerie had mentioned, and all spoke English fluently. *Good, this will be a relaxing day with the conversation flying fast, touching on every possible subject.* I couldn't wait. Once the language barrier was erased, it seemed that all other barriers melted away too.

Ann started us off with her little gem, "I'm so anxious, ladies, I'm trying to get pregnant again, this time with a boy. If I don't have a boy, Mohammad will probably divorce me. Anyone know how to use the basal thermometer to figure out when you're ovulating?"

Wow, this is pretty intimate. Well, I guess she can't bring it up to her Saudi mother-in-law. Nothing like letting your hair down immediately.

A British woman wrapped in a plush terry cloth robe chimed in, "I wish I had a boy, too. My husband has suddenly decided that our twelve-year-old daughter has to wear an *abaya* everywhere she goes. Can you imagine? I feel so bad that I had a daughter–I signed up for this country, and now she has to pay the consequences."

I can't imagine being a teenager and having to hide under a veil…

A South African voice from the far side of the pool interjected, "Patricia, your husband allows you to wear a bikini? My husband won't let me out of the house unless he inspects my clothing! In fact, he buys everything for me when he's away on business. He won't even allow me to shop for myself. I am forever doomed to wear one-piece suits. What I wouldn't give to have some sun on my stomach."

I started to respond to her comment, when another British woman interjected from the wading pool.

"My husband definitely is having an affair with someone. He refuses to have sex with me. For the past few months he's been arriving home so late at night, I hardly ever see him. I'm not sure what to do."

*How sad...*I watched her walk back to her lounge. *She's gorgeous! What's his problem?*

A German blonde rubbing tanning oil on her legs groaned, "Oh, I wish my husband would do that. He demands sex with me two or three times a day. When we wake up in the morning, after lunch before he takes his nap, and of course at night. Forget the weekends, it's non-stop boning and I can hardly walk straight by the time he leaves for work on Saturday morning."

Oh my god, that's even sadder...

An Australian brunette popped her head up from a mass of pillows and nodded in sympathy, "Wow, that's horrible. I live in my in-laws' house and every time I have sex with Omar, he insists that I wash my hair. It's Islamic law, written in the Koran, but who on earth would follow that law except an idiot? Of all the laws they willingly ignore? Now, the entire family knows when we fuck by when I take a shower. My mother-in-law keeps asking me when all this playing around will result in a grandchild. I still can't seem to get pregnant. I hope we don't have to adopt."

I hope my in-laws don't start pressuring me to have a child...

"Consider yourself lucky. I wake up every goddamn morning dreaming that I'm still in London and all this never happened. Then reality descends and I remember I'm married with a kid living in Jeddah, Saudi Arabia. You girls without babies, you're lucky! You still have time to escape."

I knew that Derby accent. It was Valerie! I turned to her in disbelief. *Valerie? She feels that way? She never said anything to me about it... especially not when she advised me to join her Saudi family. I guess she was lonely and wanted another foreigner to come. Maybe that's why she brushed over all the hard stuff.*

Ann set her drink down and sighed, "Mohammad says that if I ever leave him, he'll take my four daughters and I'll never see them again. Valerie, do you ever worry about losing your child?"

This guy Mohammad is sounding more and more like a monster...

Two Ethiopian servants appeared, one carrying a platter of assorted sandwiches, the other with bite-sized quiches and a green salad. The ladies didn't even stop to take note that lunch had arrived. They continued telling their woeful tales.

"Well, forget adoption, honey," an American voice piped up from the other side of the pool. "These Saudis never fully accept adopted children.

The entire family will contest it when the kid inherits money. The family usually wins in court. Islam doesn't approve of adoption."

"Yes, in my husband's family, the grandfather died and his one adopted son was driven from the family house, disappeared to Egypt and no one has heard from him in years."

Awkwardly, I reached forward for a sandwich. *I might as well serve myself…not that I'm feeling particularly hungry. I thought this was supposed to be a fun luncheon, not a gripe fest…*

"Lucky he got away alive," added another British bather as she cooled off in the pool. "Not everyone does. Rather than relinquish inheritance money to an adopted son, in our neighbor's family they all accused him of theft and had him locked up in jail. All it takes is four accusers and you're guilty in this place. He couldn't have been more than twenty years old. He's still there, as far as I know. Whatever you do, don't adopt. You can't guarantee your child's welfare upon your death."

What? How heartbreaking–that's so young to be betrayed by your family. I put the sandwich down quietly. I had completely lost my appetite.

"Speaking of death, did anyone hear about the Filipina housekeeper found dead in her room? Important Saudi family with a huge house in the Hamra section of town? It seemed to be strangulation, but the family claims she hung herself. Didn't like living in Jeddah. My housekeeper knew her and said she complained that the master of the house was raping her daily."

Not another one of those horror stories…

"Yes, I heard that story too," added a statuesque blond bombshell. Swedish perhaps? "One never knows what to believe. I heard that the newest fad with the upper class here in Jeddah is Saudi married women having affairs with Saudi married men," the German blonde leaned in for emphasis, "I hear there's lots of swinging going on too."

No way. If Rahman even suggested that, I'd die! I noticed the other women were finally helping themselves to the food. No one seemed at all bothered by the conversation. Just another day in Jeddah.

"Swinging? I seriously doubt that. What Saudi man would allow his wife to have sex with another man? My husband is so jealous, he won't even allow me to visit his brother's place without him to see my own sister-in-law! He prefers that I don't step foot out of the house when he's traveling for business. The servants monitor my whereabouts and the driver won't take me anywhere," the South African woman shared before exiting the pool. *Swinging? Jealousy? Throwing a kid in jail so he doesn't inherit? No one seems to know what's true and what's not. But everyone's paranoid…*

"My married Saudi friend had an affair with her British tennis pro. She's pregnant and isn't sure whose baby it is. The tennis pro is blond with blue eyes and if the baby comes out looking like that, she's doomed. We're all keeping our fingers crossed."

*The guy must have been really hot for her to take a risk like that. I hope no one spills the beans...*I started to feel my skin burn in the hot sun. I reached for more suntan lotion to douse my discomfort. Or maybe it was the sordid conversation that was making me sweat. I lay back and closed my eyes. The cautionary tales tumbled out of the group in such quick succession, I lost track of which lounge chair they were coming from.

"My Saudi sister-in-law told me that her unmarried cousin was caught having a secret romance with a Saudi boy. They were in their early twenties and wanted to get married. Her father handed her over to the police and she was *beheaded.*"

Thank God I helped Lallo and Jamila...they could have been killed.

"My mother-in-law watches everything I do and tells my husband if she doesn't approve. Abdullah and I are constantly fighting about this. I can't take much more. The old witch searches my closets and pulls out inappropriate clothing. Can you imagine? She took one of my newest Chanel dresses and threw it in the garbage because it was see-through."

What a waste of a gown. Thank God I no longer live with Mama Inja...I can see her doing that...

"My mother-in-law drags me to every baby shower, every engagement party, every wedding with her. She wants to keep an eye on me. I have no time of my own and I hardly ever see my husband. We meet in bed every night when he gets home. That's about it. It's like we're strangers! He never talks to me. I can't even bear to look at him anymore."

I can understand why she would start to hate him...

"My mother-in-law burst into my room one evening when I was in bed with a headache and ripped off the covers, telling me 'Get up, you lazy girl, get dressed and fix your hair and make-up. Your husband is coming home soon and he should never have to see his wife looking like a cow in bed.' I lost it and threw a lamp at her. My husband was so angry, he wouldn't allow me to use the car for a week."

Hah! Serves that bitch of a mother-in-law right... I hope she got a clean hit.

"My in-laws found out that their oldest daughter was dating an American boy at college in California. They hired thugs to pull her out of the school and return her to Jeddah permanently. Right in the middle of a semester. Poor thing. Now she's doomed to the Girl's University in Jeddah and an arranged marriage shortly thereafter unless she can find a way out of here."

What do they have, spies? She'll never get out of here...

"Well she can forget it, unless she figures out a way to swim the Red Sea over to Africa. No one can come or go from Saudi without going through passport control, and those guys are just dying to abuse someone. Even private planes have to deal with them."

Took the words right out of my mind!

"Well, STDs seem to make it through customs alright! Have you ladies heard about the newest STDs that are circulating through the British Air hostess population? If any of your husbands give you a disease, you'll know for sure where it came from. Some of the symptoms are absolutely horrifying."

STDs? Where would I even go to get treatment here?

"Get this–my sister-in-law invited me over to her apartment in the family house to check out some new bedroom furniture. I walked in there, and she was lying in bed, dressed in a scant nightie, with two half-naked women, one on each side! They were rubbing each other with musk oil and they suggested that I join them. Thank God my mother-in-law has such hawk eyes. She called up and told the servant to get me, just in the nick of time. I think she knew what was going on up there."

So they turn a blind eye to that? But they execute the girls who date men?

"Have any of you heard from Madelyn Zahed? No? An American. She was married to Fahad Zahed and he brought her here for a few months. She couldn't stand it, left and never returned. No one knows where she is. She's probably hiding out somewhere back home in the States. California, I'd guess. Smart girl. I wonder if she got a settlement."

An American? Why haven't I heard about her before?

"My husband has been coming home stoned lately, so wild-eyed and delusional, he's scaring me. I heard they are importing tons of cocaine into Jeddah. Who knows what else...it used to be just alcohol, but now, with all the money, you can get anything here."

Sounds like Rahman...coming and going as he pleases, showing up in the middle of the night... I wonder if he's also doing drugs.

"You might be able to get any drug or forbidden substance here, but you still can't import art. We tried, unsuccessfully, to bring in a few land-scape paintings with us last time we traveled. No luck. They were confis-cated and Ibrahim can't even find out what happened. Perfectly beautiful French landscapes."

How hypocritical! As if a landscape painting could do any harm...

"Khalid's cousin was walking in the old souk the other day and two policemen approached her, shouting that her hair was sticking out the side of her *tarha*. When she ignored them, one of the policemen pulled his leather belt out of the loops and started to whip her with it. Right there in the street. She threatened him, calling him a fool for daring to touch a woman from such an important family. 'You will be hunted and killed by my brothers!' Thankfully that stopped him. I don't know what I would have done."

Serves those cops right! What did she ever do to them, to deserve a whipping? I'll never go back to that souk again — at least not without a bodyguard...

"These Saudi women can be very tough. They have to be. It's a survival game here."

The comments slowed down just enough for me to finally interject my thoughts, "Well, I used to consider myself tough, but since living here, I'm scared to death of everything. The idea of getting raped and dying in a Saudi jail just doesn't appeal to me at all." A few of the ladies offered me knowing nods, and the conversation continued.

With each passing comment, I sunk deeper and deeper into the pillows, absorbing each statement like a sponge. As each woman rattled off another proclamation, I felt a new sting of disappointment. Hearing their complaints, my hopes of ever creating any kind of lasting, positive life here seemed utterly impossible. I clung to the idea of Georgetown and Washington DC, a place I had never even been, as my last hope for my marriage with Rahman.

As the sordid conversation continued, I laid there pretending to nod off, tuning out the rest of the loathsome comments, and wishing I hadn't accepted this lunch invitation. When the luncheon was finally over and I could escape to my waiting car, I sat back, ruminating on the sad thoughts and sickening stories, over and over in my head. Stonings, beheadings, jailings, stranglings, beatings, cheating, drugs, and married women of means, wishing they were back home...I didn't like the sound of any of it and it occurred to me that my experiences in Jeddah were not unique. Horrors like the stoning, the funeral, and the gatekeeper at the beach house *would* keep happening. Jeddah was not for me.

Chapter Ten

Georgetown

"Lourdes, can you please come over here and give me a hand?" I asked, struggling to center a black marble cube in my newly renovated entry.

"Be careful, Meesus! Don't hurt yourself!" She rushed over, nudging me aside before easing the two-hundred-pound cube into place with the help of her stout, muscular body. *Lourdes is amazing.* I felt fortunate to have her help.

"The glass top is scheduled for delivery this afternoon, and I want to make sure everything is perfectly straight. Between the weight of this cube base and the thick glass top, this table's not going anywhere!"

"Oh Meesus, everything is so beautiful! You have beautiful taste," Lourdes bubbled, taking in our ultra-modern, urban foyer. "Everything looks like in Europe. Like my country. In Portugal, even the poor people, they have marble floors and marble bathrooms. And the marble, she lasts forever," she pronounced with an approving nod. Lourdes was very pleased with her new job, and I was very pleased with her.

As Lourdes resumed her feather dusting of the crown molding, I thought back to the interview, one year ago. Debbie Doyle, the real estate broker who helped me find the house, had recommended Lourdes as a loyal, skilled, and willing housekeeper, newly freed up after her long-time elderly boss had passed. Lourdes came equipped with a wardrobe of black uniforms, white aprons, a lifetime of experience. Nothing escaped her expert attention. She was "old world" and absolutely perfect for our household. Not only was Lourdes a much-needed new addition to my life, so was her referral source, Debbie Doyle.

From the moment I had stepped off the plane in DC, everything had come together effortlessly. Debbie appeared at the baggage claim to pick me up and we got along like a house on fire. She had helped me set up absolutely every part of my new life in the Capital City from an insurance agent, contractor, and gardener, to a car dealership, doctor, hairdresser, and potential new acquaintances. Debbie advised me on where to shop, where to relax, and where to eat. She even convinced me to enroll in a real estate class, get my sales license, and record it with her firm, should any Saudi friends want to buy a house nearby. She suggested I could work with them and share the commission. I was comfortable in this bustling city and by the end of our first year, it felt like our forever home. It was certainly a vast improvement on that purposeless life in Jeddah where I couldn't even trim my own damn palm trees without getting scolded. Finally stateside again, my brain atrophy subsided. Maybe I could even start thinking about a career.

The doorbell rang and I looked up from my daydream to realize that the glass tabletop had arrived. *Great! Everything is going as planned.* I stood up to open the door but Lourdes beat me to it. *How does she move so fast?*

While Lourdes was helping prop open the door and cover the floor with drop cloths, I looked outside and noticed a young man on the sidewalk, gazing intently at the front of our house. He noted the house number and then swung open the low wrought-iron gate to come up our front walk. He was carrying a package and even though the door was propped open, he knocked on the side of the frame, not wanting to walk in unannounced.

"Hello?" he shouted, as he looked straight at me through the doorway, along with Lourdes, and two burly men carrying the wrapped glass top. "Is this the residence of Rahman Abbar?" he asked, insecurely.

"Yes, how can I help you?" I approached him, presumably to take the package from his hands.

He looked at me curiously, puzzled by my appearance and perhaps, by the delivery he had interrupted. Instead of answering, he just stood and stared, looking rather confused.

"We're having a glass top delivered," I offered, to clarify what was happening. "But, how can I help you?" I said again, now curious as well.

"I go to law school with Rahman. I'm delivering a case study to him. We're working on it together."

I took another deep look at the preppy young blond man. He had to be Rahman's friend, James, one of the few classmates Rahman had mentioned. "Might you be James?" I asked, smiling.

He seemed even more flustered and confused by my words. He fumbled with the package, took a step back, and mumbled that yes, indeed, he was James. "Would you like to come in? Can I offer you a cold drink?" He shook his head so I added, "Rahman isn't here, he's at school, but that's really nice of you to hand deliver these papers. He'll be home at 7 and I'll make sure he knows you dropped them off." But James didn't budge, still looking around the entry as if he had seen a ghost.

"We are having a tabletop delivered," I explained again.

"You mean this whole house is his? This isn't an apartment building?"

"Yes, this is our house. We live here." *Could I be clearer?*

"But who are you? His sister? You live here too?"

Now I was getting confused. "No, I'm not his sister. I'm his wife. And my name is Patricia." I reached out to shake his hand, not knowing what else to do to make his acquaintance.

His eyes widened and he asked me if I was Saudi Arabian.

"No, can't you tell I'm American? Come on. Don't be ridiculous!" I was getting annoyed. What on earth was going on?

"Sorry, Rahman never told any of us he was married. I had no idea...I'm very sorry. Did you just get married?"

"No, we've been married for three years."

James, looking desperately uncomfortable, tossed the neatly wrapped package onto the marble cube, before uttering an awkward "thank you, goodbye" and backing out the door. When he hit the sidewalk, he started jogging away before disappearing behind a grouping of parked cars. *That was weird.* Thank goodness neither Lourdes nor the delivery men noticed our strange exchange, instead busy struggling to center the heavy round glass top on the even heavier marble pedestal. I excused myself, sprinted up the stairs to our home library, shut the door behind me and settled in a chair to reflect.

We had been here for almost a year. Rahman spends most of his time at Georgetown with his fellow students, yet none of them know I *exist*? This must be true because I've never met any of them. Come to think of it, the only reason I even know of James is because I'm constantly asking Rahman about whom he's met or whom he studies with. And his answers are always brief and reluctant.

I felt myself starting to cry and realized that I needed to talk with someone. Who would be sympathetic? *Not Debbie Doyle, that's for sure.* She had her husband wrapped around her finger. She was the breadwinner and he was a stay-at-home dad. She would probably laugh at me for being such a fool.

But Basha would have some solid counsel for my husband's odd behaviors. She was my newest friend and someone I trusted. She was an interior designer and managed a successful business in the DC area. We had met months ago at a party and right away, realized we had many things in common and consequently spent a lot of time together. I started out as her client, accompanying her to the D.C. design center to work on my new house. But recently, she had been pressing me to work with her, as an apprentice of sorts. Given my art history graduate work and my natural love of color and composition, Basha's offer made perfect sense. I had always been drawn to good style so interior design was a natural fit for my skills set. I also love meeting new people and enjoyed the networking aspects of interior design work. And since my own house was completely renovated and decorated, I had nothing else to do with my days. I loved the idea of meaningful work.

To my delight, I found interior design to be enormously gratifying and challenging. And Basha was so easy to be with, great to talk to, professional but also very mellow and understanding...Basha knew me and she knew Rahman. I trusted that she would understand my prickly dilemma.

"Hi, Patricia. Great to hear from you. How's the table delivery going? Does it look fabulous?"

"Yes, the glass top is absolutely perfect. But I'm not so good."

"What? Why not? Something happen?" Her intuitive nature made it easy to unburden myself. I proceeded to describe my encounter with James, careful to include all the details. But describing it only made me feel even worse.

"Can you believe that all this time, he never once mentioned me to any of his acquaintances in school? Why do you think he would hide the fact that he's living here with his wife?"

"Well, he obviously doesn't want anyone to know he's married. That's not good. Do you think he has a girlfriend?"

"Whoa! Wait a minute. I never thought of that. How horrible!"

"Do you have any other reason to believe there's another woman? Has he done anything suspicious?"

"Not really. He's just being his usual weird self. He seems to spend the bulk of his time out of the house, presumably at school, but maybe he isn't at school after all...I have no way of knowing unless I start following him. But I don't know if I'm up for that."

"This heavy conversation requires some good fodder. I'm hungry. Let's meet at Houston's in fifteen minutes."

What a great idea. A fun place like the brand-new Houston's would definitely cheer me up and make it easier to talk. Jumping into my cute little Fiat convertible, I made my way down Rock Creek Parkway to Georgetown. I prepared myself for a tell-all session with Basha, replaying the past year in my mind with all its signs of change in my husband and our marriage—troubling things that I had kept inside for too long.

Those last months in Jeddah were unremarkable. All I could do was pray for Rahman's acceptance at Georgetown. When that finally arrived, I spent the remainder of my time dreaming about my future in Washington, DC. It seemed like everuthing vibrant and colorful in our lives had left our household once Lallo was no longer a daily fixture. He became a Muslim, closed the deal with Jamila's parents and no longer needed our phone. They were married shortly after, then embarked on a honeymoon in Italy. That was the last I saw or heard directly from Lallo. After our departure from Jeddah, Rahman kept in touch with him, and reported that Lallo was very happy, doing well at work and already had a baby on the way. I was glad for him but sad for myself. I wondered why Lallo went from being my dear friend, to only speaking with Rahman, his boss, to share the joys of his family life.

Without Lallo's cheerful presence, I was lonely, and would constantly pester Rahman to come up with some activities for us to pass the time, even though we only had a few months left. One Friday morning, I convinced him to take me to the beach house after lunch, just to have some fresh air and sun. I felt like walking out on the dock and jumping into the sea for a swim. Surprisingly, he agreed. We packed a few necessities, called for the driver, and started out on our journey. At the point in the road where our car was supposed to turn off and drive on the sand, a new paved road had materialized, with an actual road sign and an arrow, pointing to the beach.

"Look, they built a road! And signage! When did that happen?" I gasped.

"Yes, *Amati*, the government has started its development project for the city. They plan to build hundreds of new roads, extending the city all the way to the sea," Abdullah offered enthusiastically.

Rahman seemed unfazed. "Yes, yes, they have a huge plan to transform Jeddah, including a harbor, airport, residential neighborhoods, recreational areas, and all the required infrastructure. Several German and American urban planning firms have been hired to figure it out. Our company has won quite a few of the contracts for building and management of the port. Everything should be completed in the next five years. It's good for business."

"You never told me that…" I responded, surprised but also somewhat hurt.

"I never tell you anything, Patricia. I don't like talking. I don't like sharing. I like keeping things to myself. Get used to it."

"Well, you weren't like this when I met you…" I didn't want to argue about it on my one day at the beach, ruining the cool swim in the sea that I had been relishing, so I shut my mouth and let my inner monologue take over. *I never win these arguments anyway.*

Looking out the window at the seemingly unending flats of packed dust that will soon anchor new industries, workers, and modernity, to Jeddah, my eyes finally found the Abbar beach compound.

"There it is! And so close to the new road…wait a minute, Look! There's a big hole in our wall! Look, Rahman! There's a huge hole in our wall and the road goes right through it!"

Rahman snapped to attention, motioned for the driver to slow down, and all three of us stared at the sight in front of our car. Our beach property, formerly surrounded by a high privacy wall, had been breached! It appeared that the government had broken through the wall, bisecting our land, and paved a four-lane highway right through it. As we slowly approached, instead of heading to the gatehouse, we realized that we could just drive right through the hole and into the center of our property. We came to a stop quite close to the back of the house. The new gatekeeper, spotting us, ran over to tell us what happened. Apparently, an entire team of bulldozers, rollers, and pavers, owned by the government, had burst through the wall and started to pave a road, in order to complete a new recreational shopping area. Since the King has rights to all the land, regardless of property ownership, nothing was to be done. I realized that there is little one can do in a kingdom, even if you are a so-called important famivly.

Another upsetting matter was once again left up to a resigned shrug. One more reason I couldn't be happier to head off to Georgetown in a few months. *Good riddance to this backward place! This is the final straw. You can't get attached to things in this country. My house may be next.*

Our departure from Jeddah and settling into Washington, DC was surprisingly smooth. Rahman's first semester was underway and he was rather pleased that the student body was both mature and diverse, the professors worldly and interesting. He was the only Saudi at Georgetown Law and loved the status and attention it brought. Still, our bright and hopeful new September gave way to his usual antics by October. Each day, including weekends, he was presumably on campus from 7am-7pm, with no way to contact him for those twelve hours. Our new norm was looking strangely similar to the structured days in Jeddah. He was almost never home. I was again missing him and feeling alone, often frustrated that he didn't want to spend time with me, despite our new freedom in the United States. He insisted that the coursework was daunting and required all his time, not unlike in Jeddah when he would insist that we had to remain separate to satisfy Muslim propriety. Why did I again have a nagging feeling that those restrictions were a fabrication and he didn't actually want me around?

Often, the phone would ring and Rahman refused to let me answer it, laughing when I asked who had called. It seemed like he enjoyed keeping me in the dark. I recalled that first party in Jeddah. I had arrived in the country that morning, yet he greeted every single person in the room before finally acknowledging me. Had that been deliberate? I wondered how I had ended up with a man who spent such little time with me, especially now that I was in the U.S. and could no longer blame his behavior on Saudi Arabia.

I found parking a block away and made my way into Houston's. Upon entering the restaurant, the hustle and bustle snapped me out of my deep contemplation. I found Basha at a table near the window facing N Street. She was anxiously awaiting my arrival, primed for the skinny on Rahman. She was not disappointed. I had a torrent of infractions by my husband to share with her. I went over the past year, my life in Jeddah, and the strange behaviors that were no longer coinciding with Rahman's given excuses. Basha listened dutifully, as I shared for hours just how bizarre our homelife had gotten.

At first, I thought it was just Saudi. But the further I reached back, the more I realized that despite our change in latitudes, Rahman's behavioral patterns followed us everywhere. I started with what had happened with James. Then other evidence of Rahman's wrongdoings crossed my mind, often things that I had forgotten about entirely. When he was out and I answered the phone, I would get frequent hang-ups. When I waited up past midnight for him to return from studying on a Saturday or Sunday night, he claimed that the library was open 24 hours. I had no way of knowing otherwise without showing up at the library, which would horrify Rahman. Then on Halloween when he was "out studying," I found sequins in his car the next day. *Remnants of a costume?* He was probably out at a party. Just like in Jeddah!

Basha was quick to try and find a solution. "Should we follow him? I'm happy to oblige. We can go in my car. He won't recognize that. Just tell me when."

Following Rahman might prove that I have nothing to worry about, so it was worth the risk. The alternative was doing nothing except slowly go mad. For my sanity's sake. I agreed. "Ok. Let's do it on Wednesday night. He usually comes home very late on Wednesdays."

"And," added Basha, "maybe we should try to meet his friends. Why don't you throw a big holiday bash at your house and have Rahman invite all his law school friends? I'll invite some of my friends, we can include some clients so they can see your fabulous house. Let's not forget my neighbor, Lorraine, and her new boyfriend. They just started a production company and will bring a whole crew of artsy types. Debbie knows lots of fun people, and I'm dating this new guy, Tommy. He's a lobbyist and has loads of interesting people who would love a good party. Everyone will get something out of it. At the very least, you can plant your flag. Come on. This sounds like fun."

I liked her scheme. It would allow me to meet the law students without confronting Rahman. That evening, when he arrived home, I floated the party idea to him. To my surprise, he liked it and agreed to include all his law school friends. He even suggested inviting the dean and his wife. I congratulated myself for being positive and proactive instead of sitting around, moping and hoping.

The invitations were sent out and very well received! Within a few weeks, we had pulled a crowd of over eighty people together for a fabulous holiday fete. We put the finishing touches on the house the day before our event. Flowers everywhere, wood in the fireplaces, every pillow fluffed, every accessory placed, just so. I was very proud of my new home and I was sure it would drum up lots of business for Basha and me.

The evening of the party, I chose my dress very carefully. I wanted to look gorgeous and very "New York." I chose a new Moschino black number with sequins the size of quarters, at once flirty and whimsical. My body looked like it was covered with large undulating fish scales. In 1981, it was the ultimate fashion statement. Guests flipped when they saw me and I was so excited to greet everyone that I stood at the top of the stairs for the first hour of the party, not wanting to miss one single entry. Basha circulated around, showing anyone who asked to see the rest of the house. She took advantage of every opportunity. The caterer was spot on, with creatively prepared and presented hors d'oeuvres, served by stellar looking young men all clad in black. Rahman had purchased cases of the best champagne for the event and the guests were guzzling it like water. Waiters passed by, collecting the empty glasses and plates left behind, making sure everything was in perfect order. We had plugged in our best disco tapes, recorded at the famed Regine's nightclub, currently the rage in Paris, and people started dancing to the irresistible playlist.

A handsome man grabbed me and pulled me away from my entry perch to the makeshift dance floor on the landing. Basha was already dancing with another equally handsome man, and she shouted an introduction. I could hardly hear, but I gathered that my dancing partner was a lobbyist from Tommy's firm. We twirled around for a song or two, then I begged to leave. I was on the lookout for the law students. The long-awaited students finally arrived in a pack, moving slowly through the foyer, taking in a scene that grad students aren't generally privy to. In with them blew a cold gust of wind, twisting up the stairs to the second floor. There were at least a dozen, and to my chagrin, all dressed in jeans and sweaters, seemingly straight from the stuffy Georgetown library. Bewildered by the expanse and the expense of our decadent rowhouse, they were moving at a sluggish pace up the stairs, clearly stoned out of their britches. I was instantly annoyed. *Ugh. Childish kids. They get invited to a formal party and won't even be alert enough to enjoy all the effort we put into this!* They won't add much to my party, but at least they'll see and know that Rahman's very much married. I introduced myself to each and every one of them as they passed me on the steps, with little more than a nod. Nothing but blank stares with bloodshot eyes. *What a bore! Rahman can have his law students.*

Basha and her glamorous Potomac friends were cutting up on the dance floor. One of them, svelte and athletic, made rather loud small talk over the booming stereo, inviting Rahman and me to the polo games in the spring. Apparently the Potomac crowd were all polo players. I wasn't sure at the time what polo was, but I promised him that we would be there to watch. "We have great after parties and celebrities show up all the time. It's very international. Not as great as this party but still lots of fun." he winked.

"Just let Basha know when. We'll come!"

My mother would be proud of my hostessing skills—circulating, smiling, introducing, filling drinks, and passing around the beautiful food. The catering team had hit a home run and the night was a huge success, folks lingering til the wee hours. But the law students were nowhere to be found. As the party began to dwindle, guests thanked me for a stellar evening.

Debbie, inebriated but somehow still vertical, was hanging on her boss' shoulder, dragging her husband close behind. "Patricia! Fabulous evening. You must come work with us! You'd be a natural at selling real estate!"

"Ok, glad you had fun. Drive carefully." *Or perhaps walk home?*

Basha edged up to me, "I'll stay to the end, I don't want to miss one moment," she murmured, before wedging herself between two eager men on the sofa and giving me a coy smile. The house was nearly empty but I hadn't seen Rahman for over an hour, even after searching the other lounging areas on the main level.

"Have you seen him lately?" I asked Basha, still blissed out on the sofa.

"No, but I did notice him walking up the stairs about an hour ago."

"Don't tell me he went to bed without even saying goodbye to anyone… that's so rude!" I stormed up the stairs to our bedroom and tried to open the door. It was locked. I could hear music playing inside the room and I knocked hard on the door, but no one answered. I started pounding, but still, no answer.

Basha came up the stairs, confused by the banging. "What's going on?"

"Whoever is in this bedroom, MY bedroom, won't open the door. And I hear people in there. What the hell is going on?"

One of the doors above us on the third floor slammed shut. Basha and I ran up together and started jiggling doorknobs on all three bedrooms. "Hello? Hello? Can you please open the door? Whoever's in there, please open up," I shouted. No answer. Basha tried the two back bedroom doors, and they, too, were locked. I put my ear to the keyholes and could hear voices. Yet, no one bothered to acknowledge me.

"Oh my God, there are people locked in every bedroom in the house. Where's Rahman and who are these people?"

I turned and rattled the hall bathroom door. This was the smallest bathroom in the house and the only one I hadn't renovated. It still had the old door on hundred-year-old hinges with a skeleton key lock. I tried the knob. It was locked. "Someone's in this bathroom. This is too weird. Hello? Hello? Who's in there? Can you please open the door?"

Rahman's voice faintly called out from within, "Leave me alone. I'm busy."

I called over to my friend, "Basha, Rahman's inside! Why would he come up here and use this old bathroom? He's not been up here this entire year! Do you think there's someone in there with him?"

Basha shrugged, confused and not sure what to do next. "Knock again and ask."

"Rahman, what's going on in there? What are you doing?"

"None of your business," he replied, muffled and uninterested. He sounded weird. Probably drunk? Or something else?

I went nuts. I was certain he had a woman in there. All those hang-up calls flashed through my memory. I would break down the door if he wouldn't open it. Basha helped me. We pushed our shoulders against the door, but it didn't budge.

"What are you trying to do?" Rahman shouted. I didn't care what he said at that point. I was going into that bathroom no matter what.

"I'm breaking down this door unless you open it." I hesitated for a moment, giving him a chance to unlock the door, a task that I felt was simple and easy to do if he didn't have something to hide. He remained silent.

"Ok, have it your way. I'm coming in!" I kicked in the bottom panel of the door. Within seconds, the entire door splintered and gave way. As I charged through the opening, there sat Rahman on the toilet with his trousers around his ankles. He was so stinking drunk, but that was no excuse. Still searching for his female companion, I yanked open the linen closet, before checking the shower. Both empty. Ditto for the tub. I looked up at the skylight. Could she have slipped out up there? It was locked so I instead focused on the window with a small fire escape. I was sure she'd be out there, hanging on for dear life. I threw open the window, stuck my head out, but nothing. Nothing and no one.

Even after cooling down a bit, I felt no remorse whatsoever. He deserved it. He asked for it. This was a game for him, a cruel mind game to drive me crazy, and he was succeeding. Just as he laughed instead of telling me who was on the phone. Or his refusal to acknowledge my presence in Jeddah. I was sure that something disgusting had taken place in my home, whether or not I had caught it. Rahman was so drunk he could barely get off the toilet. I grabbed Basha and made my way down the stairs. I wanted Rahman's trashy classmates out of my house and I'd need the police to do it. I pushed the two distress keys on our burglar alarm system, which made a direct call to the police station.

"Patricia, what are you doing?" cried Basha.

"I'm getting the police to clear all this shit out of my house. Come on, let's get outside and watch the show."

The two of us disappeared out the front door while two police cars were just pulling up. I approached the first car and said, "Officer, there are unwanted people in my house and I need your help clearing them out. Please. They're on the third and fourth floors."

"Did they do any harm to you or threaten you in any way?"

"No. No threats or actions but they refuse to leave my house and I want them out now. Please."

More out of curiosity than fear, the group of policemen, now numbering four, made their way slowly into the house. I watched as they walked up the stairs and into the living room. Through the windows, I witnessed them spread out and go further up the stairs. A light went on in my bedroom, and two people jumped out of the bed, naked, probably startled by the officers at the door. Scrambling for their clothes, they unlocked the door and police streamed in. All the rooms were cleared like this, methodically.

Basha and I silently stood on the front lawn as the first officer escorted a disheveled couple down the stairs and out the door to the street. They were both arguing about being invited guests and their rights.

I looked at Basha and winked, "Law students. Good, they'll know how to defend themselves!"

Then we watched as the next two sets of couples were escorted out of the place by two more officers. Behind them stumbled Rahman, telling the cops that these were, indeed, invited guests, and behind him came what appeared to be the last straggler couple, still buttoning their clothing.

"All law students. Rahman looks angry," Basha noted. "What are you going to say to him?"

"Nothing. I'm not sleeping in this house tonight either. I'll stay at a hotel."

I pulled out of the back garage while those morons were still arguing on the front lawn. Basha and I checked into the Four Seasons then sat downstairs at the bar, recounting the night's events, and I realized that although it ended badly, there was quite a bit of fun, prior. Pretty soon, we were cackling so hard that tears rolled down our faces. And I would call the cops on Rahman's friends again in a sec. It felt good to finally get a leg up on his extracurricular activities and friends that underestimated my craftiness. Revenge is indeed sweet.

Chapter Eleven

Reluctant Jet-Setter

Looking back, I often question my actions and judgment at that time. Was I an idiot, lost, or simply immature? Why would I build my life with a man that I couldn't trust to be honest or loyal? He made me crazy–kicking down doors to see who he was with in the bathroom at our party. Sneaking away to a hotel with a friend after calling the police on his stoner friends. Secrets, lies, other lives…

Mocking me had become Rahman's favorite pastime. Why would I put up with this? Love? Rebelliousness? Stubbornness? Masochism? Temporary insanity? I've beaten myself up for years asking this question. Years of therapy, years of anguish, years of confusion, years of regret for not sticking up for myself. And, years of emotional pain for our children as a result.

Basha is still my close friend after three decades. She lived through it all with me, her friendship and loyalty never wavering. Her simple and straightforward response when I was questioning myself now, as a mature woman, was at once comforting and gracious.

"Patricia, it felt normal then. We were young–in our twenties! You two were the perfect couple…so together, so gorgeous, and so rich–everyone in Georgetown admired you. Rahman was handsome, smart, polite, and so well mannered. Nothing really seemed that crazy, until things got unbelievably weird."

She was right. Things suddenly got weird.

After the night of the party, Rahman, the house, and I, somehow recovered. Even the DC police let us off the hook. But my newfound affinity for truth (and retaliatory behavior) prompted me to finally mark a hard line in the sand. I was ready to leave, told him so, and meant it...I had mentally prepared myself for the possibility of divorce. But instead of resuming his M.O. of benevolent dictator/puppet master, Rahman made a complete about-face, tenderly begging me to stay. Rahman, who despised drama and emotional outbursts, put his tail between his legs and prostrated himself to me for the first time. He was desperate to keep me, to keep us, and promised we could work it out. His sincerity was hard to miss, so I relented, again excusing his recent behaviors as a result of too much partying.

In hindsight, on some backward, deviant level, I think my outraged behavior somehow excited him. My husband was a gambler, and so he countered me, just to prove he would again, win. Rahman continued pursuing his law school studies and I pursued my newly minted career as an interior designer. Things went smoothly and despite my initial reluctance in letting him in again, his behavior actually did improve. He curtailed his studies to a few nights each week so we could make plans to go out together. And the timing was perfect, as we'd been flooded with enticing invitations from many who had attended our party. New friends introduced us to more new friends and our network of fun grew exponentially. Odd as it was, our relationship hitting rock bottom was a blessing. We were finally growing individually and with each other.

***

Spring is perhaps the most beautiful season in Washington, DC. One morning in April, while staring out the window, admiring all the flowering trees along Massachusetts Avenue, I remembered that polo matches were beginning at the club in Maryland. I was curious to see this new (to us) sport that had so intoxicated our new friends. It's all they talked about and we'd been invited too many times to count.

"Rahman, wouldn't it be fun to drive out to Potomac and see a polo match today? Remember that fun group of guys from our party? Friends of Basha? They said there are games every Sunday starting in April."

Rahman was enthusiastic and all in.

"Great idea. The weather's perfect. Call Basha and see if she wants to meet us there. She knows everyone. Find out if we have to buy tickets."

I was thrilled at his reaction and started to get excited about seeing my first polo match. I snapped into action, not wanting to waste a moment. After making a few calls, we packed the car and made the forty-minute drive along beautiful country roads with the top down. Caught up in the moment, Rahman announced that he'd like to learn to play polo, just a few minutes before we arrived.

"Since when?" I queried. "You haven't even seen it yet!"

"Since I read about it in *Washingtonian* magazine. And Kamyar mentioned playing it in France. Seems like something I would enjoy. I miss the physicality of my old soccer days. I'll speak to the club manager when we get there. Maybe someone there could teach me. We're going to stay in DC all summer, it's too hot to return to Jeddah, and I only scheduled one class for myself at law school. I'll have lots of free time."

And sure enough, he succeeded in scheduling himself for lessons the very next week. I was surprised that Rahman wanted to learn how to play polo, just as I was surprised to find out he wanted to attend law school. But I was getting used to his impulsive and unilateral decision making. He didn't even ride horses, but who was I to stop him? This was all great news for me. Anything we could do together, far away from that law school library, was a welcome change, and I eagerly got involved with the Potomac Polo Club.

I quickly connected with a whole new group of friends. The membership consisted of mostly young and carefree people, all looking quite glamorous: men in white slacks and ladies in flowy sundresses. Just my style! I made the club the center of my life. We bought box tickets to all the Sunday games, and a seasonal parking space next to the field so I could host tailgating parties all summer long. My tailgate spread dazzled the crowd, complete with tablecloth and napkins, fruit and cheese platters and a fully stocked bar. I volunteered to help with the new Polo Magazine, generating interesting articles and interviewing anyone I could. And I picked up a new talent and title in the process, purchasing a Nikon camera package to rival Nat Geo. I was the volunteer photographer and historian of the club as well as Rahman's official cheerleader, groupie, and wifey supreme. I shared my high-speed action photos with the other polo players and within a few months, I became a club favorite and a must among the spectators. After the matches, our outdoor tailgates would continue long into the evening, ending with the requisiteArgentinian barbeque asado, willingly and lovingly cooked by the grooms in a large earthen pit. This was their national culinary tradition—slow roasting all parts of the cow, (including pancreas, brain, ribs and more the common cuts of beef) and they loved sharing it with us all. We would linger for hours, listening to guitar music, savoring delicious meat sandwiches, drinking sangria. and discussing all things horse, in this new and exclusive equine society.

How lucky we were to have ventured out here that first Sunday. I was having the time of my life and for the first time in our marriage, Rahman and I fully shared a healthy social life. I even attempted polo lessons, but soon realized that my arms were too weak to wield a mallet. So instead, I volunteered to warm up the horses before the practices, then clean and pack them up after. Having worked with horses year after year in summer camp, I was a natural. That summer passed quickly as we settled into the club, finally finding our place and people.

I worked every morning in DC with Basha, then spent every afternoon with Rahman at the polo club doing all sorts of activities that complimented his polo lessons. We were once again the perfect tag-team, working like a well-oiled machine. He and I had found the same easy rhythm when we partied at college in Boston. I would reserve the best tables at all the clubs and Rahman would simply fly in, enjoy, and foot the bill. And now again, we were intrinsically tied by a shared passion. Our time in DC was one of the happiest periods of my life.

After a few months of training, Rahman became a rated player, not surprising given his amount of freetime, physicality, and of course, finances. He eagerly purchased six polo ponies from an older player who was retiring. With horses of his own, he was eligible to join in with other players, forming teams for interclub matches. Polo teams consist of only four players, but require several horses per person because of the rigor and fast pace of the gameplay. Finding willing and available young men with the free time and finances to support a polo hobby is a rarity. By the end of the summer, we were invited to play at every polo field within 200 miles of DC, traveling as a tightly-knit entourage for weekend excursions.

We met several Argentinian professional players in our regional travels who recognized Rahman's keen interest and determination to become a good player. One particularly smooth pro instantly took Rahman under his wing—a middle-aged athlete named Anibal Garcia who had been immersed in the polo world for a very long time. Anibal's English was perfect, convincing Rahman that he would be my husband's polo guardian angel. The two trained each day at the polo field, practicing every possible shot, strategy, and even different horses to find the perfect pairing of skill, will, and might. As the weather grew cooler, our evenings were commandeered by notions and dreams of warm-weather travel that winter to Wellington, Florida, where the most ambitious polo club ever built had just been completed. Located ten miles west of Palm Beach with every possible convenience including a nearby international airport, travel back and forth was easily manageable from DC. Of course, an unlimited budget was also a requirement, but that, too, was doable. It didn't take much talking to convince Rahman that his future in the sport depended on establishing a winter base at the Palm Beach Polo Club in Wellington. We sat around the bonfire as fall approached, eagerly making plans to dominate the upcoming winter polo tournaments.

I was completely on board with the idea of traveling back and forth from Palm Beach all winter since that would nix a winter visit to Jeddah. Indeed, Rahman had forgotten that Jeddah even existed and we had not yet returned. We hadn't even planned a visit! Our house stood empty. It was as if our life in Jeddah had never happened. I started to feel like it was some long-forgotten nightmare. The idea of never returning relaxed me in ways I couldn't explain.

The deeper into polo we got, the greater my skills toolbox expanded. I was a petite city girl trucking a thirty-foot gooseneck rig full of six horses down Interstate 95. I felt like a badass behind the wheel of that GMC 6X6! I could tack and untack a horse in less than two minutes, braid their tails, clip their manes, and pick their hooves. I could clean and store all the leather equipment, help administer worming fluid down a horse-nose-hose, and pack the horses into the truck tight enough so they wouldn't fall down during the ride. I even started teaching them tricks. I had never seen myself scooping shit from the hooves of a half ton animal covered in mud, but I couldn't have been happier, and manual labor helped me feel more capable and strong than I ever had. And the fact that I could be squashed like a bug by one of these strong, magnificent animals at any time just added to the excitement. We were still young and shared this drive to push ourselves and each other beyond the safe places, both in life and love.

Not only was I relishing my new vocation as a barn hand, but my career as an interior designer, in partnership with Basha (of course), was also blooming. DC was experiencing a housing boom and we were flooded with job offers. When law school was back in session, I worked alongside Basha each morning, meeting clients at their homes and visiting the newly opened Design Center to shop for merchandise. Our roster of projects included fabulous residences in Georgetown, new homes in the posh, suburban communities like Potomac and McLean, and even country estates in nearby Middleburg, Virginia. Color, composition, and every detail that creates a tasteful space, came to me with ease under Basha's tutelage.

I enjoyed every minute of this work. Still, my favorite time of the day was at the farm. Rahman took a lease on a beautiful seventy-five rolling acre horse farm on River Road in Potomac, Md. He had decided that sharing space with other players was not convenient. His horses had to be cared for just so and he preferred being the boss of his domain. The farm had a charming barn large enough for his growing needs and huge fenced pastures where the horses could graze and decompress between matches. It was paradise to me. Each day when I arrived, I would call out to all the horses grazing in the big field, open the gates, and shoo them into the barn and down the aisle to their respective stalls. They all knew which stall was theirs, as I had painstakingly trained them, and each would enter obediently, waiting for the afternoon feed. Unlike humans, horses seldom make mistakes finding where they belong. I was very proud of my accomplishments as a barn hand, and were it not for Basha encouraging me to keep working with her, I might have dropped everything for those horses. I loved each one as if they were my children. I discovered their personalities, one by one. I made friends with all the other equestrian neighbors along River Road and would ride over to their barns for a visit. We would go on extended trail rides on weekends without scheduled matches.

Horses are not just a sport, they're a lifestyle. And like the horses, I had found where I belonged. I loved everything about them and Rahman was right there with me. I quickly learned that there's nothing better for a marriage than a shared purpose. We now had fourteen horses and were planning to spend the winter with them in Palm Beach. Anibal advised us on all arrangements and I followed his orders to a tee. At his behest, I rented a two-bedroom condo for us at the Palm Beach Polo Club, starting in December. Anibal and I also arranged and secured accommodations, right on the club grounds, for our growing family of very pampered half-ton babies. Anibal drove them down after Thanksgiving in preparation for the winter polo season. Our plan was to stay in DC for work and school Monday through Thursday, then to fly down to Florida for the weekends.

Winter polo in Wellington, Florida was a whirlwind of sporting and social life. Rahman was at the barn each weekend morning, riding and practicing until the sun was down. After he hired two grooms to do most of the barn work, my pre and post prep services for our steeds were no longer needed. I decided to use that spare time to indulge in my love of photography. My Nikon was out of batteries often as I snapped everything that moved. When I wasn't still with the camera, I was on my favorite horse, galloping down the sand racetrack at warp speed to keep our ponies game-day shape. It felt great to be part of the team, mingling with other riders at the barn and making dear friends with people who shared our passion. Rahman tirelessly pushed himself, improving his polo skills, entering more challenging tournaments, buying even faster horses, and perhaps taking a quick trip to Argentina for an immersion clinic with Eduardo "Eddie" Moore, the undisputed top polo player of the world at that time.

Rahman made many trips to Argentina in years following, and developed a close friendship with Eddie, a legendary horse broker of the finest and fastest horses that unlimited money could buy. Anibal was quickly dismissed. We went full monty on horse life, purchasing a small house in the Palm Beach Polo Club so we would be a permanent fixture rather than frequent rental guests.

Rahman only wanted the best for himself. And although his obsession with top tier everything reeked of total narcissism, I went along with our novel life, no more humdrum and ordinary, and no more Jeddah rules and regs. We were an international couple, not simply an "Arab" with an American wife. I married an international man, an unusual man, who lived life to the fullest and was willing to share that with me. I couldn't have dreamed up a more exciting lifestyle or degree of contentment.

In order to stay in Washington, DC after graduating law school, Rahman continued his studies and went back for a Master of Laws degree, then a PhD. If he dragged it out, he could keep up our East Coast lifestyle for another few years. In student mode, he didn't have to make excuses for not seeking (undesirable) employment. Working surely would have cramped his style. His family gladly bankrolled everything we did, perhaps with rose colored glasses on, hoping he would return to the family business after mass matriculation. As far as I knew, this was never fully discussed with his parents so I put it out of my mind. I didn't want to rock the boat. Everything was going my way. I believed that Rahman was too addicted to our Western life to throw it all away for awful Jeddah again.

Rahman soon ratcheted up to a new level of sneaky (read: crafty). Rather than apologizing or excusing his lack of visits home, he put a spin on the need for family togetherness and somehow convinced his blindfolded parents to purchase a summer house for themselves.

In Marbella, Spain.

I say "house" but it was more like a magnificent estate. Saying no to Rahman was exceedingly difficult and apparently, not just for me. His flawless (and entirely selfish) plan for their money also included importing a highly curated collection of polo ponies to a nearby Spanish club in

Sotogrande for the season. His advisor, Eddie, was only too happy to accommodate.

As with any number of other decisions made without my input, summer in Spain was not discussed with me prior to plans being made.

"What? We're not playing at Potomac? What about our horses and our farm? I love it there! Who do we know in Spain besides your family? We don't even have a team!" Confused and baffled, I protested him thoughtlessly throwing away our well-earned good life here. I thought of my beloved horses, tailgates and polo matches in Potomac, our tight family of DC friends, my job (Basha!), and how beautiful our splendid days already were.

But my happiness was not a concern. His next fix was. I stared at his mouth while he continued to convey his reasons. I simply could not process all that I would lose on his endless quest for worldwide recognition.

"Eddie promised it would be a great season there—and with him on my team, I'll meet everyone. Potomac? Come on, that's small time. Besides, Patricia, wouldn't you rather see my parents on our terms, this way, in Spain, rather than spend a whole month doing nothing in Jeddah?"

"Uh, I guess…" was all I could say. The option of skipping Jeddah was definitely enticing, although our departure felt abrupt. But, I complied, as Rahman always managed to lace his mandates with something beneficial to me. Namely, no unsavory trips to Jeddah. That was the carrot.

We started with summer in Spain, which bled into trips to England for polo. Always in pursuit of bigger and better goals, Eddie convinced Rahman to sponsor a team with two other international players for the summer season at the Guards Club outside of London, England. The beauty of this plan was that we could easily transport our horses to England from Spain now that the tunnel had been built. Rahman rationalized the decision as a very practical thing to do and a way to get more use out of his European string of ponies. This British club was the height of prestige in the polo world and we were both flattered at being accepted there as members. The roster of celebrities included none other than Prince Charles and Princess Diana, whom we were instructed never to approach unless spoken to.

Rahman had always loved England, having spent many years there at school, and of course, he was attracted to the idea of returning with his polo team and new found glory. All of his childhood school friends came to watch, and life sped up even more. The pace was dizzying. I could barely keep up with all the people we met and all the places we visited—The Ascot

Races, the Henley Regatta and the Opening Gala at Cowdray Park Polo, hosted by Lord Cowdray, himself. But I found myself missing the slower pace of life at the farm in Potomac. I wondered how my horses were. I had not seen them in months and was no longer their keeper. In these elite clubs, wives of the polo players didn't touch the horses. We simply sat, dressed to the nines, in the stands with the socialites, and watched. Paid professional photographers rendered my Nikon skills obsolete. Rahman and I traveled throughout summer between Spain and England, attending party after party, match after match, and when it all came to an end in September, I was delighted to get back to D.C. However, this return to our quieter life understandably felt like a letdown to Rahman.

For a fresh Guards Club inductee, DC was amateur hour. We resumed our routine of my work with Basha and Rahman's graduate studies, but all focus and planning was on attending the Florida winter polo season full time, then spring and summer seasons in Europe. Things moved quickly as we gradually left DC in the rearview. I wouldn't be able to work or have anything of my own in this new international lifestyle. I had the sinking feeling of doubt, the suspicion that my life at twenty-five was drifting off-course and I was once again losing control. I was on top of the world, but my purpose, my best friend, my joy, and my calling of caring for our hoofed ones had all been ripped away from me without any consideration or even warning.

I reluctantly broke the news to Basha that I wouldn't be around anymore come December. It was one of the most difficult conversations I've ever had, and I could hardly conceal my heartbreak. I knew what she would say before it even exited her mouth.

"What? Why would you guys do that? What about your house, and your farm? You put so much into it. You're giving up work? You're just going to follow that man around from match to match, country to country?"

"I'm not sure what the details will look like but Rahman's smitten with the polo world and convinced that this is a good move for us. He's getting set up with a lot of big-name players…And we'll keep our house here! It's not like we're not coming back. You can come visit Europe whenever you want and I'll be on the lookout for cool international decorating jobs! Maybe work will get even better for us." I tried to keep our conversation light and upbeat, but Basha and I both knew that the chances of us launching an international design firm were slim. She wasn't about to give up the life and business that she had built, and I sadly accepted that unlike her, I was relinquishing mine. Without my work or my farm, who was I anymore?

"Patricia, I'm gonna miss you so much."

I held back the tears. "Me too. But honestly, Basha, I don't know how to stop it."

The next few months flew by, Rahman wrapping up his PhD and me, finishing my last few jobs with Basha. Like a puppet, I went through the familiar motions of packing up, making all the required reservations and saying goodbye to everyone I loved. I was so disappointed in myself. I knew I was giving up on me yet again. But I felt powerless to do otherwise.

Chapter Twelve

Motherhood

Marbella, Spain was a fabulous place to be in the summer. Perfect weather, chic beach clubs serving paella and cocktails at the water's edge, parties and nightclubs starting at midnight, lasting 'til sunrise and a very hip crowd to celebrate with. At Rahman's insistence, the Abbars had purchased a gorgeous Mediterranean-style mansion, high in the hills with a view of the sea and award-winning gardens that stretched in every direction. The property itself was a behemoth, boasting ten bedroom suites, some in detached cottages, dotting the perfectly manicured landscape. The well-kept estate came equipped with every possible luxury and was fully furnished in the classic European style. There were several areas for entertaining both inside and outside, each one with breathtaking views of the surrounding gardens and the sea beyond. Upon arrival, we jumped right into a non-stop life of polo and partying.

Endless hosting of new friends and family was enjoyable at first, until it occurred to me that everyone else was coming and going but I was stuck there, a permanent innkeeper, forced to remain stationary while our guests came and went at will. It was like being on an all-inclusive vacation at Disney World for an entire summer, but without being allowed to leave the park, even briefly. And given the generous amount of adult tomfoolery at our place, the Marbella home was feeling more (to me) like Hotel California than Disney.

I was tired of mindless entertaining. I had never intended to be a full time bartender, and was again struggling with no sense of purpose. Rahman would not discuss future plans with me, as he preferred to live for the moment, drifting from one high to the next. I was again nothing more than his shadow (and perpetual cheerleader) and I missed my budding career as an interior designer. I missed the freedom of making my own days, and being in charge of my own formerly flourishing and enriching life.

No matter how many times I mulled it over in my head, I couldn't see a possibility of an optimistic outcome for me, both personally and professionally. I simply couldn't replace the creative high of designing with Basha with the static station of perpetual host and partygoer. I had outgrown that exhaustive lifestyle. And, I wanted to be at my farm, in rubber boots and leather gloves, running my big beautiful equines in open expanses without an audience. My life in a Spanish mansion overlooking the sea could not compare to the peace I felt in that barn in Potomac.

What was supposed to be a summer was looking more like an extended stay with no plans to return. Rahman's studies were finally wrapped up, and the summer was ending, yet we were still firmly planted in Marbella, with no return tickets home. I was afraid this might happen, but I couldn't bring myself to argue with him. Things were good between us and I couldn't rock the boat. Things were actually too good between us. And, much to my surprise and sincere shock, I realized that I was also pregnant. We'd been together for years, yet now, out of nowhere, "we" would be "three."

After recovering from the initial collision of wants and fears in my head and heart, I was wholly relieved. I wasn't crazy after all. My "out of sorts" and constant second guessing of every single thing/person/situation/future was just hormones. I'd been gifted a generous distraction from what I'd been missing, but in hindsight, this new chapter, motherhood, would bring its own unique challenges. Still, I was finally again feeling joy and purpose. Maybe I wasn't an interior designer anymore, but I was married to the man I loved and I was having our baby.

When Rahman announced the baby news to Abbars, they immediately joined us in Spain, ascending with their usual entourage. Mama Inja donned a perma-grin, from ear to ear and the Ethiopian housekeepers, all eight of them, kept us entertained, trilling like warbles, clapping and spinning for joy at our good news. They were genuinely happy for me, happy for us, happy for anyone in their fold who had good fortune. I felt closer to them, having brought a new Abbar family member into the world. With the flurry of life in the fast lane those few years, I had forgotten the warm and relaxed feel of family.

***

Months later after returning to DC for the birth, I lay in my hospital room alone, more in love than ever, staring at my son, born healthy that morning. What a rollercoaster the last 12 hours had been! The previous evening, as Basha and I sat together, enjoying a relaxed dinner at Houstons, my water broke! The baby was a full three weeks early and in my youthful ignorance, I never imagined this could happen. We both fumbled around, apologizing to the waitstaff, wondering what to do next when Basha brilliantly decided to use the restaurant's reservation line to call my obstetrician.

Smart move. When I arrived at the hospital, they discovered the baby was breech and a C-section would be my only choice. Because I had eaten a full dinner, I remained awake for the surgery, not as scared as I was shocked when they pulled a beautiful 9-pound baby boy out of my stomach! I couldn't contain my joy, my pride, my relief and the fullness that I felt as a new mom. I immediately started making calls to announce my news to everyone. First, the fifteen-digit number for Eddie Moore's place in Argentina where Rahman was spending a few weeks. My husband wasn't even on the same continent for the birth of his first child! After sharing that he was thrilled to hear we'd had a boy, he quickly switched gears. Instead of asking more questions about the birth, apologizing for not being with us, or sharing in the wonder of our child at my breast, Rahman inquired about when the baby would be ready for our trip to England. He cared for nothing above polo, even after becoming a father to a healthy baby boy.

I continued making calls to my sisters, my parents, Basha and our other friends, all of which went to the answering machine. I could feel myself getting upset, resenting being left alone, but I had to admit that at least part of this had been my own doing. Coworkers? I had quit work. Friends? I was always on the move. Family? I departed the country all those years ago, leaving everything in the dust. At that moment, I was forgotten. And the husband I'd left them all for, had not even bothered to support me in the birth, or welcome our child to this world.

I had very much wanted to name our boy "Max" but instead named him something more reflective of his father's conformist culture. Our beautiful son was named Abdelkarim, or "Karim," for short. This name is one that I had admired as it means 'generous' in Arabic. I chose the name on my own while carefully considering traditional Saudi culture and family expectations. According to Rahman, all Saudis were obligated to bear Sunni Muslim names. Names were a very political topic in Saudi and in the Middle East for that matter. If our son had an American name such as Michael or Robert, Islamic law might prevent him from inheriting family money. As I filled out the application for his birth certificate in the hospital, I savored the satisfaction of having picked the name myself with no one around to object, perhaps the one good thing about giving birth completely alone.

My new focus was learning how to care for a human baby. This was not something that I instinctively knew how to do; in fact, I found taking care of horses to be far easier. Human babies were exceedingly complicated, and unsolicited advice on how to care for them properly was both plentiful and contradictory. All of my female friends, especially but not limited to those with kids, regularly offered their extensive and highly subjective point of view.

Of course I did it the Patricia way. Instead of heeding the gospel of family and friends, I bought dozens of books, experimented a bit, and eventually devised my own parenting system. Much to my chagrin, the individual most liberal with definitive ideas and (useless) suggestions about child rearing was Rahman. When he finally arrived in DC, he at once began lecturing me about how to raise his firstborn son. I was not aware that he had opinions on this matter, given he had neglected to be present for the birth. But apparently he did have much to say, and was eager to tell me exactly how and what to do.

"You have to hire a nanny right away, Patricia. We have things to do, people to see, events to attend. You can't be sitting around all day and night, taking care of a baby. Your hair, your nails, your baggy clothing! You're a big mess," he scoffed. Not what I had hoped for, but of course, I complied by hiring a Filipina baby nurse. I wanted him to feel part of the process and share in this season of new life.

When it came to babies, a quick glance, a cheek squeeze, and a kiss were enough for Rahman. But not for me. As with most new mothers, I was obsessed. I was constantly checking on him, watching the nanny change his diapers, staring at him while he slept, folding and unfolding his clothes in the drawers, and frequently running out to buy yet another adorable blanket to swaddle him. Every baby store and every toy store in DC and the surrounding areas knew me on sight as I sought out musical wind-up toys or mobiles, combing the infant section at every department store for anything I might have forgotten. I knew my preoccupation with Karim was borderline crazy, but I couldn't stop myself. I was a changed person. Ironically, the more Rahman insisted on including me in our dizzying social life, the more I longed to stay at home and be with my new baby. He was offering me the life I had been fighting for since the day of my arrival in Jeddah, but now, it had lost its allure. I had something better.

By the time Karim was six months old, the novelty of a baby in the house simmered down and we found our rhythm. Rahman had miraculously secured a position at a prestigious international law firm and with that stability, I was able to return to my work with Basha. What a joy! After all the international travel, I had given up on returning to our steady life in DC, but this great law job offer came as a surprise and Rahman was very excited to be following through on his career plans. Things were good and nothing would make me happier than to stay in DC for the rest of my life with my international lawyer husband, my design firm, and my precious son. However, such contentment was fleeting with Rahman at the helm.

One spring afternoon, I pulled into the driveway behind our house and saw Rahman's car in the garage. Hmmm, strange. *He's back early.*

I found him at the commanding desk that I had recently designed for him, made of the very same beautiful blond burl maple wood as the adjacent library. He looked up as I approached, motioning that he was on the phone, so I quietly sat down until his conversation was over.

"That sounds good. Send me a breakdown of all the costs and I'll have the money wired to you this week. Oh? You already spoke to him about England? Great. See you soon. Thanks," and he hung up. *Is this about polo? Why is he talking about polo in England? We're staying here in Washington DC for the summer.*

After a long minute of awkward silence, I forced out a smile and looked him in the eyes. Rahman, dodging my glance, appeared uncomfortable, almost guilty, but didn't speak so I took the lead.

"Who were you speaking to just now?" I asked, as calmly as I could. I recalled that fateful conversation in his office back in Jeddah, when I crawled into his arms and he announced we were moving to Georgetown. We were such different people now—how could this be happening again?

"Eddie Moore," he offered. Nothing more.

"What about?"

Rahman shifted his weight, his arms folded at his chest in a defensive, faux-tough stance, "About making a polo team this summer in England with Ricardo. I like the idea."

"So when would you be playing?"

"This summer. Didn't I just say that?"

"For how long?"

"For the season. Wouldn't be worth bothering unless it was for the entire season. You know how many working parts are needed to put a team on the field. And I think it would be a winning team."

"What about Potomac?" There. I asked the question. I struggled to conceal my desperation—was I back in Jeddah, subject to his whims?

"Potomac? Well, I don't think a summer of polo here compares to what I could have in England. And don't forget Spain," he condescended, as if to mock my attachment to mundane life in the US. As if our marble townhouse, perfect son, and budding careers were anything close to the average American's "mundane life."

"But what about our horses? The farm here?"

"Oh, they can rest up for next winter in Florida. Maybe I'll keep two of them fit so I can practice next month. Before we leave for Europe."

My heart dropped. I didn't know what to say. He was planning for us to spend the whole summer in Europe. I felt like I had just been broadsided by a truck. He again took the liberty of commandeering my life, but this time time was different. We had a child and I had more to consider.

"What about your new job? The law firm!"

He brushed me off with a flick of his hand and said, "You worry about your business and I'll worry about mine. Have we ever had a lack of money?" Rahman had made himself clear. He had decided that he would return to the playboy polo lifestyle, living off his family's money. Karim and I would be his accessories, with no choice but to follow. There went my career (again!) just after I had managed to get it back. I turned to leave the room as my eyes welled up with tears of frustration and sadness. I didn't see the point of having another argument with him. I knew how it would end, how it always ended. My choice was now to stay with Rahman as his shadow or to seek a divorce. Only now, it wasn't just my life I had to worry about. I had Karim. The last thing I wanted was to subject my son to some messy international divorce, and I suspected Rahman would turn it into just that. So, I gave up and gave in, in an effort to keep the three of us together with minimal drama.

Rahman took my stunned silence as assent. "We leave the first of May."

The next few weeks were a blur as I went through the mechanical motions of organizing yet another new life. I soon found myself back in Spain. Karim's nanny refused to accompany us out of the country due to her visa status. I completely understood her dilemma, so I left for Europe with a baby and no help. Rahman insisted that with money, help would be easy to find. But he was wrong.

Rahman decided that we would spend the entire month of May in Madrid, a city I'd never visited. The spring polo season was said to be fabulous there, a perfect way to warm up for the June season in England. But instead of booking one of the many grand hotels in Madrid, Rahman accepted an invitation to occupy the guest quarters at a friend's property. Noel was Rahman's British boarding school buddy whom I had met a few times when we were dating in college. Noel absolutely insisted we stay at his palatial residence in the most prestigious neighborhood of the city.

"The place is enormous and hasn't been occupied for years! What a waste! We would be delighted to have you here and I won't take no for an answer," he had gushed.

But when we arrived, the welcome was less than tepid as the home actually belonged to Noel's aged parents, who were entirely put out by our intrusion, especially with a baby in tow. The grand old house, in a tired but elegant neighborhood of Madrid, was anything but comfortable. Nothing worked properly and according to Helen, Noel's mother, since the newly elected Socialist government took power, there were no willing workmen in Madrid to do the sorely needed repair work. "The unions are to blame!" she insisted. But I wondered if the family wasn't just excessively frugal and didn't want to spend the money.

The house had been neglected well before the Socialists were inducted. Most of the electrical outlets were dead. The dishwasher was dead. The washing machine and dryer barely worked, and often, when it was time to heat up the baby's bottle, there would be a complete power outage. This, Helen blamed on the summer heat and use of air conditioners, which she highly discouraged. So, at feeding time, I devised an unconventional method of heating up Karim's bottle by placing it between my blazing thighs. I tried to find humor in this situation; after all, it wasn't exactly life threatening. But being an unwelcome guest in a hot house without working basic appliances became tiresome and grated on my already fraying nerves.

Further fanning the flame of discontent was that Rahman took charge of our nanny search in Europe. Instead of personally seeking out a seasoned nanny blessed with warmth and gentleness, Rahman delegated this responsibility to Abbar and Zainy's London office manager, Mr. Oxley, a stuffy old Englishman. Rahman's instructions were clear—find a nanny who could speak Arabic. This nonnegotiable skill disqualified experienced European (read: proper) contenders in favor of an Arab nanny, a job most Arabs hand off to their foreign servants. I argued but Rahman would not budge. Mr. Oxley was well aware that in order to retain his job at the family company, he had to oblige. The crusty Englishman made several inquiries at their Lebanese branch office and within a week, a young idiot from Beirut arrived at our doorstep.

Layla was useless. No credentials and no experience with babies. And the only thing she learned quickly was how to crush on my husband. I surmised that her only reason for coming was that her father, who had dealings with our Beirut office manager, wanted to get his daughter out of the country. Lebanon was erupting into civil war that year.

I was able to get past the obvious crush, but Layla's inexperience was intolerable and laborious for me. I had to drag Karim and Layla everywhere with me, and teach her basics such as how to mix baby formula, how to put diapers on, and how to safely bathe Karim. To make matters worse, Layla had a fixation with her long, dark hair. When she wasn't washing or brushing it, she was whipping it around from one shoulder to the other, like a horse swishing its tail. She complained bitterly about not being able to use her hairdryer due to the lack of working outlets in her room. It would have been easier just to do everything on my own.

Layla did not appreciate Spain and made that clear to anyone who would dare listen. She habitually quarreled with other house staff, giving the impression that she considered herself above everyone. But it was Helen, the mistress of the house, who particularly disliked her, because Layla was a slob. She would leave dirty bottles in the sink and spill water all over the floor while cooking for the baby, which prompted Helen to detail what a pill the nanny was to her son, Noel. Noel gently informed Rahman of each infraction, carefully outlining how the new nanny was ruffling his mother's brittle feathers. I secretly gloated over Rahman having to deal with the drama that he created by his Arab nanny decree. I watched and waited, biting my tongue until Layla's behavior would catch up with her.

One hot afternoon, when Madrid temperatures rose past 90 degrees, I decided that Karim and I were better off staying home rather than packing up and going to watch a polo match in the blistering sun. We had faithfully spectated every game that month and although the match was for the semi-finals, I felt the baby would be more comfortable at home in the meager air conditioning. When I went downstairs and informed Layla of this decision, she threw a hissy fit right there in the entry.

"How could you decide this without telling me? Look! I packed lunch for Karim, here in this cooler, and I put his stroller with all his toys into the car already. It's waiting for us out front. I've been preparing all morning for this outing!"

I did look and intently noticed that she had indeed prepared Karim's things but that she had also overprepped herself for the outing. Layla was decked out, complete with a full make up job (read: war paint), hair elaborately styled (like an aspiring empress) and a flowery silk dress which plunged deeply, exposing an ample bust (and cavernous cleavage). It was apparent that Layla wanted to be noticed at the semi-finals, and I was spoiling her plan.

"Sorry, Layla, but we aren't going today. It's too hot. Karim is better off at home."

At that moment, Layla, in all her glorious hair, makeup and silk dress, went nuclear, shouting loud enough for Helen and the entire house staff to hear. The maids in the kitchen all peered out from behind the door, just in time to hear the girl lambaste me, "No wonder your husband is so unhappy! If I were married to such a handsome man, such a wealthy and important man, I would be there by his side every day! You don't know how to treat your husband. You are such a selfish lady. A very foolish lady, too! **You will lose him!**"

Layla grabbed the cooler, stomped into the kitchen, and threw it on the table, its contents tumbling out, clattering and clanging on the stone floor as she huffed and puffed, cursing in Arabic. I wondered if she was throwing things but made no attempt to find out. I was a bit stupefied at Layla's blatant behavioral outburst, so when Helen and I finally looked at each other, I simply shrugged, picked up my son, and headed upstairs to our rooms. I knew this would be the end of Layla's nannying but wanted to steer clear of the fireworks.

Rahman returned home a couple hours later, feeling victorious from his win when an unamused Helen informed him that she would no longer tolerate the nanny in her home. In fact, she presented Rahman with a bill for damage caused to her house by the girl. Layla was put on a plane the next day and shipped back to Lebanon. I gladly took care of Karim myself for the next few weeks and heaved a big sigh of relief when our sojourn in Madrid ended. London was looking better and better.

"I'm so dreadfully sorry, Madame, that the nanny I hired for you did not work out," were Mr. Oxley's first words upon our arrival in England, "If I might say so myself, a proper English nanny would be advised. I do realize that your husband wished for someone well versed in the Arabic language, but nothing can compare with an English nanny. I will make the necessary inquiries and I believe you will be pleased."

"Very good, Mr. Oxley. Please do so."

Enter Nurse Jean. A miracle and indeed a proper English nanny, complete with her slender but fit six-foot frame, thick white bobbed hair, and an unlimited supply of smart navy-blue uniforms.

Chapter Thirteen

English Life

Domestic life improved immensely once back in London. The thick tension from being an unwanted second-hand guest in an aging Madrid palace dissipated, as did my nerves over the useless Lebanese nanny who would have gladly serviced my husband in my stead. Layla was plucked (read: drop kicked) from our lives just as quickly as she ascended. And Jean, as if on cue from above, swooped in like a respite caregiver savior. The change felt surreal. In a matter of days, I was exhaling in the elegant sitting room of a very charming English country house just west of London, with a professional English nanny taking expert care of my son. For the first time in a long time, I had stability and peace. I was almost afraid to blink, as if Jean might float away into the atmosphere via stiff black umbrella a la Mary Poppins.

Nurse Jean was extraordinarily capable with over 30 years of baby care under her belt. She had nannied children in twenty different countries and worked for many celebrities, including being a nanny on tour with Eric Clapton and other rock stars. She had worked for several royal families, the Saudi royal family among them. Nurse Jean knew more about caring for children, their parents, and their households than one could imagine and I could finally have Karim with me everywhere. Travel with a baby became instantly manageable. Her confidence even brushed off on me, a still-new mama. She was encouraging and uplifting, and I instantly trusted her. She was almost like a mom to me *and* my son and easily morphed into whatever we needed at any given moment. She fit in anywhere and nothing intimidated her. Jean's ability to rise to any occasion and turn out an impossibly ideal child, impeccably dressed, perfectly fed, and supernaturally well behaved, was uncanny. I often wondered if she hypnotized the children, such a strong influence she had on their behavior. It was nothing short of miraculous.

At my urging, Jean would often recount her nannying adventures, and over the years, I came to know her story well. Much like the rest of humanity, Jean's early years shaped her path, particularly her vocation and approach to life and purpose. Jean was a young girl when World War II broke out, and her father was the fire chief of the English coastal city of Southampton. German planes were bombing nightly at one point as town residents hunkered down in the subway tunnels below.

Young children were relentlessly traumatized night after night in the cold darkness with sirens blaring and loud explosions shaking their small bodies and wreaking havoc on their fragile minds and hearts. During one of the bombings, a restless baby was crying inconsolably, the mother unable to calm the child. Though still very much a child herself, Jean moved towards them, arms open, silently offering to help. The mother, desperate and haggard, gladly handed her infant to the gangly and somber fourth grader. Jean slowly walked the dimly lit tunnels with the child in her arms, whispering and rocking until the child succumbed to rest. From that evening on, Jean assumed the task of bringing peace and comfort to the children and moms in those tunnels. Jean's gift of arresting the immediate fears and calming the tantrums of young children somehow soothed her own thoughts and stressors as well. Life in the tunnels, they all knew, could end at any time as the Germans bombarded the town with fire and airborne debris, destroying structures above and life below, but this bold eight-year-old girl was determined to keep some hope alive.

Jean's calling would bring her to future families in need of solace and rest, not in dark tunnels but in the flurry of post-war life, along with the innovations and rapid societal shifts that followed. Jean was gifted and generous enough to share her gift with many. Our family was lucky enough to experience her magic.

***

As soon as we were settled in the house, I felt ready to invite friends to visit. Valerie, whom I hadn't seen in about five years, was the first person I called. She had finally made it back to the West and had her own house in London, where she and her three children spent their summers. Valerie was delighted to come for the day, and the children were anxious to meet their new cousin. We had much to catch up on, especially my latest (and greatest!) news. I was pregnant again and could not have been more thrilled!

"If it's a boy, and I think it will be, I'll call him Sultan. I've always loved that name. And if it's a girl, I don't know," I supposed with a wide grin.

"My word, Patricia! I could hardly imagine you with one baby, and now there will be two? You certainly work fast, my dear! Mama Inja will be delighted! When are you due?"

"Next April. It feels like a long time away."

"I can't wait to meet Nurse Jean. I've heard how happy you are with her. Mr. Oxley from the office hasn't stopped patting himself on the back that she was his find."

"He owed us big time after that first abhorrent nanny! Couldn't have been worse! Luckily, Oxley redeemed himself with Jean…and this rental house! He found this too!"

"Well, Patricia, you can't do much better than Wentworth, home of the rich and famous. I always wanted to see it for myself. It's even grander than I'd imagined."

"I know! Mr Oxley explained that Agatha Christie owned this house years ago, hence the charming name: Green Hedges. I'm hoping that Rahman can make a purchase deal with the owner when the lease is up this fall. I'd love to own it and bring my children here every year."

Valerie and I sat for hours, nibbling on tea sandwiches as our children got familiar with all of Karim's multitude of toys and each other. I told her all about Nurse Jean's celebrity clients and she caught me up with the latest Jeddah gossip. For the first time in a long while, I was at ease with our living arrangement, motherhood, and our future. Magically, suddenly, everything was going to be okay. Spending time with Valerie was an elixir of sorts and the fact that I'd be a mother again, with Jean to keep things fluid, was just frosting.

That evening, after dressing Karim for bed, Nurse Jean brought him in to Rahman and me as we sat watching television in the living room. Karim reached for Rahman, delighted to see his father after a long day of play in the garden with his cousins. Joy radiated in Rahman's face as he sat our boy on his lap and bounced him around. He seemed to be more relaxed holding Karim, now that he was stronger, sturdier, and able to sit up. I wasn't the only one inherently changed by parenthood. Karim had cast a notable spell on Rahman as well. Rahman was delighted with his son, happy to tote him anywhere, patiently introducing him to the wonder of horses, and proudly displaying him to all his friends.

"I think Karim will be walking soon. He's so large, almost twice the size of an average nine-month-old. And today, he was grabbing the cocktail table and trying to stand. Showing off for the cousins—he knew they were watching and wanted to be the center of attention. Valerie was astounded by how precocious he is," I gushed.

"No one can take their eyes off him! He resembles me, of course. My boy will be riding a pony one day soon, and maybe I'll even have a miniature mallet made for him so he can start hitting the polo ball." In my head I pictured Karim accidentally whacking himself (or me) in the head with the mallet and was a little worried.

"Well, I don't know about that. It still might be a bit too soon…but it doesn't hurt to dream." I loved the fact that my husband was finally seeing our child in his life as I did—an extension of us both. Our little family was no longer a movable fixture, but a triangle with three parts, stable, equally and eternally bound.

After settling Karim into his arms, Rahman turned to me with a more serious expression on his face and confessed his new geographic intentions for our little family, "I would like to spend the winter in Florida, playing polo at the club. I've been talking to friends there and we've figured out a great team. I think I'll send the DC horses down in October, and perhaps we'll head there, too."

"You're sure you don't want to go back to Jeddah with Karim, for your family? Valerie told me how excited they are."

"No, they haven't complained yet and I want to get a good head start practicing with the horses in Palm Beach. Going to Jeddah would take so much effort and time. Let's forget it for this year."

"Fine with me. I'll be glad to get back to the States. I'd like to see the doctor, too, and make plans for the birth in DC this coming April. Your family can see the new baby next summer in Spain…"

I smiled to myself, thinking I'd hit the jackpot. Another year without Jeddah! I could always count on Rahman to be all about himself, however disruptive or impractical it was to me and now Karim. I learned quickly that he wasn't kidding about his polo aspirations for our son and had unfortunately not reconsidered Karim learning Arabic immediately, either. He was fixed on his own (uninformed) ideas regarding age-appropriate education and milestones.

Lucky for me, Rahman's self-centeredness spilled over into extended family relations as well as our small triad. The idea of him showing the Abbars his firstborn son versus the lure of the polo season was not even an afterthought. Palm Beach was in and Jeddah was out, just like that. I had quietly feared that he would insist we return with a baby to the harsh conditions of Saudi, but he shrugged off his familial obligations in favor of polo with friends. I have to confess, I was glad his lofty plans for amusement would finally benefit me for a change. No long trips and no need to deal with in-laws for the time being. All I had to do for the next few months was take care of Rahman, myself, Karim, and our coming baby.

***

Our transition to Florida was like butter thanks to Jean, who oversaw everything. She sorted and packed, shipped and scheduled. With the flick of her wand, we were prepared for the family journey across the pond. I wondered what life at the club would be like as a mom. And even Jean was keenly curious about what our new life would be like at the Palm Beach Polo Club. Sunny Florida couldn't have been more different than formal, overcast, London.

"It's beautiful, Jean. A gated equestrian paradise full of families and horse activities. So many children for Karim to play with. You'll be busy every minute of the day."

I believed in what I said completely. I was optimistic about this new phase of our lives. We had a home in England, two homes in the United States, and Rahman and I were finally on the same page. In harmony, we took our family to Wellington that winter, and started this new chapter together.

Eight months later, I was on the operating table at Georgetown Hospital, having my second C-section. My little sister, Cindy (now a woman), sat up by my head as my esteemed doctor lifted the baby from my torso and announced, "It's a girl!"

"A girl?" we replied in unison before looking at each other, stunned. Now that woke us up! For some unknown reason, we had both expected another boy. After the initial surprise, waves of excitement flooded me and I realized what a generous gift this daughter was to me. After all, I was from a robust family of girls and would be ahead of the learning curve for mothering a little girl. But what to name her?

"Let's think of a suitable name…" I mused. "I was planning on calling the boy Sultan or Rashid."

"So add an "a" and call her Sultana," Cindy suggested, beaming with pride. "It's beautiful and regal! And easy for us to pronounce. No other little lady will have such a commanding name!"

"I love it too, Cindy! Why didn't I think of that? Sultana she will be."

My first phone call from the hospital room was to my husband, once again playing polo in Argentina…"Rahman, I had the baby. She looks like you." *And by the way, this little routine of yours–not being present–hasn't gone unnoticed.*

"She?" he replied, somewhat in disbelief.

"Yes, a girl and she's gorgeous! Don't dare be disappointed. I know, we all thought it would be a boy. But now, I don't know why. Maybe because the Abbars have lots of sons? Whatever. It's a girl and I'm naming her Sultana. It sounds beautiful and it's an acceptable Arabic name. Don't you agree?"

"Yes, it's a good name, Patricia. Wait until my mother hears about this. She very much wanted a granddaughter. Do you want to phone her or should I?"

"You call your family and I'll call mine. So when can you come back to join us?"

"Not until the tournament is over. This all happened very early, again. Patricia. Why can't you do things on time?" he teased. "The due date was three weeks from now. I still need two weeks to finish up."

"I know, I know. Don't worry about it. Cindy's with me and Nurse Jean's keeping Karim very busy here in DC. He loves the place! We're all fine. Let me make some calls to tell my family the good news and I'll get back to you later."

The second call was to my mother.

"Patricia, you are an amazing woman. So strong, so independent. Going through all this without your husband, for the second time! When exactly is Rahman going to get around to seeing his new daughter?"

"Mom, I know what you're doing. Don't spoil the nice compliments you just paid me by being nasty. That's just the way he is and you know it. I can't change him. I'm used to it. I have all I need. The best doctor, the best hospital care, my sister for company, and the best nanny ever, looking after Karim. And it's not so hard to have a baby. Women have been doing it for eternity! They used to go off into the bushes and give birth alone, then cut the umbilical cord with their teeth, load the newborn on their backs and catch up with the rest of the tribe."

"This is 1987, Patricia, not some primitive movie scene. That's not reality. Reality for modern couples is men taking Lamaze classes with their wives to help coach the breathing and the push!" I could hear her eyes widening in glee, "My cousin Tony's daughter had her husband in the delivery room with her for ten hours, pushing and breathing together. Now, that's a real man!"

"Mom. Please. I wouldn't even want to do it that way, and you know that. Besides, there's no breathing or pushing techniques in a C-section... It's just slice, pull, stitch! We're done! I don't have to lift a finger!"

"Ok, Patricia. It's hard to believe that you're my daughter, but I can't change you, can I?"

"Nope! And I can't change you either, Mom." The conversation ended in a slightly uncomfortable laugh. I knew my mother disapproved of the way Rahman and I conducted our marriage, but it had stopped bothering me years ago. I accepted her opinion and I hoped that she might accept mine at some point. Was I crazy or just stubborn to a fault?

Looking back, of course my mother was right, perhaps on many fronts. Her concerns during the visit to Jeddah were spot-on. Maybe her thoughts on Rahman being MIA for the births were also valid. Since then, I've asked myself again and again why Rahman had deemed polo tournaments more important than his wife and children. I also wrestled with the fact that I secretly preferred to give birth without him. He simply could not have put new life and my health above himself and his presence in the hospital would have just caused more stress for me. The sad reality was that he didn't want to be there and maybe I didn't want him there either.

Eight weeks later, Nurse Jean was finishing packing up the children's suitcases as I sat on the floor, playing with Sultana on her mat. I was terribly excited about leaving for England with the children and Jean. For the first time, I knew exactly what I was going to find at the other end. We had succeeded in purchasing Green Hedges, that lovely English country house, and our belongings were already there. We would simply unpack and resume our life where we left off last summer. And this time we had two children! We had made a great many friends last year, and several members of the Abbar family were also residing in London, so there would be lots of familiar faces!

Nurse Jean was in full command of the children. She had already phoned nannies she knew in the area and set up playdates for later that week. I was bursting with anticipation. My husband would meet his daughter, my children would meet their Arabic family, and after two months of being with just the children and the nanny, I would finally have some time to myself and some time with my husband. I was looking forward to hitting the shops in London to outfit myself for the summer season at the Guards Polo Club. I would be cheering on my man in style!

Besides, after having a second baby, I sorely needed to pull my look together! I had been on bedrest since February, due to the baby dropping early; without being under a doctor's care, I would have risked going into labor for a vaginal birth, and that would almost certainly have ripped open my C-section scars. I hadn't done my hair, put on makeup or worn anything other than sweatpants for months. I determined that the best way to start my journey back to sexy would be to contact my hyperfashionable friend, Patricia Mansur, as soon as I had a sec.

Last summer, I became instant friends with the tall, slender Brazilian beauty. Her husband Ricardo played polo with Rahman, and his wife not only shared my name (easy to remember) but had children Karim's age. The kiddos got along like peas and carrots. This season, Ricardo was sharing the high goal team with Rahman, and no doubt the two of them were already inseparable, just as they had been last summer. I was sure Patricia would be delighted to join me for a shopping spree in London. I anticipated us always together, either watching our husbands' polo games at the club or sampling the London nightlife with a few other expat couples.

Rahman finally made a much overdue effort and was waiting to receive us at Heathrow Airport. He pounced the moment we stepped out of customs, sweeping us all up, helping with our bags, and sparing no hugs and kisses for the children and me. Once happily settled in the car, Rahman focused on our new daughter, instantly smitten, and of course, mini-Rocky (Rocky was Rahman's nickname on the polo team), the apple of his eye, received all the attention he desired as well. Karim had grown even bigger and brighter since Rahman had last seen him. As we made our way to the house, Rahman cheerily chattered about family plans for the coming week. I was delighted to experience this "Western" version of my husband and rather than look a gift horse in the mouth, I relaxed and just accepted that being back in England was doing wonders for his personality. Parties, polo matches, the races at Ascot, visits from friends wanting to see the new baby and outings to visit relatives in London, were all on the menu. I couldn't have been happier at that moment. Everything had come together and he was *finally* anxious to show off his young family.

True to form, Patricia Mansur was very willing to drive into London with me the following week for lunch and a day of shopping. She spent most of the year in Sao Paolo, where imported clothing was almost impossible to purchase. She lived to stuff her suitcases full of all the latest European fashions before heading back to her native Brazil. Ricardo treated his wife like a delicate little doll to be pampered and protected. I supposed that was the Brazilian way. Ricardo had offered us the use of his car and chauffeur for the day since Patricia was not in the habit of driving herself anywhere. But, I insisted on driving my new Audi. I loved to drive and I especially loved the independence I felt behind the wheel. Besides, it would give us more flexibility and I wouldn't have to explain our every move to a driver who felt more like a bodyguard or a babysitter than a driver. I had experienced enough of that nonsense in Jeddah. This was London and I was anxious to catch up with my dear friend, without an audience. "So, what have you and Ricardo been doing lately? You've been here for a month or two, right? Any good parties? Tell me everything!"

"The club is buzzing this season because Major Ferguson's daughter is marrying Prince Andrew. Everyone wants to snag an invitation to the wedding next month, so they're all throwing parties to catch his attention. Even Ricardo, who doesn't usually care about things like that, wants to be invited. He says the Major is playing position 4 on our team so he feels entitled to an invitation. I hear it'll be very formal. White tie, tails and top hats!"

"Wow, his daughter is marrying Prince Andrew? That must be the talk of the season. We must get invited! Let's make sure to visit all the shops on Sloan Street today. Sounds like I need a whole fetching new wardrobe!" I sang.

"How have you been doing with the new baby? What's her name?"

"She's great–I named her Sultana. Didn't Rahman tell you? And I was on bedrest the last month because I was carrying very low. Now that was a drag."

"No, he didn't...Rahman told us very little about you. In fact, we haven't seen much of him outside of polo. He has been...well, keeping more to himself." Patricia looked away nervously.

"What do you mean?" I asked, confused. I assumed he had been spending every day socializing with Patricia and Ricardo, like last summer.

"Oh, nothing...but, well, it seems to me that Rahman has been avoiding us after the games each day. He makes small talk for a few minutes and then gets in his car and disappears. Ricardo has noticed it too."

"What do you mean? What are you saying? Stop squirming and explain." I was getting impatient.

"Well, because I'm your friend, I'll tell you what I found out, but you must never let anyone know. Ricardo will kill me if he thinks I told you."

"Told me what? Please tell me. I won't say a word to anyone."

"Well...the grooms said that late one evening last week, while they were doing a night check on the horses, Rahman showed up at the barn with a very slutty English woman. A bleached blonde. He had obviously spent the evening with her. She was drunk and hanging all over him. He was quite embarrassed when he noticed the grooms were there. I think he expected to be alone. He dragged the woman off to his car without looking back and drove away fast. We had invited him to dinner that evening over at Eddie's, but he refused, saying that he wanted to get a good night's rest before the tournament. Obviously, that wasn't the case. He wasn't at home, or resting up…"

I sat speechless for a moment, my new contentment crumbling. "Are you serious?"

I was in shock at my own question. It couldn't be true. I was humiliated as a wife and woman. The grooms had seen—it was all over the club—Rahman's best friend knew—my friend knew—everyone knew but me.

An inordinate reserve of angry energy surfaced. Rahman had cheated on us. Lied and cheated on not just me but the three of us.

But I couldn't lose my cool just yet in front of my friend, and I needed time to consider how to keep my family together after such vile behavior. *Could I keep him? Did I want to?*

And under that, the first whispers of something I had been unable to voice to myself: *Did I still love Rahman?*

"Please don't be angry at me. I just wanted to warn you because you're my friend. That's what friends do, at least in Brazil…" Patricia turned away uncomfortably. "If Ricardo finds out that I said something…"

I felt like I was dying inside, but I didn't want my friend to hurt. "Patricia, please," I insisted, "don't worry. I'll tell no one. Thank you. You're a good friend. I'm glad I know about this. We'll figure it out and I won't say a word."

We awkwardly finished our meal, our conversation devolving into idle chatter. I found myself consoling her rather than consoling myself. We headed off to the shops, but no amount of fabulous hats or dresses could shake my disappointment in my husband or the dread I felt knowing that I would need to address it. The thought of Rahman showing up at our barn in the middle of the night with some other woman cut deep. That was our place. Why would he bring her there? The show of a loving husband and father that he put on at Heathrow Airport was nothing more than a lie.

Chapter Fourteen

Fractures

On my guard for the rest of the summer, I nervously waded through the weeks. While I focused on the children, I was sharply tuned into the tiniest indicators of the other woman. Not only was Rahman pulling away from us, the family he and I had created, he was detaching himself from our close circle of shared friends. This only launched me further into unwanted isolation. Unlike last polo season in London, Rahman was reluctant to spend any time with the Mansurs or any of the couples from the polo club. Consequently, our social life took a big hit, or at least mine did. For whatever reason, we did not attend the royal wedding, though many of our friends did. Instead, Rahman made frequent unconvincing excuses, sometimes twice a week, that he must go to London alone for business dinners. He'd later stumble into our home snockered, incoherent, and sweaty.

His behavior infuriated me, but I could not bring myself to confront him. I was afraid again, a stranger to myself and others. No more close friends to share meals and a good laugh, only high drama as Rahman's behaviors became increasingly unsavory and well-known at the club. I knew there were whispers. I knew people were looking at me with pity and that sense of relief good gossip always provides: *thank God it's not me.* I was humiliated and couldn't tell anyone how I felt or what I was going through. My best friend Basha and my family were across the ocean. And once again, my mother's comments on Rahman's frequent absenteeism rang true.

Having children changed me. I needed to manage my increasing rage and paranoia. I couldn't simply kick a door down or set off the fire alarm because I was angry. We were a family, with young children at home and staff watching. I was terrified that if the house was unsettled, Nurse Jean would quit, and I needed her the most. Jean was my only source of calm.

I hoped that things might change when we returned to the US that fall. Perhaps his affair would not make it across the pond. But on a Thursday morning in August my eyes opened at 5 am, as they did each morning, and I looked over to find his pillow still fluffed, tightly tucked sheets fully intact on his side of the bed. Rahman had not returned home. Despite everything, this wasn't like him at all. He absolutely never slept elsewhere. He always showed up at some point, in some condition, to sleep the remainder of the night in his own bed. Perhaps so the girls he was with wouldn't get too comfortable? I had a feeling that he had either been injured in a car crash or had been caught drunk driving.

London was very strict about DUIs and the police were everywhere along the M4 highway, patrolling and breathalyzing anyone who appeared intoxicated. I started calling the police stations in each town, one by one, tracing the route from the center of London to our house in Wentworth, a stretch of thirty miles. I phoned Chelsea, Fulham and Hammersmith precincts, but no luck. I anxiously asked if there had been any traffic incidents because my husband hadn't returned home. My last call was to Chiswick Station. Bingo.

When I described him as a Saudi Arabian man in a yellow Ferrari, they said I was in luck, he was fine, but being held at the police station, due to being quite intoxicated. They had planned to release him when he was alert and sobered up. I sent Alex, our houseboy, to pick him up that next morning because I was in no mood to go myself. The Ferrari was impounded. As a result of that evening, Rahman was prohibited from driving in England for one full year. Alex, our trusted Filipino houseboy brought from Jeddah, was given a chauffeur's uniform and promptly upgraded to driver, thus ending Rahman's late-night romps. So in reality, the drunk driving (however reckless) worked in my favor. Rahman was not about to do anything illicit with Alex, a gentle and decent member of our household, present; and it was certain that Alex would not keep such secrets from me. Disgust smoldered inside me when I thought about it, but I felt some degree of resignation given my new set of eyes.

I didn't have the stomach to confront Rahman about the night away, the impounded exotic car, or his new need for a babysitter/driver. He had already been caught and disgraced so thoroughly that I stepped back and held my tongue. To be held overnight in a police station for drunk driving was about as humiliating as it could get for a Saudi Arabian. It was certain he was terrified his family or countrymen would find out that he was a closet lush. I hoped that he had learned his lesson, but it soon became obvious that these unsavory behavioral patterns were going to follow us wherever we went, be it Jeddah, Europe, or home in the US.

Our departure from England ended what had become the summer of distrust, and once back in Florida I felt like I could breathe again. Being in my home country gave me a greater sense of control. The children and I adjusted and our marriage did normalize for a short time; perhaps I could forgive and forget? We bonded again over the milestones the children were making; learning their little individual personalities kept us both proud and amused. Our children were the glue, and I hung on for them, even if their father didn't notice or acknowledge my pain or that his habits were chipping away our happiness.

True to his promise, Rahman bought Karim a small, jet-black pony named "Taffy," and our amazing boy learned to ride at only two-and-a-half years old. It was a joy to see. We would spend hours at the barn, feeding and grooming the pony, watching Karim take riding lessons. He really did take after his father. He was a natural.

My relationship with Rahman, to say the very least, was strained. I still hadn't confronted him because I couldn't prove anything, except that he had been drinking heavily. The only proof of cheating was what Patricia Mansur had divulged, and she had sworn me to secrecy. No use ruining her marriage as well. I had no interest in fighting about suppositions. It would sour our household and he would deny everything, so what would be the point? Since the summer in England, his drinking had only gotten worse. Often, I would come home with the children in the afternoon and find him sleeping on the living room sofa, drunk, an empty bottle of champagne sitting in a melted ice bucket on the floor. When he wasn't riding or playing polo, that was how he spent his time. No work, no outings with us, no purpose. Just alcohol, then sleep.

I worried sick that Nurse Jean would object to working in a household where the father was a willing, useless drunk, bankrolled by his family in the Middle East. But somehow, she either didn't notice, ignored it, or she simply maintained her professionalism and didn't interfere or comment. Perhaps because there were no arguments or detectable friction, she was tolerant of his behavior. She was busy all day, accompanying the children from one activity to another, and that was a relief to me. As long as she was happy, so were my children.

I desperately needed a real friend to confide in during those days. I yearned for someone to talk to, to tell all. But somehow, my relationships with the women I knew in Florida were not those kinds of friendships. I needed someone like Basha, but sadly, none materialized in the Sunshine State. As the months went by, I waited for the hammer to drop. Something had to give. It was only a matter of time.

"Mama, mama! Watch me," Karim shouted proudly as he glided past on his new bicycle. Suddenly I realized that he was riding without training wheels. Pretty amazing, for almost three years old. When did that happen?

"Karim, good job! Jean, I have you to thank. You have done wonders with Karim. I don't know what we would ever do without you."

"Well, now that you've brought up the subject, I must speak to you about my taking a few weeks' vacation to visit England. I haven't really had a vacation in over a year, and I want to see my brother and his family in Southampton. I told them I would come later this month, before polo season gets in full swing and we get too busy. I hope you can agree to that." Her request was thoughtful but she wasn't really asking permission. She needed to go and her decision was firm and non-negotiable. I had no choice but to agree.

"I can have the agency send a replacement nanny for you in my absence..."

"Oh Jean, that's unnecessary. It would be more work getting to know the new nanny and teaching her everything. I think I can survive for three weeks on my own with the children. As long as I know you're coming back," I half-teased.

"Well then, good. It's settled. I will book my ticket and get on with it."

This would be a welcome opportunity to visit my family in New York with the children. Knowing his response would be an unequivocal "no", I didn't even bother inviting Rahman. He was too busy with his own diversions in Florida, and I needed some time apart to think.

The visit to New York went better than I could have imagined. My entire family was overjoyed to see Karim and Sultana, and all pitched in to help with their care. It was wonderful to be fussed over and I realized how much my life had changed, somehow diminished, over the last few years without them. I got a glimpse of perhaps how my life would have looked if I had never left.

"It's fun having adventures and doing exotic things, but there's nothing like home sweet home," I gushed, tucking into the soft chenille sofa in my parents' den. Even the sofa felt like a hug after being tense and isolated for so many months.

Karim was busy rocking back and forth on a huge wooden horse that my parents had brought to the apartment for him. It had belonged to a cousin and my dad borrowed it from their garage.

"I knew this would be a big hit with Karim," Dad beamed. "From what you told me about his riding, I figured it was worth the trouble of getting it up here. Look at him go! This kid hasn't stopped rocking yet. We might have to serve him lunch on that horse." It was so good to see Dad smile. I hadn't seen him smile in so many years.

"Dad, you should see him on his real pony. I'll take a video and send it to you next time I get a chance. I got a new Sony camcorder."

"So exactly where is your husband these days, Patricia?" My mother always went right for the jugular with her meaty questions.

"He's in Florida, at our house." I was equally adept at deflection.

"And why couldn't he come up with you and the children to visit us?"

"He's busy with his polo ponies, prepping for the tournaments."

"My goodness, one would think he was headed to the Olympics, at the rate he's going. Isn't there any other endeavor worthy of his time? Just fun and games always...what about work? What about being a father?" she pressed, digging further into my nerves and cracking my permasmile.

"Mom, not in front of the kids..." I begged her.

Before we dissolved into an argument, Cindy saved the day with the novel idea of taking the children and me to the Central Park Zoo. We escaped the apartment, the four of us crossing Fifth Avenue at 68th Street, Cindy pushing Sultana's stroller while I gripped Karim's hand in mine. It was a glorious, sunny day as we made our way down the grand tree-lined avenue, a scene that hadn't changed since my childhood. Meditating on my children's laughter echoing off the ivy-covered, old rusty red brick walls, I felt at peace. "I love this place, Cindy. I never get tired of it."

"I know. We have good memories, don't we? I wish you lived here, Patricia. We could have so much fun together with the kids."

"I wish I did, too. This jet set life isn't all it's cracked up to be. I'm really struggling. And Rahman isn't making it any easier. But let's not talk about it now. Let's just enjoy the zoo."

Our three weeks with my family flew by. I never realized how many things one could do with young children in New York. Parks, zoos, movies, theater, museums, it was never ending. To my surprise, it was even more fun seeing everything as an adult. Difficult conversations aside, the simplicity of that time offered healing to my crumbling homelife and a confidence that I needed to stick up for myself, and for our kids. In New York, my children and I were loved and accepted, without compromise, complication, or pain. It gave me the strength I needed for what was to come.

***

As the taxi from West Palm Beach Airport pulled into our driveway, one glance into the garage and I knew Rahman wasn't home. *He's probably at the barn riding.* Karim will be disappointed. He had talked incessantly about his father on the plane.

"Is Daddy here?" he inquired, scanning the front of our house for his dad's car.

"No, I'm sure he's riding, though. Why don't we go in and change into riding clothes? We'll surprise him at the barn!"

Karim dashed into the house while I paid for the taxi and gathered up Sultana, the stroller, and our suitcases. I could have used some help. *Oh well, it will be fun to watch Karim ride. I can unpack these suitcases later. I'll just change Tana into a romper and we can go.*

I glanced at the mailbox and realized it was bulging, half-open, with letters. *Mail. I'll grab that.* It always amazed me how Rahman was so attuned to details about things that interested him, but he was completely oblivious to anything else. As if mail didn't arrive in the mailbox, it just magically appeared on his desk. *Must be nice to live that way.*

Maneuvering Tana's stroller over to the curb as I reached out to open the box, I noticed out of the corner of my eye, my newish older female neighbor approaching, leaning heavily on a cane. I had not yet met her. *She's probably one of those Northern Snowbirds.* I didn't even know her name. I straightened up and extended my hand, ready to greet her.

"Hello. You must be our neighbor. I'm Patricia Abbar."

She looked nervous and slightly off balance. *She didn't expect me to be so friendly?*

"Hello, I'm Helen Campbell. Yes, I recently moved in, although I've seen you and your children coming and going over the past few months. I just recovered from hip surgery and don't go out much. But I do watch everything from the front window and saw you drive up. I didn't want to miss an opportunity to speak to you, privately."

"Oh. How nice…" *Wow, she's very bold…* "Well, Helen, I hope you make a full recovery." I turned back to the mailbox, reaching in to retrieve the large load of mail. Two hands and good balance were needed to carry it all, and somehow get the stroller with my squirming toddler inside, back up to the house. Helen watched me struggle and juggle but there probably wasn't anything she could do to help. As I finally reached my front door, she insistently called me back.

"Wait, I really would like to speak with you about something that's been bothering me. This might be my only chance, dear. You look like a very nice young woman."

I waited, at once alarmed and disarmed.

"I don't know how to begin…but I'll just tell you straight. I noticed that you've been away for a while with your children. While you were away, a young Barbie-doll of a woman was living in your house with your husband. She drove up and parked her white Mercedes in the driveway a few weeks ago, and today is the first day that her car isn't here. At first, I thought it might be a relative, but I saw her kissing your husband on the back patio." She flushed. "They did other stuff, but that's when I stopped watching."

"What? A blond woman? A Mercedes?" I stepped back, nearly losing my balance, the mail scattering across the grass as it fell from my arms.

"I'm so embarrassed at all this, but you looked so sweet, going in and out with your precious children, and I had to let you know…I'd want to know. I am so sorry if I upset you, but what else could I do? I have daughters… Oh, I hope I did the right thing." She turned and shakily walked back to her house.

The shock kicked me into autopilot. *Pick up the mail first. Bring Sultana into the house. She's still dressed in winter clothing and must be getting warm. Karim is in the house, probably changing his own clothing. I promised to take him to the barn. Just go through the motions and figure this out later. I have two young children who need me to be there for them. I can deal with this later. I can do this. But how?*

Luckily, when I turned up the long driveway approaching the barn, Rahman's car was nowhere in sight. *Good.* I had no desire to see him right then, despite how disappointed Karim would be. In fact, I was hoping he would never come home. Wouldn't that be wonderful?

The grooms and several other riders were there, so I decided to relax and make the best of the afternoon. No telling what would happen tomorrow.

Taffy was out grazing in one of the paddocks and Karim leapt from the car as soon as we parked, quickly slipping his little body under the fence. The pony was just as thrilled to see Karim, the two of them nuzzling like old friends too long apart. Karim grabbed the pony's halter and led him closer.

"Mama. Mama. Look! Taffy's here. I want to ride him right now."

José, our groom, waved hello to us and rushed over to help Karim. *Good, José will take care of getting Karim ready to ride. I can just sit with Tana.*

I lifted my baby girl from her car seat and settled into a large spectator chair at the edge of the riding field. A few minutes later, out bounced

Karim on Taffy's back, José leading him to the grassy riding field. I waved and cheered them on, then noticed one of my club friends, Anne McKeckney, had spotted us and was approaching. I hadn't seen her yet this season, but she and her husband Doug were in our close circle last season, before Rahman started acting like a fool. Anne greeted me enthusiastically but after catching up about our respective summers away and how big the children had grown, Anne looked around nervously, stretching her neck to survey the far parking lot.

"So, Rahman's not here, right? You're alone?" she asked.

"Yes…" I replied hesitantly.

"Because I want to talk to you, Patricia. It's serious."

"Oh no. I hope it isn't bad. I don't think I can take any more bad news today." I supposed, choking out a nervous laugh.

"I'm not joking, Patricia."

"Neither am I, Anne." I held my breath, frozen, not wanting to hear what she had to say, but so, so curious…I waited, although in hindsight, I already knew what was coming.

"You know my friend Sandy has been here all summer. She said that your husband has been seen all over the club with Laura Parton, a young real estate broker, who lives with her mother in the village. Laura's kind of a gold-digger, like a cheesy man-eater type…Apparently, she and her mother both hang around the polo fields looking for stray men. He probably met her there. Rahman has been driving around with her in his yellow Ferrari, and one of the players warned him that the wives were all talking about it. Well, yesterday, Rahman showed up here in his car and guess what? He had put some tacky dark film on his windows so now you can't see inside. He ruined the car! Wait until you see it! The rumor around is that he rented her an apartment in the tennis lodges on the other side of the club. Patricia, everyone is talking about it. I feel so bad for you. And your kids. You've gotta do something." She grabbed my shoulder, as if to put emphasis on my doing something, and shook me several times.

Anne furtively glanced over at Doug, who was riding alongside Karim in the field.

"Don't tell Douglas. He didn't want me to get involved. Rahman is his good friend and they play together, but I had to tell you. Remember her name, Laura Parton."

Anne sashayed off, smiling and waving at Doug, "I'm coming, honey."

I was numb.

On the way home, I instinctively pulled into the Publix parking lot. *The kids need something for dinner.* I grabbed a shopping cart, strapped Tana into the seat and Karim into the front.

"Karim, we're going to do something new. We're making dinner! Just sit tight and I'll put the food in your lap."

I quickly wheeled the two of them through the store, pulling whatever I needed for the evening from the shelves, and dumping it into the cart with Karim. He eagerly inspected everything as it arrived, delighted to be playing this new cart game. Tana held onto the front bar and rocked back and forth, kicking her chubby legs, also delighted to be sitting up so high and moving so fast. Thankfully, the kids were oblivious.

When I finally got to the check-out counter, something caught my eye: Two young women, peering out from behind the fresh fruit stand. They were whispering and looking at me. Was that my imagination? Or were they two "gold-diggers," spotting me and knowing that I was "the wife?" *Don't let your imagination run away with you. Why would anyone be following you around?* But I felt like everyone's eyes were on me suddenly. I had to get home.

I headed straight to my car in the parking lot. A careful glance to the side while I was buckling in Sultana revealed that the women had followed me out of the store and were watching me from behind a column. *Well, I guess I'm not actually paranoid...*

At home, I settled the children in the playroom, Sultana in the playpen and Karim on a bean bag chair. I turned on one of their favorite videos and grabbed the phone. No sign of Rahman yet.

First, I called our housekeeper, who obviously had not been to the house in a while.

"Peggy? Hi, it's Patricia Abbar, from the Polo Club. I just arrived home today with the children and I see that you haven't been here lately. Are you ok?"

"Yes, Mrs. Patricia, I'm fine and I can come tomorrow morning. Your husband told me that he wouldn't be needing me to clean the past few weeks, so I didn't come."

"Oh? Well, that makes sense. Please get here early tomorrow morning and plan to spend the entire day here. It's a mess."

My response was tempered, but I practically smashed the phone when I hung up. The mounting pressure from "well meaning" neighbors, the jeers of the two women in the supermarket, and now, the evidence that Rahman had deliberately let our house descend into filth while he romped around with his not-so-secret lover was too much for me. I didn't care if Peggy ever cleaned up the house. I was leaving.

Tears swelled in my eyes as I dialed the friend I needed most: Basha. I prayed she wasn't out to dinner yet, and I was in luck. She answered on the second ring.

"Hi, Basha. It's Patricia. Listen, I want to talk fast. Before Rahman gets home."

"Patricia! So good to hear from you. How was New York?"

"Never mind that. Can you pick me up at the airport tomorrow morning if I arrive with the kids? I could use some help handling the luggage and the stroller."

"Of course I can. Are you staying long?"

"I might stay forever…"

"What are you talking about?" Basha's voice rose.

"I'll tell you when I get there. I can't talk now. I'm frantic. Rahman could walk in any minute."

"Don't tell me you're going to keep me in suspense!"

"OK, well… I think I'm gonna leave him. There's another woman. In fact, there have been a few. And people are noticing. I'm getting too old for this shit. I need to get away from him for a while."

"Okay, okay," Basha spoke in hushed tones, "It's probably better if you slip away quietly, tomorrow when he goes out. No telling how he'll react if he sees you leaving. He could try to stop you!" She always had my best interests in mind, and she was quite the schemer. I knew I could count on her.

"Exactly my thinking. I'll call you from the airport. You're the best, Basha," I hung up.

"Mama, I'm hungry," Karim had walked in, still in his riding clothes.

"Sorry, honey. I had a few phone calls to make, but now, I'm going to make you and Sultana some delicious baked macaroni!" I tried to make it fun for the kids since they didn't often see me cook. They were mesmerized, tasting noodles and cheese, patting the pan with butter and salting the top with breadcrumbs and spices. We sat down to eat and still no Rahman in sight. *Act blasé. He could show up any minute.*

As I spooned the warm, creamy macaroni into Sultana's mouth, she smiled and closed her eyes. "Mmmm." *Of course she loves it. Why don't I cook anymore? I remembered the first meal I made for Rahman in our first private home together in Jeddah….Was it chicken livers? Lallo had taught me.* I idly wondered where Rahman might be. *Perhaps enjoying foie gras at the Palm Beach Grill or perhaps at his new sex pad down the street?* I felt sick at the thought of him with his bimbo realtor blow-up toy but even more queasy over the idea of confronting him because I knew it would be over. All those years of pushing us forward, wasted.

"Karim, would you like to watch a movie after dinner? I have that new tape of Annie. Or we could watch Ninja Turtles again…" *The kids need a distraction.*

When the children were back in the playroom, with the TV on, I ran to my bedroom to quickly change into my robe and PJs. *No sense in staying dressed, Rahman probably won't be coming home until the morning.* Reaching into my vanity to get a rubber band, I found a mess of items that did not belong to me. *Maybelline mascara? Cover Girl eyeshadow? What is she, fifteen?*

I slammed the drawer shut, stumbled over to my dresser, and pulled open my undie drawer, convinced that there was more evidence. Lo and behold, there were two pairs of unfamiliar panties and one rather large bra which definitely didn't belong to me. *She's really been living here with him. In my bedroom. Don't get upset, you're leaving. This is just validation.* I quietly inspected the bra that had made all this real then sat on the edge of the bed before my legs gave out. I felt smaller than I ever had in my life. Not only rejected by the man I left everything for, I was thoroughly humiliated and would have to shield my children from the man I thought was the best father I could give them. I remembered the children and returned to the TV room, finding a spot next to Karim. *They need me. I shouldn't be searching drawers like an obsessed maniac, I should sit here and watch the Ninja Turtles…Oh God, how will I get through tonight…I can't wait for tomorrow to come.*

Rahman finally rolled in, stinking of alcohol, late at night while I lay in bed. I pretended to be fast asleep, listening while he struggled in the bathroom, then vomited in the toilet. Nice. *He better not try to touch me.*

I was in luck. He could barely even crawl into bed, and I remained motionless, feigning sleep. Eventually, but not without effort, I did fall asleep, a much-needed break for my tired brain.

I awoke in the early morning with a jolt after hearing Rahman stumbling around in the closet across the room. I quietly waited in the dark and listened. *Is he getting dressed? What time is it?* The alarm clock read six-thirty. But I couldn't think of a reason why a man who sleeps until noon would be awake now, still hung over, only a few hours after returning home. I held my breath, hoping he wouldn't realize I was awake to notice him.

Rahman moved like a cat, out of the bedroom and across the carpet to the kitchen. *Making coffee? Or an Alka-Seltzer?*

Then I heard the garage door open. I slid out of bed, made my way to the kitchen and listened for more sounds. He was fumbling around in the garage. I crept to the door and opened it a crack to see what on earth he was doing out there. When I finally spotted him, I yanked the door open wide to better see the inconceivable.

There was Rahman, thirty-two years old, clad in shorts and a tee shirt, halfway down the street on Karim's new bicycle, one designed for a four year old. Furiously pedaling in the direction of the apartment where he was reported to have been keeping his Barbie. As I watched his long, hairy legs moving faster and faster on that tiny bike, waves of disgust swept over me. This vision of him pedaling away, looking utterly ridiculous, would sustain me for years, through all the horror which was to come. I didn't know how bad the outcome could possibly be. All I knew was that packing up the kids and flying to DC that day would be easy now that I've seen how low he'd stoop to cheat.

Chapter Fifteen

Flight

After what felt like an all-day flight, the children and I finally landed in D.C., just a short skip up from Palm Beach. Basha was waiting for us at the gate, eager to help with the bags and the children.

"How did it go? Any trouble?" she asked, breathlessly. But I was leery of speaking out loud at the airport given the sensitive nature of our situation and wanted to hurry to the car to avoid people who might recognize me or the kids. Rahman's network was extensive. Once in her car, I gave Basha the child-friendly version of the last rather enlightening twenty-four hours. When we arrived at our DC residence minutes later, I immediately called Jean. She was finishing up her last days in England so I provided a quick debriefing before rerouting her return plans to DC.

The children finally settled into their playroom after letting out some initial excess energy from the two-hour flight and bracketing taxi rides. So much more to do, but I took a much-needed moment to sit on the floor, quietly enjoying my children's smiles. Finally, some calm. As I sat there, quiet and content for that brief moment, it occurred to me that I had underestimated myself and took the liberty of giving myself a quickie pep-talk. *I am indeed capable and exactly the mother I needed to be for my children, even without Jean here today! I did it!*

***

There was no going back to Rahman. I had finally escaped his intentional hurting of me, mercilessly grinding me down. I had no doubt that he would find a way to blame me for breaking up our marriage and family. He was faultless in his own mind. As sad as I was to give up the promise of our future together, that wouldn't stop me from shielding the kids from his behavior and after-hours company. How bold these women were! Would they follow our children around? Could I ever leave our house for an hour or two without someone else in my bed with my husband? Such are the problems of a woman with an idle, untrustworthy, but otherwise desirable husband. *They can have him. I'm done.*

I debated in my head the best way to tell Rahman that we were no longer in Florida before it occurred to me that I might simply wait until he figured it out himself, which could take days in his current state of stupid. Besides, after packing and flying on such a tight schedule, the idea of having a few days of peace and quiet was appealing, so I paused, taking time to gather my thoughts and forecast what might be next in my marriage evacuation plan.

Despite the likely wisdom of my chosen course of action, I was too rattled to stick to it. After twenty-four hours of nothing from Rahman, anxiety set in. I called the house in Florida. I felt it was the right thing to do, and needed some nominal amount of closure to the last few days. He wasn't answering. Basha came back to check on us and watched as I unsuccessfully tried to contact Rahman a few more times. Nothing. I felt so many things at once. Anger. Jealousy. Anxiety. Paranoia. Sadness. Neglect. Fear. But also nominal traces of remorse. In my heart, I knew that he left me no choice but to leave, but part of me would forever miss our family intact.

"I haven't heard from him, and he's still not home! These are his children—does he even care?" I felt so betrayed and furious that the kids had a father who didn't notice their absence or wonder how they were.

"Why don't you try calling him at her place?" she suggested. "Then you can catch him in the act. It'll blow his mind."

"What? Her place? That's crazy...but now that you mention it, that might be a great way to start the divorce talk." I erupted in hysterical laughter. I was so tense, and the outrage of it all struck me as hilarious. I needed the release.

We got the number easily from the operator, after recalling Anne's portentous warning: "Remember her name. Laura Parton." I dialed impatiently. Nothing could stop me now. Four rings and an answering machine took over. "Hello, you have reached..." I hung up.

"What do I do now?" I asked Basha, in disbelief that we were actually going through with this.

"She has an answering machine. We'll listen to her messages. Then you'll really know what's happening. Let's try the factory preset code. 4321. No one ever changes their passwords!" Basha urged.

I dialed again, waited for the outgoing message to begin and then punched in carefully "4321." I could feel my heart beating out of control. *Please, please, please be right!*

We both listened into the earpiece of the phone as the outgoing message stopped. The glorious whirring sound of the machine rewinding the messages made us jump for hesitant joy.

"This idiot never erases her messages. We've hit the jackpot. It's still rewinding," Basha whispered, not wanting to drown out the whirring of the machine.

We crouched over the receiver as if it were a precious relic, listening to ten minutes of messages, most of them from my husband, but others from her tacky friends and unscrupulous mother, all outlining their recent romps and trysts around the club and elsewhere. Yuck. Basha and I were able to create a timeline to the entire affair through that string of recorded messages. How they had met, who was complicit, what they were doing, where they were going.

Her mother offered, "Honey, of course you can borrow my Chanel shoes. I'll leave them out for you. I know you have an important date with Rahman…"

Her friends reported, laughing, "We spotted the wife driving in with the kids," and "We followed the wife at the grocery store." *I was right. My family is a game to them. Some sort of sick amusement.*

And of course, there were messages from my pathetic husband, "My wife is returning tomorrow, so I must see you tonight," and "Be ready at six, I'm coming to pick you up," and "We need to talk. There are rumors about us going around the club. Call me when you get in."

When the messages were finished playing, I grabbed some paper and a pen, and started furiously jotting down notes, names, dates, and places, in case I had to use this information as proof of his infidelity for the divorce proceedings. I knew Rahman would deny everything and I needed solid, detailed evidence. Anything to bolster up my case.

"What do you think he'll do when he hears that you want to leave him?" Basha asked.

"Strangely enough, I've been feeling so distant from him these days that I don't know. Can you believe that? I don't know how my own husband will react. I don't know what he wants or expects from me anymore." Suddenly, I could not hold back. It all came spilling out." I can't reach him—between the drinking and the women. He let that creep put her clothes in my house! Bras, undies and all! She brazenly parked her car in my driveway for two weeks! My neighbor saw them…Not to mention our friends at the club…I can't go back. I mean, maybe he's really in love with this woman and wants to be with her instead of me. Wouldn't that be convenient? She can have him, as far as I'm concerned. They can live in our house down in Florida. I could live up here in peace and sanity. Pull my own life together…"

"Sounds like it was really bad, Patricia. What happened in England? You didn't enjoy your summer there? Here I was imagining you floating around at that elite polo club with Princess Diana…" *Ugh. Nothing further from the truth. It was just as humiliating as yesterday….only in a barn with a floozy rather than in my bed with a floozy….*

I told Basha the things that I had been holding in for the past year, even longer, never wanting to confront any of it. The more I spoke, the more I felt committed to looking out for the kids but also the person I'd been neglecting since I was first tethered to him. Me. My sanity, my dignity, and my dreams, all of which I had willingly set aside for Rahman to chase down every new passion, place, or people that coincided with his new fix. I had given him so many chances. My thoughts, late in coming, were better late than never. But it was hearing the words in my own voice, outloud, that made the decision very rational and real. It was done, and I somehow felt relieved. I would never regret leaving.

Later that evening, after putting the children to bed, I resumed calls to reach Rahman. Finally, around 1 am, he answered.

"Hello, Patricia?"

He sounded drunk. I sighed, realizing that whatever I told him tonight, I would have to repeat tomorrow when he was more coherent. Why waste energy having an argument that would no doubt happen again? So I hung up.

The next day, when he finally called back, sort of sober, I outlined everything I knew about his activities of the past few months, trying hard not to call out anyone in particular. I stuck to the script I had rehearsed, relying heavily on phone messages in his own voice, that he could not deny.

At first, he ridiculed me. "You're imagining things, Patricia. There is no other woman." But after my barrage of evidence, he stepped back into a 7th century pile of BS, claiming that as a Saudi, he could have up to four wives, as was his birthright. Never before had he voiced such absurdities, which sounded all the more ridiculous spoken in his acute British accent. The hypocrisy of it all broke me and there, at my kitchen phone, while watching my children play outside on the patio, I lost my patience, attacking head on with all I had left.

"What? Four wives? Are you kidding? Do you even know one person in your vast circle of friends who has even two wives? You know damn well your family would never fund it! Maybe this Muslim rap works on other people but I know you too well. Dragging us around the world, living out your Western fantasy life? Disrespecting your children and me? Fine. Have all the wives you want, but I won't be one of them. Unbelievable. See if your new girlfriend wants to be wife number two or three," I screeched before slamming the phone down so hard the plastic receiver cracked.

The next week, at my parents' behest, I met with a well-reputed lawyer who specialized in International Family Law, a fairly esoteric field, as I was soon to learn. Mr. John Long, Esq. was an older, mild-mannered and bookish gentleman. I wondered whether he would be up for this nasty task. Recent conversations with Rahman had gotten ugly and made me realize that he would not make this divorce easy for me or the kids. With each day, his attitude had become more belligerent, more menacing, and more desperate to win. It would be a new game for him to beat me at. A new challenge in an arena he knew well. He was a Georgetown educated PhD in law. And he had two definitive advantages—endless piles of money to fund his fight and endless hours to find new ways to drive me further into the ground. It was game on for him.

"Dream on, Patricia. You have no way to defend yourself from me. I can hire a dozen men to track you down, take my children, and teach you a lesson. You won't even know what hit you and it'll be over," he often threatened. But beyond the cheating and the lying, it was his cold, calculating voice that forced me to confront the fact that he didn't love me. Even worse, he was capable of murdering me, or so he claimed.

As I explained all this to Mr. Long, in his quiet and unremarkable office I began to slowly lose my sanity, and repeatedly asked myself what everyone else was thinking: why would I have married a man like this in the first place? Why have two children with him? Didn't I realize that he was capable of this behavior? Was I blind? Mr. Long routinely reassured me that Rahman couldn't get away with any unlawful plans he'd threatened me with. We would get a restraining order and Rahman would only be allowed to see the children in supervised visitation. "This is the United States, after all," he concluded, "Good thing you didn't decide to leave him when you were in Saudi Arabia. That would have been far worse. Once he gets himself a lawyer, and I hear he has made inquiries, Rahman will simmer down. His lawyer will help explain to him what his rights are.

People involved in a divorce often begin with unrealistic expectations. They start out emotional but later clarity sets in and they eventually settle. Don't worry, we'll negotiate our way out of this, and things will turn out well for you and the children. Now remind me of what their names and ages are..." he asked as he took notes on our conversation, jotting everything down on a yellow notepad.

I was not feeling hopeful. Mr. Long was too nice, too confident, and was forgetting that Rahman had studied at Georgetown Law School for six years. Rahman lived to punish me and I had a feeling that he knew just how far he could go and what he could get away with. When Rahman finally hired a DC lawyer, we were bombarded with motions, objections, accusations, and all sorts of ludicrous demands, causing my already fragile nerves to further fray and legal bills to skyrocket. Overwhelming me, knocking me sideways with legal noise and needless harassment was his first chess move.

His second attack was financial. He refused to send us any support, claiming he was unemployed, expenses were adding up, and I found myself wondering how on earth I could withstand incoming waves of mounting bills. Karim was enrolled in Montessori nursery school and both children needed winter clothes. I doubled down with work, desperately trying to keep up with expenses. Thankfully, Nurse Jean's salary was paid directly from Amm Abdullah's bank to Jean's account in England. Otherwise I would have had to let her go.

Rahman then began demands to see the children, unsupervised, using every trick in his backward playbook to bend the law. He claimed that the entire next month was made of holy days and he had a right, as a Muslim, to be with his children to celebrate. He claimed that I was trying to convert the children to Christianity, and the court entertained these unfounded fantasies. Forcing me into endless hearings at my expense, he flung lies from every direction, harpooning my character, portraying me as a cold fish, a calculating and unfeeling woman, and a shrewd opportunist looking to cash in on the marriage. However absurd the accusations sounded, I had to pay my lawyer to defend me against every single claim.

Time dragged on, and Rahman's demands intensified. He wanted the children to travel down to Florida, where he was residing in our house with his girlfriend, so he hired a second lawyer in Florida, claiming Florida as his state of residency. This new aggressive Florida lawyer sent a sheriff to my DC house late one evening with a divorce subpoena, and suddenly I was entangled in two legal battles. I, too, had to hire an additional lawyer in Florida to combat the charges, and we started litigation afresh down there. I soon learned that his Florida lawyer was quite comfortable utilizing sleazy tactics that the DC lawyer never would have agreed to. Things heated up and became ever more outrageous. I was now stuck paying my DC lawyer to speak with my Florida lawyer and they were fighting in both state courts about which domicile was true. The laws were unclear about this and specialists were brought in, which necessitated additional retainers (read: lots more zeros).

Rahman's demands to see the children had heightened to such a pitch that Mr. Long sheepishly confessed that I would have to agree to visitation or risk contempt of court. In desperation, I requested that Rahman instead come to Washington DC. I was even willing to allow him into the house with Nurse Jean present, to pay a visit to the children. I reasoned that it was infinitely easier for him to fly up than for both children and the nanny to fly down. For once, I got my wish, and the following week, we set up a day for the big visit. I left the planning to Jean, as frankly, I could not imagine Rahman spending an entire afternoon with the children unless it was them watching him play polo. Knowing how upset I was, Basha offered to pick me up and I cleared out of the house with her early on visitation day. The idea of facing Rahman, after all he had been doing to me, was too much. And I didn't want the kids to see us sparring so I avoided his visit altogether.

Upon my arrival home in the evening, I was relieved to find that the children thoroughly enjoyed their father's visit. Karim happily recounted his escapades on the bike path behind the house.

"Daddy was so surprised to see me balance on the back wheel. He said I looked like a big boy!"

"Well, Karim, you are a big boy!" I gushed.

"And Daddy wants me to come to Florida to ride Taffy. He says that he'll buy me a bigger pony because I am getting so grown up. Then I will have two ponies."

Bribing Karim with the offer of a new pony? How cliché. Just buy your kids like you buy everyone else....

"That sounds very exciting, Karim! Perhaps we can go down there next month." I tried to sound cheerful but my heart was sinking by the minute.

"Why can't we go next week, Mama?"

"Karim, we can talk about this tomorrow. How about some ice cream at that new shop that opened down the street? C'mon, let's ask Nurse Jean and Sultana what flavors they want and we'll bring it back for them."

Jean was dressing Tana for bed and was delighted to hear that ice cream was in the plan. After taking everyone's order, Karim rushed to the garage to get into the car and I silently followed, deep in thought.

"Mama, where is the car?" Karim called from the garage.

"What are you talking about?" I answered, following behind him.

It was empty. I pushed the opener and waited there in confusion, as the door went up. I strained my neck to see if my car was somehow parked in front of the house. Not there, either. Together Karim and I walked around the driveway to the side of the house. No car was in sight. I rushed back in to ask Jean.

"Jean, why isn't the car in the garage?" Nurse Jean looked up, slightly disoriented, from diapering the baby.

"The car? Your car?" she asked.

"Yes, my car. Do you have any idea where it might be?"

"No, Madam. No one has been here except your husband…" she stared at me then stood very still; the only breaking of tension was Tana kicking her little legs on the changing table.

"Do you think he took it, Jean? How did he arrive here? Did he come in a rental car or a taxi?"

"A taxi. He arrived in a yellow cab, I assume, from the airport."

"And how did he leave?" I asked, holding my breath.

"Well, I didn't watch when he went out. He got up to leave and I stayed down in the playroom with the children. They were still watching the movie…"

"So, I can assume that he took my car. OK. I no longer have a car…" I said in desperation. *No car. Now what do I do? How could Jean be so careless? Why didn't she watch him leave?*

"Mama, does that mean we can't get ice cream?" Karim's eyes welled up with tears. My heart fell, again, as I realized that Rahman's arsenal of thuggish behavior now included auto theft. *The worst may not yet be over. He was just warming up.* "No, sweetheart, we'll call a taxi. No big deal," I said cheerily as I dialed the number for the taxi service. "Maybe we'll bring back an ice cream cake too! For the weekend!" I took his little hand and pulled him out to the curb to wait for our taxi. I would have to deal with this nonsense the next day. For the moment, my children needed me.

The next day was full of drama and confrontation. First, I called Mr. Long and informed him that my car had been stolen.

"Well, I must admit, I didn't expect this from him. And I can promise you that he will not get away with it. This sort of behavior never sits well with the court." Mr. Long was completely taken by surprise at this most recent event. I remembered my first impression of him and it was spot on. He was wholly unprepared for an opponent as crafty and resourceful as Rahman. Mr. Long was a gentleman, an old school attorney for average people, not hardball tactics with ruthless operators.

We agreed that a motion would be filed immediately to address the auto theft and perhaps enlighten the court as to the likelihood of a kidnapping. This offered me a glimmer of hope. Perhaps some good would come out of the theft of my car.

"Find another lawyer, Patricia!" my mother insisted, over the phone later that day. "This guy is too prissy! You need a street fighter."

"How am I going to change lawyers now, Mom? I've already sunk a small fortune into this one and a retainer to the second lawyer in Florida! I cannot afford a third retainer! Mr. Long knows the case. I'll just have to push him more. At least now he realizes how sneaky and dishonest Rahman can be. I'm almost glad it happened. It will give the court insight into his character. His bad character. Maybe it'll help me keep the kids from going down to Florida for a visit."

"What are you talking about? A visit where?!" She challenged.

"I didn't tell you because I didn't want you to worry. Rahman wants the kids to stay at the house with him in Florida for a week or two."

"Don't do it, Patricia! You'll regret it for the rest of your life," she demanded. Her voice was at once motherly and terrifying.

"I know, Mom, I know. Please! I'm trying to remain calm. I can't function in a state of panic."

"You cannot send those children down to Florida. Under no circumstances should they go down there! I don't care what he says or does. I don't care if they threaten to arrest you. I am warning you..." she concluded the conversation in complete exasperation. And sadly, I knew she was right. The walls were closing in.

Mr. Long's assessment of the situation at our next meeting echoed my worst fears. "Patricia, your husband has now filed claims that he has the right to see his children at his home in Florida. He's a parent. Florida law is strong on this point. I suppose that's why he decided to file there. You're being portrayed as a very unreasonable woman, and I am afraid that we must negotiate something or else you could be held in contempt of court. The Judge appears to be leaning more to his side, saying that your husband hasn't done anything wrong yet. We have a hearing next week. Acting irrational will do you no good."

"Irrational? He stole my only car. He threatened to send men to hurt me. He's not supporting us. He threatened to kidnap my children! Several

232 - Jeddah Bride

times! How much clearer does it have to be? He's planning to kidnap them when they get down to Florida. I'm completely convinced of that."

Mr. Long appeared quite uncomfortable at hearing my words. Again, he insisted that the court didn't see it that way. Perhaps neither did he. We had a planned hearing, I would get another car, everything would be negotiated. Every father has the right to see his children. Rahman had succeeded in charming everyone involved. Was he paying them all off or did he call in favors from his extensive network of ambassadors, law school professors, business associates, or any other party that owed his family something? I would never know and my children were slipping through my fingers.

"Perhaps you can send the children down there for a week next month. If only we could get past this issue of a visit. I believe it's more his ego talking than anything. He might behave more reasonably when he feels that he has won something. It will be a big help with the issue of temporary child support, too. Didn't you say that you're running low on money? I'm trying to help you. We must tackle this issue first, then I can finally negotiate the other issues of the settlement. We simply must get past this visitation. Would the nanny be available to accompany the children? Or perhaps your mother?"

"Forget my mother. She would probably hit him over the head with something." *Not a terrible idea.*

"So let's talk about the nanny, Ms. Jean. Is she capable of handling things without you if she were to accompany the children to Florida for a week?" I could feel his frustration with this case and I wondered if perhaps I was acting in the wrong and making things harder for him. *Maybe he knows what he's doing. Or maybe he doesn't.*

"Nurse Jean is certainly capable, as capable as I would be. She would have to watch his every move. He's very sneaky and clever..." I responded. But I knew that I wasn't being heard. Mr. Long stubbornly insisted that all I had to do was give in a little and allow the lawyers to settle the case for us. So, against every instinct, I decided to put my faith in the legal system.

***

"Mama, look at the jumbo jet landing! It's British Airways!" Karim shouted, as he stuck his head out of the car window.

"Karim, get your head back in the car! You could get it chopped off if you're not careful!" I answered. I had allowed Karim to sit in the front seat with me as we drove to the airport. He was usually in the back with Nurse

Jean and Sultana, but not today. Today was special and I wanted him close to me for as long as I could have him.

***

After a few weeks of rather infuriating negotiations, all parties agreed that the children and Nurse Jean would fly down to West Palm Beach for a week's stay. I simply could not win that argument despite all my efforts and pleading with my attorney. On a positive note, Karim was beside himself with excitement at the prospect of seeing his father and, of course, his pony, Taffy.

I was the only sad one in the car. Even Jean was talking a mile a minute about how lovely it would be in Florida and how many activities the children would be doing over the next week. It was irritating. *Why is she so happy? For the kids' sake? Maybe I should get used to this. I suppose they'll be visiting their dad regularly, from now on. I can't act like I'm walking to death row every time, can I?*

I snuck a quick glance at Karim, all dressed up in a new pair of jeans, a fresh white Polo t-shirt, and his favorite sneakers. What a beautiful boy he had become! I marveled at the gleam in his eyes and his huge smile, studying the dimples on his perfectly round little face. He was so happy. I was glad about that.

Sultana was chirping happily in the backseat, a true delight. Her hair was finally long enough to put a little bow in it, which delighted her that morning. At almost two, her developing personality, mellow yet determined, was finally showing itself. Not surprising, she was a very bright child, speaking prematurely and putting simple sentences together with ease. She was wearing red patent leather shoes of her choosing–with a sense of style leaning towards shine and sparkle. I had wanted to buy her black shoes, but she refused to let me put them on her, instead gesturing wildly at the red ones on the shelf. Of course, I relented. She loved those shoes and was so proud of them.

Again, I needed a pep-talk and a positive outlook. I'd never been away from the kids. Staying home was my favorite thing to do ever since they entered my life. *Maybe I'm just being overdramatic…Why am I acting like I'll never see them again? Before I know it, they'll be back and we'll finally be able to move forward with all the legal matters. I can use this next week to organize things at home and to catch up on my work.*

I pulled into the short-term parking lot and grabbed the ticket out of the machine. But as the traffic arm went up, so did my anxiety. I pulled into the first vacant parking spot, not wanting to drive around anymore. I felt dizzy and was crumbling inside, out of nowhere. But I had to push on. *Just breathe. Don't let them know you're getting upset.* I plastered a phony smile on my face and got out to open the trunk of the car before barking orders to feel some semblance of control of the situation.

"Jean, stay there and hold Sultana, I'll set up the stroller for you. Karim, stand by me, sweetie, there are cars driving by and I don't want you getting in their way."

Karim came around next to me and together, we lifted out the stroller and the luggage.

"I can open the stroller, Mama, watch!"

"Amazing, Karim! Who taught you to do that?"

"I saw Nurse Jean do it so many times, Mama. It's easy."

"Since you're so grown up, I think you should wheel your own suitcase to the terminal. I can handle the other two. Okay, here we go!" We made our way through the parking lot, into the elevator and up to the departures desk where I checked in the luggage and received boarding passes for everyone.

As we approached the gate, I realized that I wasn't ready to relinquish my children just yet so I looked around for some excuse before spying a fro-yo stand. "Since we have a little extra time, why don't we get you all some frozen yogurt? We can eat it while waiting to board."

"Mama, I want to see the different flavors. I'm not sure which one I want."

"Okay, I'll lift you up to take a look. Hold on tight." I bent over and hoisted him up so he could peer through the glass into the refrigerated cabinet containing vats of yogurt. *Wow, he's so heavy! I haven't lifted him in months, maybe even a year. He is four and a half. He was so tiny when he was born, I was afraid to hold him at first. The first newborn I had ever handled...*

"Mama! I asked you what flavor is this green one? Mama?"

"Oh, sorry, I was thinking about something else, Karim. That flavor is pistachio."

"That's the one I want. With chocolate sprinkles."

We found some empty seats and ate our frozen yogurt, ignoring the first call for families with children and disabled people to board. Then came the calls for row-by-row boarding. We were just finishing up, so I asked Karim to throw all the empty cups and spoons in the trash can. He did so proudly, returning to pick up his backpack before we meandered over to the ever-dwindling boarding line.

It was time to board. I couldn't delay it any longer, so I bent down and gave Sultana a hug and a kiss, again noticing how long her hair had grown.

"Jean, let's get Sultana a haircut when she returns." I suggested, as if making plans for next week would make right now any easier. We approached the gate, where I handed the three tickets to the stewardess in charge.

"We're going to see my father in Florida," Karim boomed, as she inspected the tickets.

"That sounds like an exciting trip! Maybe you'll be able to visit the pilot in the cockpit during the flight if there's no turbulence. I'll come over to your seats once we've taken off and let you know what he says," she said with a big smile.

"Did you hear that, Mama, I might meet the pilot!" He was beside himself.

I bent down to give Karim a hug and a kiss, fighting back the tears, trying to laugh along with him but I felt sick at the thought of letting go.

"That will be fantastic!" I exclaimed as I clung to his body, wishing I could have a few more minutes. But my time was up, and I backed away, wishing Jean a safe trip, cheering them on for this big adventure, blowing kisses and waving my hands until they disappeared into the tunnel. My last words were, "Kiss Taffy for me!..."

I stood there in silence, not able to move. The stewardess smiled and asked, "First time with visitation?"

"Yes, first time they've been out of my sight for more than a few hours."

"Don't worry, you'll get used to it. We see this all the time. Cheer up," she encouraged. She picked up her carry on, turned and followed my children down the jet way to board the plane.

Chapter Sixteen

Kidnapping

I think we have a problem, Madam." The tension in her voice knocked me from a deep sleep.

"*What?* Jean, it's the middle of the night!" I didn't mean to be short with her, but it was 1 am.

"Your husband hasn't brought the children home yet," Nurse Jean continued, clearing the hoarseness from her voice.

I blinked a few times before realizing my contact lenses were still in. I sat up, scanning my bedroom in a fuzzy-visioned, sleepy stupor, the green toile wallpaper dancing in the flickering light of late-night TV. I must have fallen asleep, emotionally drained.

"Jean, what are you telling me?" I asked, throwing off the covers and turning on the light. "Did Rahman take them? Did he take them somewhere without you? Do you know where they went? What time did they leave?" I didn't give Jean a chance to speak. My breath was short and I felt my chest tighten, crushed with overwhelming panic.

"Your husband told me to dress the children for dinner," Jean said, gaining composure as she recounted the facts. "He said he was taking them with him to the Arellano's dinner party, and I assumed that I would go too. I have accompanied them everywhere since our arrival." Of course Jean believed she'd be with them; Sultana wasn't even two, and she needed somebody to feed her dinner and change her diapers, neither of which were Rahman's strong suits. "But as I was getting ready to go," she continued, "he told me I wasn't needed, and I could stay home to get some ironing done…"

"You let him take them *alone*?!" I scolded.

"He insisted," Jean countered, "and at the time, it made sense to me. I did have laundry to do, and the children are comfortable at the Arellano's house, so I assumed they'd be fine. Mr. Abbar's been so pleasant lately…"

"When has he ever taken those children anywhere without you? Didn't you think that was weird?" Silence. "You should have gotten in touch with me immediately." I couldn't stop myself.

Jean said, "Madam, I didn't even consider calling you. I promise you, at the moment, it didn't seem odd. It made perfect sense." *Perfect sense? After all the kidnapping threats? She knew how hard I had fought for supervised visitation. How could this make perfect sense?*

"Okay, fine, so what happened? Tell me everything you remember." I did my best to keep my tone civil. But inside I was interrogating her, insisting she hurry the hell up and give me a clue as to where that snake of a father had taken my babies. And why she didn't notify me of Rahman's sudden interest in being a present parent.

Jean continued, "I packed a diaper bag for Sultana, then put them both into their car seats. That was the last I heard from them. About six hours ago. I assumed Anne and Douglas would also be at Arellano's, and that they would help with Sultana. After they drove away, I called Anne, but no one answered at their house, giving me even more confidence that they, too, were at the party. But I just now got off the phone with Anne. She didn't even *know* about the party."

I had heard enough. "Thank you, Jean. I'll call you back in a bit," and hung up.

I sprung from the bed and did my best to focus on the next steps. Something had happened, although I was afraid to admit that I knew what it was. I called the Arellano's house, but after twenty rings with no answer, I slammed the phone down, took a deep breath, and dialed Anne. She picked up after one ring.

As calmly as possible, I asked, "Jean just called and told me the kids aren't home yet. Do you have any idea where they could be? Did you see Rahman at the club today? Could they have all gone down to Miami to that Cuban restaurant for a late dinner? We've done that before with the kids… I just called the Arellano's, but no one answered. Maybe there was an accident on the road… I don't know. I'm sorry I woke you, but I'm freaking out." I was babbling. "Maybe I should call the police."

"Don't apologize for calling, Patricia," Anne said. "Douglas and I have been awake since Jean called us. We're both so worried. We love you, and we're here for you. We're your closest friends. We want to help."

"Thank you, Anne," I murmured, blotting my eyes and cheeks with the collar of my nightshirt. *Don't let them hear you cry. Stay strong. There must be some reasonable explanation for all of this...*

"Of course. We've been trying to remember if Rahman said anything strange today, *something* that gave *some* kind of hint that he planned on going *somewhere*, but we can't think of anything. He was relaxed at the barn this afternoon, smiling, interacting with the grooms and making preparations for coming matches. He was as normal as can be. Typical Rahman. He mentioned that Karim would be riding his pony on the main field tomorrow morning and was excited to show off his son. I didn't get the impression that he had big plans for tonight."

A dead end. No clues whatsoever. "Thanks anyhow, Anne."

"Maybe you should have Jean snoop around his desk," she hesitantly suggested. "See if he's left any papers there that might give you a clue. This is rather strange."

"I've had Jean snooping around his office all week. She hates doing it, but every day I force her. I stay on the phone with her while she's looking around. I doubt there's anything new today, but I'll give it a try." I hung up, then called my house in Wellington. Jean answered immediately, and I could tell she'd been crying. *She's thinking what I'm fearing.* I tried to reassure her that I was in control of the situation and had a plan. After she calmed down a bit, I instructed her to go into the library and look through his desk drawers.

"You mean you want me to go through his *drawers* now? It's enough that you made me snoop around his office, but to actually open the drawers and rummage around there..." she huffed, rather put off by my request.

"Of *course* I want you to go through his drawers. Don't you think this situation calls for it? He disappeared with my children, so go to the damn library, open the drawers, and *tell me everything that you see in there!*" I screeched.

I had finally lost my cool and didn't care to offer her the English niceties as they were of no use. My children were falling farther from my grasp by the minute yet Jean was stuck on proper nanny ethics and etiquette.

She sighed, "Fine." I could hear the soft opening of the rather commanding double doors to Rahman's office library. I listened intently, fully tuned in to each sound. Metal drawer. Open. *Hurry up!*

"I'm in the top drawer. Lots of papers, but nothing looks important. Oh, let's see here – There's a pad with notes on it. Some handwritten things...flight schedules – Monday, April 3rd to Cairo on TWA...Tuesday, April 4, 10:45 to Casablanca on Air Maroc...there are a few more here, too..."

"Is there anything with today's date? Anything that says Saturday, April 1? Come on, Jean, hurry!" She was moving and speaking with absolutely no sense of urgency, and it was making me crazy!

"No," she said, "nothing for today…but…wait, here's something… Sunday, April 2…Saudi Arabian Airlines…2:00 PM…leaving from Kennedy Airport…going directly to Jeddah…there's a receipt for those tickets…and a schedule of flights from West Palm Beach up to Kennedy Airport…some are for today, some are for tomorrow."

"Is there anything else??? Is his passport in the drawer? Please look carefully, Jean. He always keeps it in the top…"

Nurse Jean interrupted, somehow thinking it was a good moment to argue with me and rationalize any imprudent behaviors on Rahman's part, "But Madam, he was hardly prepared to take the children on such a long journey." Jean continued, "All their clothes are here at the house. And you have their passports, don't you?"

"Jean, one doesn't need a passport to leave the country." I thought back to that first trip to Jeddah, the men who came up and bundled me into the limousine, whisking me off to a private home. And with Rahman's money and his family's influence, he could easily pass right through. As for luggage—half of the contents were stolen anyway. Rahman could easily replace anything necessary.

"It looks like all his belongings are here, too. As far as I can tell, he left the house with only the clothes on his back. Maybe he's just keeping his kids out to an ungodly hour because he's so irresponsible."

Ok, she's right about that…he can be unbelievably irresponsible. Especially when it comes to putting what he wants above all else. But he had never taken care of the kids alone. Never. He'd never touched a clean diaper, much less changed a dirty one. Still, I could not ignore the fact that my children went missing and there was a receipt for three seats on a flight to Saudi. Rahman, Karim, and Tana. Three. No nanny, no helper, no luggage.

"Jean! Please answer the question. Do you see Rahman's passport in his top drawer or not?"

She took an extended pause, feeling the gravity of the situation, finally. "No, Madam. I don't see it."

"Did you look everywhere?" I implored, begging for some semblance of hope.

Another pause. "No. I didn't. Because he always keeps it in the same spot. Always."

"Well, I will assume that it's missing for a reason. Please stay by the telephone and call me if you hear anything." I slammed down the receiver, breathing hard.

During our eleven years together, Rahman had demonstrated (with great precision) his high capacity for low behavior and certainly threatened me more times than there are numbers for. But I couldn't fathom the level of hurt he would cause me or the children by taking them back to a land that he didn't even care to be in himself. A culture of backwards thinking that would extend zero rights for our baby girl, Tana. He had humiliated me at every opportunity–attending parties like a singleton after we were married…Going through a year of law school before being forced to admit he was married…And finally, disgustingly, keeping a slut Barbie realtor as a sex pet in our house while I was in New York visiting the grandparents. Even so, it was hard to believe he would actually just steal my children from me. But I had to assume the worst. That meant flying to New York and camping out at the Kennedy International terminal, patrolling for him and the kids. *How could I make sure he didn't slip by me? Would I have to tackle him? He's twice my size…maybe I could get an airport security person to pinch hit?* I had no idea what my next step was. Should I call the police? The FBI? Maybe calling my divorce lawyer would be the most logical move. *This is going to be a long night.*

Still reeling, I slowly slipped into some comfortable jeans and a loose sweater. I attempted to calm myself by meditating on my children's faces, reassuring myself that a good outcome was still possible. I'd need all my wit and grit to beat the world's biggest winner at his own gamble—and if I couldn't relax and think clearly, I'd be useless.

After an attempt at steadying myself with long, slow breaths, I sat down at my bedroom desk and picked up the phone. My first call was to Basha, who was just returning from a night at the Kennedy Center. "Patricia, I'm sure it's nothing! Rahman is having too much fun down there in Palm Beach to return to Saudi. His polo ponies are all there! His friends! Come on!" I felt a little better.

I then rang up Debbie Doyle, who was dead asleep. She woke up enough to offer her bleak take on the situation. "He kidnapped them. I'm sure of it. You get your ass over to Kennedy Airport as soon as you can and bring help." Now I felt worse. Because unlike Basha's rosy (and liquored up?) conclusion, Debbie's assessment was highly probable.

My baby sister, Cindy, who had recently moved to DC and was living only fifteen minutes away, was the last on my list of calls. After I spilled the story, she said, "Debbie was right. I'll go with you to Kennedy in the morning. Just come over now and spend the night. It's not like either of us will be getting any sleep. I'm so sorry, sis."

"Thank you," I whispered, trying to hold in the tears, "I'll be there in a few minutes." After hanging up, I threw some clothes and toiletries into a duffel bag and headed down to the garage.

My new Taurus wagon had been purchased, by order of the court, several weeks prior, so I didn't have to catch a cab at 1:30 am. But leaning up against that very plain wagon was something infinitely precious, Karim's blue two-wheel bike. I instinctively took the little handlebars into my own hands, holding them tight as if I were indeed headed down a steep jagged mountain with no path and no breaks. As I held on ever-tighter, my nails dug deep into my palms. That small bike had prompted an unexpected response, shattering the poker face I had put on in an effort to fool even myself.

I might lose my children forever.

Leaning into the side of the car, I eased down onto the cold concrete floor as emptiness took over and the floodgates opened. I'd never cried so hard in my life.

I pulled myself together—more or less—to the point that I was able to get into the car and make the fifteen-minute drive to Cindy's house. She was waiting for me at the front door with her arms open wide. We spent the early morning hours ruminating on every possible scenario and devising a plan. Cindy asked, "Didn't he have that girlfriend down there? I thought Anne told you she was going around the club, bragging that he promised to marry her once your divorce was finalized?"

"Yes...no...I don't know. The girl's been saying all kinds of things for the past six months, and as far as I know, none of it's true. But even if that's what happened, I find it hard to believe he'd just up and leave his polo ponies, his house, his clothes, and his friends. He has been making investments in South Beach, and he invested in a Florida bank. It sure felt like he was staying..." I continued, "And, to make matters even more confusing, Anne has been bombarding me with stories of other women who crawled out of the woodwork, also claiming to have had affairs with him. Can you believe it? There were at least two others, and apparently he told them all he would marry them and bring them to Saudi Arabia once our divorce was finalized. How crazy must they be to get involved with him, considering all the rumors? I guess cash is king."

"Wow, what a mess!" Cindy said.

"Yes, a mess. You know, if he kidnapped the kids, he can't return to the United States. He would be arrested. He would have to remain in Saudi Arabia."

"I didn't know that."

"Yes, he would be stuck there. That's a big sacrifice, just to steal the kids. He never even spent that much time with them in the first place," I said. "He was so busy with his own stuff." After a bit, I added, "And the work he was starting with his investments in South Beach, that would all go down the drain, too. Just like the law job in DC. Do you think he's ready to go that far, to burn that bridge? I don't know, maybe we're jumping to conclusions."

Cindy said, "Patricia, to be honest, I've never been able to get a handle on what's going on inside Rahman's head. He's always been so secretive and closed. As far as I'm concerned, anything is possible. And I know he was angry that you wanted a divorce." She paused. "He sure never missed an opportunity to show us all that you'd lost your senses."

"What could he expect to gain by doing something so, so, so extreme? I know he hates me, but this won't be good for him either. It won't be good for anyone. I mean, Karim just got his acceptance letter from the Beauvoir School in DC. He's supposed to start kindergarten. You can't take a child away from his home once he starts school. You can't ever take a child away from his home. What is Rahman doing?"

"I don't know. I can't believe it." Cindy stifled a yawn. I realized it was almost dawn.

"Go to bed," I insisted. "It's okay, really. There's no way I'm going back to sleep, but you should get some rest, even if it's just for a few hours. I'll need you awake for tomorrow when my mind is scrambled."

Cindy stood up. "If you hear from Jean or anyone, knock on my door and wake me up. We can take the first available shuttle up to New York," she mumbled, stumbling off to bed.

I stared out the den window, biting my fingernails, regretting that I'd sent my kids to Florida in the first place. I winced as I remembered a recent conversation with Mr. Long, "You have to let them visit Rahman, Patricia," he'd said. "The judge ordered you to do it. He's their father and has the right to see them. If you don't, you'll be in contempt of court."

"Contempt of court," again and again, Mr. Long's favorite warning. But what power does "contempt of court" actually hold? Would it make any difference now that I was hightailing it to Kennedy Airport? Would I get fined or thrown in jail after intercepting the kidnapping of my children? Would the judge look unkindly at my side, after all of this? I wished

I had never heard that phrase and had never complied. My mother was right—it was all empty legal threats.

At 5 am the phone rang. Speak of the devil, it was my mother. "Patricia! Cousin Tony and I are meeting you and Cindy at Kennedy. We'll be waiting for you whenever you show up. What time does your flight land?" she asked. My father was away on a business trip, and my mother enlisted the help of her older cousin—she couldn't handle it alone.

"Nine. We're going right to the Saudi Airlines terminal when we get there. Pray we're not too late."

"What did your attorney have to say? Did he tell you to call the police?" asked Mom.

"I haven't called him yet. It's too early. But he always talks about filing a motion with the judge, more papers, more money, more waiting. We need to stop Rahman ourselves if we can. It's just another case to the attorney and the judge! Their lives will be no different tomorrow either way. We need to make this happen and worry about asking permission later!"

"Good idea," she affirmed. Mom was tapping my enthusiasm and seemed to like my new approach. Less talk, more walk.

"I remember Rahman repeating the phrase, 'Possession is nine-tenths of the law.' If we can get them back, nothing will ever make me give them up again. *Nothing*."

"I'm calling the FBI right now," my mother said. "I'll tell them my daughter's going through a tough divorce with her Saudi husband, who's scared that he'll lose control over his two children. He's taken the children against your will, and booked a flight to Saudi Arabia with them, and…and…and *has threatened to blow up the plane*. That'll get the FBI to the airport!"

"Um, Mom, that's a little much…" *Though it may work more quickly than calling the regular cop shop…*

"You're an American," she yelled, "and those two children are Americans! I'll give them a call right now. We need all the help we can get!" Before I could explain to her why it might not be a good idea to call the Feds with a fake bomb threat, she hung up. *Oh well. Like I said, ask permission later.…*

Cindy came out of her room and joined me on the couch. She looked as drained as I felt. I told her about our mom's plan, "She thinks that as a grandmother and as an American, she has special privileges. She's determined to get the FBI over to that terminal to help us."

"I hope she doesn't get in trouble."

"If she gets in trouble, she'll just wiggle her way out. She always does. And nobody messes with her. I'm so desperate, I think it's worth a shot."

Cindy suggested we confirm Rahman's flight plans, "Do we have all the flight information? Should we call Saudi Airlines and ask about Rahman's reservation? We can pretend you're his secretary checking up on his flight status. Make sure that he and the kids are still booked on this flight."

"Great idea!" After kicking myself for not having thought of it in the first place, I picked up the phone and dialed. "Hello, yes, I'd like to check on the flight status for my boss who's booked today to Jeddah...yes, flight 3524 to Jeddah...yes, three people...yes, is he still in seat 3B?...the other two are in seats 3C and 3D...okay, and the flight is scheduled to depart on time?...great, thank you."

"I guess we'll be having a little reunion at the airport," I suggested, hopeful but terrified of what could happen to my children or family in the process. I had to take that risk.

Before noon, my family convened at Terminal 1 in Kennedy Airport, close to the Saudi Arabian Airlines check-in counter. Mom showed up dressed to the nines in a tan Missoni pant suit with matching shoes and bag—elegant as usual—with her cousin, Tony, ready for a showdown (or throwdown?). From the expression on mom's face, she was ready to rumble. If we saw Rahman, Mom would hold nothing back. She was just itching to take a piece of his ass home for a souvenir.

She approached me with a warm, enveloping hug and said, "Patricia, I got in touch with the FBI this morning."

"The bomb threat?" I replied in a whisper.

She nodded. "I gave them the flight number and everything. They seemed quite interested."

"I bet they did." *Holy Shit! This just got real.*

"They said that two agents would be waiting in the terminal."

My heart skipped a beat. This could get us all into a heap of trouble... but it was too late to do anything about it now. *And it might work...*

We spread out in the waiting area, anxiously watching travelers check in. Most were well-suited businessmen, both Saudis and Americans, probably going to Jeddah to make money. A few Saudi families were in the mix— men wearing long white robes, and their ladies, clad in modest but expensive dresses that grazed the floor. But no sign of Rahman, who would have stuck out like a sore thumb with his sleek hair, expensive Italian loafers, cashmere sweaters, and tight designer trousers. He looked like Rome or Paris, not Jeddah.

If Rahman showed up, I imagined that he'd be surprised we were there...but maybe he wouldn't. Maybe he expected something. Maybe he wanted a fight and was prepared to deal with a law enforcement officer or flash his diplomat card and waltz onto the plane. Maybe he'd play the wounded, indignant father who was exercising his right to visit his native country with his children. Perhaps he'd even invent a story of a dying relative. Rahman had spent six years at Georgetown learning how to bend the law in his favor. He always said that our legal system was the most absurd, twisted mess he'd ever studied, but he could figure out how to play it to his advantage. And Rahman lied for sport. He loved an opportunity to win a situation or argument.

About an hour before the flight was scheduled to depart, we saw two men wearing nondescript dark suits standing off to the side. With the cheap suits, they didn't look like international businessmen, so we decided they were probably FBI agents. I walked over to speak with them, thinking that the more information I could give —a photo, a description, anything—the better. I hesitantly approached the two static men and said, "Um, excuse me. I'm the wife of the man you're looking for. It was my mother who called your agency today. She's the one who reported my husband's strange behavior. You're from the FBI, right?"

They glanced at each other, then glared at me. The taller of the two said, "We'd like you to answer a few questions, ma'am. But not here. Please come with us."

"No, please, not now. I must stay here to watch for my husband in case he shows up with my kids." *Why on earth would they suggest I leave my post?* My eyes darted all over the terminal, scanning in every direction, looking for Rahman, my children, or anyone else that I recognized. "If you'd like to see a photo of him and the kids, I have one." As I reached into my handbag to get my wallet, I noticed the shorter agent tense up. Did he think I was going for a gun? He calmed down after I showed him the pictures. "My husband has taken my children from our house without my consent and he's booked to leave on this flight. We're afraid that he might do something crazy. That's all I know. I'm here to stop him."

The taller agent said, "You're saying he threatened to blow up the plane? Do you realize that to make that statement falsely would be a federal offense?"

"No," I said frantically. "I never said that he threatened to blow anything up. My mother was the one who made the call. He told Mom that he intended to harm himself and my children, and that he's booked on this flight with the children, without clothing or their belongings. Not even carry ons for this long journey…" I desperately tried to blur the details of my mother's call. "I don't know exactly what he plans to do. I mean, I'm not a mind reader. I'm just a mother standing here trying to keep my children from being kidnapped out of the country." *Play on their sympathy… although they don't seem to have any. Just don't say anything to make this situation worse.*

Again, they glared at me, and my heart sank as I realized they weren't on my side, and wouldn't be helping me save my kids. All they were interested in was finding someone to blame for the phony phone tip—and I was the easiest target. I hoped that when Rahman appeared with the children, they would understand. But I wasn't optimistic given they were not interested in the safety of two American citizens under five years old.

I took another long look at the two agents, then, without saying goodbye, walked back to rejoin my family. "Don't say a word to those two guys," I told everybody. "I think they want to arrest us for committing a federal offense." Mom waved her hand in the air defiantly, as if to dismiss the entire thing. Tony, obviously more aware of the sensitive situation, gently put his arm around Mom and led her out of the agents' eyeshot.

We went back to watching the passengers check in. It was getting dangerously close to boarding time and still, no Rahman. My heart sunk even lower, and again, my mind barraged me with questions. *Was he booked on a different flight? Could he have possibly booked himself on more than one flight? Had he purchased several tickets to hedge his bets? How could I have allowed things to get to this point? Was there a way I could have resolved this more peacefully?*

I had no answers. All I could do was to keep looking through the crowd for a glimpse of my kids or Rahman.

And then came the announcement: "At this time, I'd like to invite all passengers on Saudia flight number 3524 to Jeddah, to please…" They were calling for boarding and Rahman still hadn't shown up.

Cindy said, "It's getting late. Are you sure that this was the flight?"

"He definitely purchased these tickets, Cindy. But anything is possible."

Mom and Tony wandered back over. Tony said, "I'll go take a look in the first-class lounge upstairs. He might be waiting there until the last minute." As he walked away, the two agents eyed him suspiciously.

"Cindy," I said, "Take a look at those two FBI creeps. They're more interested in what we're doing than in watching the passengers. Why don't they keep their eyes on the boarding gate?"

"Patricia, calm down, just forget them." She said to my mother, "It was a bad idea getting the FBI involved."

Mom nodded sheepishly, then shot the two agents a nasty look.

And then came the announcement inviting the first-class passengers to board the aircraft. Cindy suggested, "Maybe you should call Nurse Jean to see if she's heard anything. I'll keep my eyes glued to the line."

I hadn't spoken to Jean in a few hours, but perhaps something had developed at home in Palm Beach. Maybe the kids had appeared with their dad. Maybe they'd simply spent the night somewhere and were returning home. Or, maybe he devised this entire charade just to further mock me. *Like the time he made me break down the bathroom door, only to find him on the toilet…*Anything was possible.

I walked over to the closest pay phone, which afforded me a clear view of the departure gate and dialed our home number. Jean answered on the first ring and, from the sound of her voice, I could tell that something wasn't right.

"Mrs. Abbar," she said, "you'll never guess who called the house just an hour ago. I've been trying to get in touch with you. The phone rang, and…"

Out of the corner of my eye, I saw the two agents move quickly toward the boarding gate. I dropped the phone and tried to see what had caught their attention. Coming from the far side of the terminal was a Saudi man with two children…but it wasn't Rahman. Since the agents hadn't bothered to look at the photos I'd shown them, they didn't know that.

As the man and his children neared the boarding line, the agents blocked their path. *"Cindy,"* I called, *"tell them it's not Rahman!"*

Too late. The poor Saudi man was pulled aside and questioned. He showed his boarding passes to the agents, after which they gestured for the man and his children to step away from the gate. The agents ripped the carry-on bag from his hands, and he looked horrified.

I motioned to Cindy that she should keep watching the boarding gate, especially now that the two agents were preoccupied with detaining these innocent people, then I grabbed the dangling pay phone receiver and said, "Jean, the plane is almost done boarding and the kids still haven't shown up."

"Well, they probably won't show up," she said.

"What?"

"About an hour ago, I got a call from a strange woman with an Arabic accent. She said that Karim and Sultana were safe, on a flight to Morocco with their father, and they'd be arriving in Casablanca shortly. I tried to ask her questions, but she said that she'd been instructed to say that and only that, then she hung up."

"A woman with an accent?"

"Yes."

"And the kids are on a flight to Morocco?"

"Yes."

"You're sure that's what she said?"

"Yes. That's *exactly* what she said. I'm so sorry, Madam." Jean broke down and cried.

My entire world stopped. I couldn't hear a thing but my own beating heart. My kids were on a plane to Morocco. Rahman had taken them. My children. My legs gave out and I sank to the floor. I sobbed, with my arms around my knees, burying my face for a moment of privacy as curious onlookers gaped at me, shaking and wholly broken. My children were gone.

Gone.

Cindy and my mother ran over. They attempted to pick me up, but I begged them to leave me on the floor. My children were gone and I didn't know how to go on.

Cindy noticed the receiver of the phone still dangling in mid-air and picked it up to see who was on the other end of the line. She hesitantly said, "Hello," and listened silently for a moment, then looked down at me, horrified. She hung up the phone and said to my mother, "Jean says the kids are on a plane to Morocco."

"What?!" my mother shouted. *"Oh my God!"*

Cindy continued "Jean got a phone call from some anonymous woman who claimed they were flying to Morocco this very minute. We missed them."

After hearing the chilling update from Jean, Cindy and Mom joined me on the floor as we huddled together and cried. A crowd gathered. The passengers who hadn't yet boarded the flight stared. A ticket agent left her counter and walked over to see what was happening. The two FBI agents finally stopped interrogating the innocent man at the gate. They walked over, but before they made it, my mother shouted, "Go away, all of you! Please leave us alone! My grandchildren have been kidnapped and none of you can help us! Just leave us alone!" She glared at the agents and said, "*Useless.* You're *useless!*"

Had it not been for Cousin Tony returning from his stake-out point and literally scooping us off the floor, we might have stayed there sobbing indefinitely, so impossible was it to get up and walk away, empty-handed and empty-hearted. I was paralyzed, all but the staggering heart, broken but beating in my chest. It was the only evidence that I was indeed, somehow still alive.

***

Hours later, I realized it made sense to contact Mama Inja and Amm Abdullah in Jeddah. Rahman had not yet communicated with them. They were astonished and obviously disturbed to hear that their son had gone rogue with my children. It was a very difficult conversation with my in-laws, but from their noncommittal tone, I sensed that they were not willing to throw their son under the bus at my word, instead withholding judgment until speaking with him, directly. I fully understood their allegiance to him as was customary in their culture. Saudis always side with family.

The next call was to Mr. Long. How I wished I had listened to my mother's advice and hired a "street fighter" instead of this stodgy, by-the-book counsel. "Don't worry. Tomorrow, I will file a motion with the court and he will pay long and dearly for his actions," was his response. Again, an empty promise from a limp lawyer.

I was the one who paid long and dearly for the ensuing two-and-a-half year legal exercise in futility, one that bore me no fruit whatsoever. Not only did Rahman refuse to answer all legal pleadings, even those from his own American lawyers, he also stopped payments for our many homes, left exorbitant credit card bills unpaid, and had one of his law school "buddies" secretly sell the horses and exotic cars on his behalf, wiring the funds to Rahman in Saudi Arabia. I found it hard to believe that an American would assist him in his shady endeavors, but it happened. Perhaps his "buddy" was reimbursed for his illicit fiscal activities.

I had to endure frightening calls at all hours from collection agencies over his unpaid, $100,000 Amex bill, charges that weren't even mine. All my personal credit cards were canceled due to his debts and it took months for me to replace them. When my meager savings were used up trying to keep current with the unending legal and mortgage payments, my family, who maintained they never supported my marriage in the first place, refused to help. They insisted I first sell my extensive collection of jewelry, which they claimed I wouldn't be needing in the US. I followed their instructions, and when that money was used up, because my parents had started a divorce litigation of their own, they suggested I sell both houses. I countered by demanding where we would live when the children were returned to me?

"Patricia, you should face reality. You're throwing money away by holding onto those houses. Sell them! Worry about where to live if and when the children are returned," my mother insisted. They would not budge from their position, even after I discovered the American courts wouldn't permit any home sales before the divorce was adjudicated. So I rented out the houses to pay the mortgages, and I lived with Basha. I worked day and night, taking on whatever work was available to supplement my earnings, utilizing skills I hadn't deployed in decades, including sewing all the curtains for lucrative decorating projects in Northern Virginia that Basha and I had designed.

The unending divorce proceedings ground on as did the related bills. I went without health insurance and auto insurance, keeping my fingers crossed for better days, instead of my current constant cycle of hope and fear. Hope that I would be reunited with my Karim and Sultana and fear that I, too, would be kidnapped, or even worse, killed. Some nights, I would lie awake in bed, unable to sleep, my imagination running wild. I heard noises in the house and hid under the bed, in terror that someone was coming for me. I would remain there, sleepless, until dawn. Rahman continued to taunt me at will, calling me angry and drunk with more threats to my life. What else could he possibly take from me? He had already won.

***

When the final judgment on the divorce case came two years later, I awarded full custody of the children with a large cash settlement, none of which I ever received. By that time, I was completely emotionally and financially bankrupt but finally able to sell the DC house. The proceeds of that sale barely covered my still mounting debts, so a week before the closing, I opted for a complete tag sale of all my furnishings and belongings in hopes of raising some cash to fund my new custody fight with the State Department.

The day of the sale left me feeling numb and violated but with $15,000 cash, mostly in small bills, in an white envelope. The excited public had swarmed into my house at 9 am sharp and within six hours, the place was picked clean, every belonging carted away by opportunistic, eager neighbors, none of them shy nor civil or even remotely well-mannered. At one point in the afternoon, a rather crass woman broke into my storage closet and came out waving my fur coat in the air, "How much for this coat?" she barked.

"$350." I retorted. "It's all for sale. Take it all if you want."

Not that I was attached to all those material goods, but having hordes of strangers pillaging through my memories was hard to watch. None of it mattered anymore and it was all weighing me down. I needed those resources desperately to continue the fight for my kids—the parent who was granted full custody by a government that was too lazy and inept to follow through.

But then, governments don't love children. That takes a parent.

Despite everyone else moving on, I stayed the course for fourteen years. Having my children safe in my arms again was the only thing keeping me alive. I never relented.

Epilogue

After the original devastation passed, I wandered around, dazed, confused and thoroughly broken for many years, trying desperately to reclaim my children who were held captive in that padlocked foreign land of still desert air and antique customs. The State Department, after endless costly meetings, was unable to do any more than put my ex-husband on a useless international "watch list." He circumvented all their restrictions by obtaining a diplomatic passport with an altered name.

With no other options, I resumed desperate calls to the Abbar household. The only options they offered were self-serving—reconcile with their son or plan a solo visit to Jeddah, knowing that both options would likely end in my death. I offered to meet them in Marbella, but naturally, they wouldn't agree to that.

Early on, hearing from Noura that the children were bewildered in that foreign land and couldn't speak the language, I convinced Nurse Jean to fly to Jeddah and live with the family; the Abbars eagerly took her in. I couldn't bear the idea of my kids suffering. But my mom had strong opinions about that and let me know it.

"Patricia, why on earth are you making it easier for them to keep your children? You've handed them the keys!"

"Mom, I can't sleep at night worrying…what they're wearing, who's dressing them, who's feeding them, who's helping get them acquainted with the place, who's explaining my absence…What does Noura know? Not a whole lot, mom. She's never been a mother. Mama Inja sent hers to be raised by grandparents and an English guardian! Not much love or motherly instinct there! At least with Jean my children would have a loving, seasoned…"

"So make it more difficult! Turn their household upside down! Make them uncomfortable! Two stolen American preschoolers, crying for their mama! Maybe they'll send them back…where they belong."

"Mom. Stop right there! Is that what we really want? Crying? I can't live with that!" Tears were streaming down my cheeks at the thought. Yes, I had made the Abbars' outrageous behavior easier, but at least my darlings had one familiar person who loved them and knew them in the household.

Jean stayed for over two years in Jeddah. I had secretly hoped to use her as my informer but no matter how many times I made contact, Jean offered meager information, not nearly enough for any degree of peace in my heart. At times I wondered where her allegiance was. But any attempt at passing information to me would have been met with serious consequences. At best, she would be shipped back to England. At worst, she would end up in a Saudi jail.

To my surprise, my children did not live with their father in our old house. Instead, they were sent to live with Mama Inja and Amm Abdullah while Rahman used our place as his bachelor pad, for girlfriends and parties. Noura stepped up and stood in as a surrogate mother, with Jean as her assistant and the grandmother figure. The children attended Arabic private school, and Noura fussed over them daily. I was never allowed to have direct conversation with either child, but occasionally I would score a secret conversation with a member of the household.

I randomly called weekly and sometimes someone sympathetic answered, allowing me five or so minutes to ask a few questions. Once, Thahab answered the phone and I quizzed her for about fifteen minutes. Although I learned that both children were alive and well, her answers didn't scratch the surface of all I needed to know. One time, Lallo answered the phone, but even he was deathly afraid to be caught speaking with me. Maybe Rahman had financed his new restaurant, or he'd threatened his immigration sponsorship. As crazy as it sounds in today's world of social media and instant communication, that was 1990 in Saudi Arabia.

The onset of the Gulf War only further complicated my intercontinental communications. I continued to barrage the Abbar household with phone calls to no avail—crying, begging and attempting to reason with any live person who would listen. As war escalated and the US and Saudi governments allied with Kuwait, Iraq reflexively retaliated by dropping bombs on Jeddah. Most of the Abbar family evacuated the country, but not my useless, self-centered, oblivious former husband.

I spent day and night glued to the television for news on Jeddah. In the midst of the bombings, I made attempts to reach the house by phone, praying and desperate for information. Thahab answered, and in hushed whispers, informed me that she was still there and so was my husband. When asked, she called him to the phone. Rahman's tone was blase, perhaps drunk out of his mind, when I questioned him, "Why are you still there? Jeddah is being bombed! What about the kids? Who's taking care of them? Where are they?"

"With me."

"Are you crazy? Why haven't you left? Why haven't you sent the children away with the rest of the family?" I pleaded hysterically. *Of course I knew the answer—in another country, I could fly in and steal them.*

"Don't be so dramatic, Patricia. Death isn't so bad. If I die, I'll take them with me."

I didn't have an answer to this evil, this insanity. He was beyond reason and I was utterly helpless, so I hung up. He had added yet another torment to my increasingly fragile emotional state–the very real possibility of my babies lying dead in heaps of rubble while he's pouring himself another stiff drink.

By this time, friends and family had for the most part moved on and encouraged me to do the same. They were incapable of understanding my anguish. By law and by nature, the children belonged with me. I was their mother. I would never be whole again without them. And a mother cannot simply move on, ever. But as one might expect, many well-meaning friends took turns giving me wholly ignorant and unsolicited advice over the years...

"Just move on and forget about those children. You'll never get them back. And if you ever do, they'll be completely brainwashed by Arab culture." *Forget about my children? Impossible! I will love them until I die.*

"Can't you lure him over here and hire some thugs to break his legs? Get him to listen." *And get arrested? Thrown in jail? The Abbars would hunt me down. And how much would the kids hate me for doing this to their father? Maybe they love him...*

"I know a person who knows a person who knows Ted Kennedy. If you give him a $100,000 donation, Kennedy can speak with his dear friend, the King of Saudi Arabia, and help you get your children back." *That probably wouldn't help. He could take the money and do nothing. Besides, I don't have $100,000.*

"Now that the Gulf War shifted to Saudi Arabia, why don't you try to contact General Schwarzkopf and pay the military to go in and get your kids?" *The military cannot be hired. I would have to find mercenaries for hire and put my kids in harm's way. That's crazy!*

"Can't you go over there and kidnap them back? It shouldn't be that difficult." *A visa is impossible and I would be caught and killed. Great idea.*

"Can't get in without a visa? Surely you can sneak in some other way. Why don't you try parachuting in with the military?" *Because being shot out of the sky is not on my to-do list...Does this "friend" want me dead?*

"I know a lady who runs a safe house somewhere in the Midwest. She takes in women who need help going off the grid to escape their abusive husbands. If you could get Karim and Sultana and flee there, no one will find you." *I cannot run, penniless and nameless to the Midwest. Living like fugitives is not a life for little ones or for me...*

In retrospect, these unrealistic and poorly executed attempts at good advice were the most frustrating and hurtful words of all. Granted, there is no guidebook for this incomprehensible situation, but instead of compassion, absurd advice was forced on me. As a result, I became more and more hesitant to discuss my two children's whereabouts. After a while, I completely stopped speaking of them, outwardly pretending those years never happened, just to avoid the unsolicited comments and insinuation that I was, somehow, inadequate, complacent, or simply not doing enough.

I discovered that people are incredibly naïve and ignorant of international law and how governments behave when there is a conflict between citizens of two different countries and cultures. My experience was that people were comfortable with their assumed narratives and not open to any conflicting information. No one wanted to consider that the United States couldn't or wouldn't help me. Period. Not only did it add to my sadness, it made me very bitter.

As far as I know, Rahman never resumed his DC or Florida polo playboy lifestyle. He did, however, continue riding high in England, Spain and Argentina, then popping into the Midwest, USA, to drop his son off at Culver. Although I'm sure we were both in attendance at the stadium college graduations of our shared children, I never saw him or spoke to him again. And he has never been brought to justice.

It was a full fourteen years before I succeeded in seeing Karim then Sultana. I was lucky in that both chose higher education in America and were willing to connect with me after I found them here. The outcome could have been far worse with no resolution whatsoever.

Karim did agree to meet me again for dinner a month after our first encounter, and although he was reluctant to discuss any details of life back in Jeddah and would not volunteer any information about his sister, we continued to see each other regularly throughout his college years and beyond.

I was able to connect with Sultana online in a very fortunate turn of events a year later. I was sitting in my office one afternoon, working. The phone rang. On the other line was a friend of Rahman's, a lawyer who had gone to Georgetown with him. He had visited Saudi and was astonished and distressed to discover that although Karim seemed to be flourishing as the prince of the family, Sultana was languishing there without a mother. She was lost. It broke his heart, and although he was Rahman's friend, he felt moved to contact me and give me an amazing, miraculous gift: her Hotmail address.

Personal email was becoming a common way of communicating and Saudi Arabia had allowed its citizens full use of the internet. This changed the entire playing field. No more failed calls to the house phone. Sultana and I started an MSN messenger thread that lasted over a year. Every afternoon, while she was ostensibly doing her homework online, we would email back and forth with each other. I finally got to know my daughter. Whereas Karim was more protective of his father and family, she was very willing to discuss the details of her bleak life as a female in Saudi. I learned that Tana was artistic and loved to paint, and that she was so bright that she had skipped 5th grade! She was a great rider and had two horses. She was a ravenous reader and we exchanged book suggestions. Despite her intellectual gifts and the level of comfort that family wealth had afforded her, she did not have the unconditional love of a father. Not like I did. Rahman instead lavished endless privileges on Karim, none of which she was privy to. Sultana dreamed of attending college in the US, and in fact was planning to apply for early acceptance to Wellesley the coming year. I counted the days until her arrival, and patience again rewarded me with a wonderful and willing daughter who wanted to rekindle the bonds of mother and child. This was another miracle; anything could have happened.

It was as if we already knew each other; Amanda and I waited for her with our Maltese puppy and open arms, as Tana arrived at Logan International Airport in Boston to start college. I finally had both of them in the US after all that time apart, and I worked hard to rebuild the relationships.

When my adult children and I were finally reunited, Rahman was less than pleased. He had warned them that I was "a silly woman," that I "wasn't worth knowing," shrugging his shoulders at their interest in me, and ridiculing their decision to include me in their lives. I suspect that his marginalizing of me was really just a cover for his outrage that I had never returned to him and his abuse. Despite his reactions, they somehow knew they had the right to know their own mother and pursued a relationship with me. I believe that many in their Saudi family encouraged this and urged them on, but did so quietly, afraid of retribution from my ex-husband. I know, from my daughter's own tales, that Noura spoke of me constantly, throughout their childhood, keeping my memory alive.

No one did anything concrete to help me all those years. Certainly not the Abbar family. They stuck together, as I knew they would. Considering how many women I had befriended, confided in, felt closeness to, and shared with, one could assume someone would offer me a small tidbit of information about my kids over those 14 years. Instead, no matter how many pleading letters I wrote or phone calls I made, I received nothing, not even a photograph. Imagine not even knowing what your kids look like. No one wanted to get involved, not Niggi, not Tasnim, and not even Valerie, each very afraid of her husband's reaction if he ever found out. Breaking the rules in Saudi came with big consequences. I struggled to come to terms with that, at times drowning in anger and contempt for these women whom I had considered my friends—yet trying to remember that they lived in fear in a way that an ordinary American could never understand. Even so, I would have risked helping them, much like I did with Lallo and the woman he loved. I would have found a way to help if a friend needed me, no matter my fear.

Never wavering in my efforts to reach my children in Saudi, I did attempt to rebuild my life. I had no choice. Fourteen years is a very long time and I needed to soothe the ever present pain in my heart. I pursued my career, grateful to have creative and meaningful work. I remarried with a man I had known in college (that felt safe) and we had one daughter, Amanda, a precious gift from God, all the time watching and wondering when my opportunity would come to have my first two children in my arms again.

***

Many years later, in the summer of 2010, my ex-father-in-law, Amm Abdullah, set out for London in need of an ophthalmology consult and surgery. When an elder of a wealthy Saudi family traveled to a foreign country seeking medical attention, it was customary for family to join him. And because Mama Inja had recently passed away, Karim and Sultana, now well into their twenties, along with many other relatives and friends, gathered in London to keep Amm Abdullah company while undergoing treatment.

Out of nowhere, Rahman's brother, Ghazi, called, urging me to join the family for a dinner in London. Amm Abdullah said it would give him great pleasure to see me and my other daughter, Amanda. According to Karim, his grandfather had specifically arranged a dinner party in hopes of bringing me together with the family. For me to refuse would have been viewed as an egregious insult. Since it was summer and Amanda wasn't in school, we flew to London for a few days, with the purpose of seeing the Abbars. After so many years, I admit, I was overcome with curiosity.

The dinner party was held the day after our arrival with a posh Middle Eastern restaurant hosting our gathering in a private room. Sultana informed us that Amm Abdullah was greatly looking forward to the party and had shared his excitement to meet his granddaughter, Amanda.

"Granddaughter?" I repeated incredulously, thoroughly confused.

"Yes, he said that you are his daughter and Amanda is your daughter, so by default, she is his granddaughter. I think he's just curious to see what Amanda looks like," she said, chuckling.

"And I'm curious to see what he looks like!" Amanda piped up. "And the rest of them, too. I've heard so many stories growing up."

"So, I guess you now have another grandfather, Amanda. I told you the family ties go deep and strong in Saudi," I mused. It was flattering and I was also looking forward to this dinner, but on the other hand, I was nervous, not knowing what to expect. These were people whom I'd not seen in over twenty years, people who had failed me and my children in so many ways.

At the restaurant, Karim and Sultana waited for us by the front door. They looked relieved when they spotted our taxi pulling in, probably because they weren't sure we would actually show up. After exchanging greetings, I asked who would be at the party.

"Everyone in the family who could come. It was Amm Abdullah's request. He said it was important."

"Is Noura here?" I asked eagerly. I was hopeful but couldn't seem to get a hold of her before the event. *Was she avoiding my calls?*

"No, Aunt Noura said she's not comfortable traveling. You know she hasn't left Saudi in so many years, she didn't even come to our college graduations, so…" Sultana's excuses and her tone suggested that Noura had a choice to leave Jeddah. I took the hint and did my best to keep the conversation light and moving forward

"Too bad. I was dying to see her. If only I had been able to contact her. I might have convinced her to come to London, for old times' sake."

"No way. Aunt Noura never leaves Jeddah. She has her own quirky life at the Bin Zagr house and it's almost impossible to make her change or do anything new," stated Karim with strong conviction. He was often exasperated by Noura's eccentric behavior, not having the patience and compassion of Sultana. I wondered what went on in Noura's head. To this day, I'm not sure if Noura is still barred from leaving Jeddah, or if she's spent so much time in the Bin Zagr compound that she gave up on the outside world. Perhaps both.

Next I inquired about Valerie. Sultana filled me in with great enthusiasm, "Yes, of course she's here. She still has a home in London, where she's living most of the time. She's looking forward to seeing you!"

I replied just loud enough for Tana to hear, "I haven't spoken to her in years. You know, she refused to pass a letter to you kids years ago. I had mailed it to her and begged that she slip it to you at lunch when no one was watching, but she was too afraid..."

Sultana eyed me tensely. "You're not going to call her out tonight, are you?" she pleaded.

"No, of course not. I promise I won't do or say anything controversial. Sorry to have mentioned it." Sultana exhaled deeply then took my arm and moved Amanda and me into the dining room. We weren't sure what to expect but what we found was a roomful of people who truly believed my youngest daughter and I were part of their family. And that's the Saudi way. Blood ties run deep.

Eager to greet us, the company of guests surrounded Amanda and me, showering us with kisses, handshakes, hugs and back pats, words of admiration, and whatever appropriate affections their culture would allow. They all expressed, in one way or another, their joy in seeing Sultana and Karim reunited with their mother. Of course, with each declaration, and I do believe their words were sincere, I held back the retort sitting on the tip of my tongue, "If that's the case, why didn't you do anything to help me for fourteen years? Why did you ignore my phone calls? Why didn't you answer my letters?" Something inside of me wouldn't let me call them out. Was it forgiveness? I had promised Sultana, and I didn't want to ruin the moment.

My children were relaxed and enjoying themselves. I allowed myself to get swept up in their buoyant moods, as if nothing abhorrent had ever happened. On some level, it was supremely comforting to smile, nod, and remain silent, as I had discovered my first hectic night in the Abbar sitting room. I stood there experiencing true, whole joy, for the first time in 15 years, surrounded by all three of my children, Karim, Sultana and Amanda. I never dreamed this day would come.

Generations come and go so quickly in Saudi Arabia. Children I had known were now adults whom I hardly recognized from across the restaurant table. There were even children of the children I had known when I was there. Others were of my generation and behaved as if it was just yesterday that we had dined together at the big house. Still others stared at me curiously, seeing for the first time the American lady who was the mysterious mother of their cousins, Karim and Sultana. It occurred to me they had all moved on with their lives, yet I had remained, frozen in space, for so many years. Fourteen years. I began to feel resentful again. It was overwhelming. I struggled to tear myself away from any negative thoughts. *I can be mad about this later. Focus on the present.*

As everyone enjoyed the pre-dinner festivities, a very elegant looking couple approached, smiling broadly. They were introduced to us as the owner of the restaurant and his wife who had come to greet Amm Abdullah, one of their most frequent and beloved patrons.

"What a beautiful lady you are, and how lovely it is to see your children gathered around you. We can tell they are yours. They have your presence and grace. You've raised them well. It is always a joy to encounter such a family. Count your blessings, my dear," crooned the owner's wife warmly, in her thick Lebanese accent. "We are delighted that you're here in our restaurant. Do you live in London?"

"No," I answered, "we're visiting from New York. We flew in to see Amm Abdullah."

"How wonderful! What I would give to have my two sons fly somewhere with me! They are so busy with their own lives; we hardly ever see them. Again, count your blessings. Please ask for me personally anytime you call for a reservation. Pleasure to meet you." She nodded her head, grabbed her husband and moved on to the next guest.

Count my blessings…count my blessings…Twice she had said this to me and I couldn't stop thinking about it. She didn't know our story, or what we had gone through to get to this moment. She didn't see me as I did, a defeated person, vanquished by a womanizing husband who was above the law and made use of every attempt to mortally wound me. She did not see my loss. Instead, she saw who we were today.

At last I understood. I had to make a choice. I could see the glass half-full or I could see the glass half-empty. That was no choice at all. I knew immediately that the better option would always be to take the glass half-full and be thankful for that. This would be my mantra.

262 - Jeddah Bride

The headwaiter rang a small bell, announcing that dinner was being served at the table. Amm Abdullah motioned for me to sit at his right side, a place of honor. I did so, keeping Amanda to my right. Karim and Sultana sat across from us. It was a very long table, reminiscent of the one in the big dining room in Jeddah, and it filled up quickly with guests of all ages.

The dishes were served Arabic style, all brought out at the same time and lined up, down the center of the table. As soon as the last platter was placed, everyone dug in, serving themselves. I giggled to myself, recalling my first family dinner in Jeddah, a swift sprint to the finish line, with every man for himself once the food hit the table. I do miss those family meals. As we plated our favorite delicacies, Amm Abdullah made comments, both in Arabic and English, so that every guest at that table was aware that the patriarch, Amm Abdullah, an otherwise stern and serious man, remembered me and that I was important to him.

"See, Patricia? I ordered grilled chicken livers because I remember that those were your favorite!" and, "Oh, I notice that you still serve yourself a huge portion of salad. And I remember you always said you eat so much salad because it helps keep your weight down." He continued warmly, "Why don't you have some Basmati rice, Patricia. I made sure they included that because I remember you don't like long grain rice."

He paused, smiling, meeting my eyes and assaulting the anger that I had buried deep. With these simple words, he ordained my role in his family. All were astonished as he continued to ingratiate me with a devout tenderness, "Patricia, I see you still cut the meat off your lamb chops with a knife and fork instead of picking it up with your fingers. Just as you did in Jeddah. I recall when everyone in the family would tease you for that. Remember, we would say that you were leaving all the juicy pieces next to the bone, and you insisted that your knife skills could extract everything worth eating." Some of the guests had never heard him make a joke or speak so freely. Everyone nodded, looking at me as if I was the luckiest girl at the table. Again, if they only knew. But Amm Abdulla's act of loving diplomacy was sincere, and he was successful in what he had set out to accomplish that night, both with the family and in my heart.

I glanced across the table at Karim and Sultana and understood from their surprised but pleased expressions that they had never realized their grandfather knew so much about me or paid me any heed.

While waiting for dessert to be served, Amm Abdullah scooted his chair out a few inches, then pushed himself up to standing position before clearing his throat, signaling immediate silence and his intention to speak. I don't recall him having done anything like that before, as he was a man of few words. His world was that of short, to the point, declarations or orders, which everyone would instinctively obey. He never needed to do more. But that particular evening, as he studied the room, making sure that all eyes and ears were on him, he spoke slowly and carefully in his best English.

"I want everyone in this family to know that I am very pleased to welcome my daughter, Patricia, and my granddaughter, Amanda, to our table today. I want everyone to know that Patricia is a fine woman, a true lady, and that Karim and Sultana have a beautiful, intelligent, educated, and graceful mother. Mama Inja and I recognized this from the first moment we set eyes on her. When I look at my two grandchildren, Karim and Sultana, so attractive and intelligent, I know, and I want them to also know, that she is the reason why they are the way they are. They are her blood. They are lucky to have Patricia as their mother and we are proud to have Patricia and Amanda in our family forever."

Then he turned and looked me straight in the eye, "Patricia, I have a photograph of you and Amanda, which Sultana gave to me, on the table next to my bed. I keep pictures of all my children and grandchildren there and every night, before I sleep, I ask God to bless all of you. I am thankful to have you in my family. Please remember these words, now and when I am gone."

He nodded and sat down. Tears welled up in my eyes, and I struggled to hide the emotions I was feeling—anger, sorrow, shame, pride, regret. I was again overcome, but somehow embarrassed to let the family see me cry. I understood what he had said and what his purpose, as the head of the family, was in saying it. Subtly, his speech had put all conflict which might have existed for my children, to rest. He acknowledged me as their unquestionable mother and he demanded that all in the family should accept that fact, overshadowing the lies and ridicule which Rahman had spread.

At that moment, I was reminded that their culture, harsh, cruel, and ancient, does not bend or change for anyone. There are no exceptions. A father's claim to his children over the mother is his undeniable right. Everyone had acted the way they were supposed to act, and no one had transgressed. In their traditional culture, it was simply a tragic turn of events, and we all had to accept that. There was nothing anyone could have done differently. This is the very same ancient system that has kept so many women veiled against their wills for centuries.

With Amm Abdullah's justification of me as his daughter and mother of his grandchildren, he somehow showed me that I could forgive the women sitting with me who did not have the will or even awareness to fight for themselves. How could they possibly have fought for me? How could I have expected them to, with so much to lose? As for the men, they simply accepted the sovereignty of the father, the man, over all females and children in the family. Right or wrong, it's their religious law, the law that has governed their society for centuries. In their minds, a good woman must accept that, and in their eyes, I had.

I had behaved as a decent, worthy woman, hence they embraced and welcomed me again as part of their family. More importantly, they encouraged my children to respect me and spend time with me. I could see that watching their family accept me was helping Karim and Sultana come to terms with their situation. Had I chosen to take a path of continued anger and scorn, hurling accusations at their father, family, and friends, my children would have been torn apart over and over again. It wouldn't have been worth it.

I was only twenty-two when I joined the Abbar family. There was no way I could have fathomed the deep roots of their culture, and how wholly I had to embrace it to be an Abbar. Their moral code was not movable. Although it was in direct contradiction with what I believed in, namely freedom and equality in a union, I could not forcast the dismal outcome of my marriage with such young eyes. No matter what continent we lived on together, I would not escape Rahman's hardwired, soul-deep, elitist, entitled, and sexist thinking. Forgiving him may or may not be beyond my mortal power, but I can be at peace with his family as they intended to increase rather than further diminish me as a human, mother, daughter, and friend.

Theirs is a culture of contradictions, a faith where everyone is equal while twirling around ancient otherworldly stone relics, and then they aren't. I had married into this rigid world, misunderstanding my situation, and eventually paid dearly. They would accept me as long as I understood my place in the family fold: they could love me and my unrelated child as their kin, all the while having aided my husband in separating me from Karim and Sultana for fourteen years.

As a mother, my own feelings will always come second to those of my children. After more than twenty years, I must admit it was healing to hear Amm Abdullah's words, acknowledging what I always believed—that I was loved and appreciated by my in-laws—but more importantly, my children needed to hear that. It was empowering for Karim and Sultana to see their grandfather, the patriarch of the family, stand in praise of their lost mother. I believe that was the true purpose of the gathering. In the only way his culture would allow, without ever mentioning any blame or wrongdoing, Amm Abdullah had acknowledged my loss, and was offering me an apology by making sure my children knew I was legitimate.

Did this grand gesture ease the pain of fourteen years apart? Did it answer my boundless questions, or make up for precious irrevocably lost moments? I'll never know at what age Karim lost his first tooth. I never enjoyed the wonder of Sultana's budding personality as she grew into womanhood. Even with a perfectly preserved photo diary, those invaluable moments in between, the non-milestones of favorite songs, fleeting friendships, bedtime stories, cuts and bruises, are all lost to me. There is no making up for that. My two oldest children were raised without a mother, and I missed the miracles of their growing up—something that can never be fully righted by any amount of apologies or regrets in this life. But for what we are now, I am grateful. And just as I felt hope and courage flood over me with my vision of the pink sky, that early morning so many years ago, I look to the future with unbounding optimism. We will live new, inestimable memories and milestones together, my three children, all gifted and good, under my wings.

THE END

Acknowledgements

It is a rare writer who can create a book in a void. In my case, I owe thanks to several people in my life who kept me going and ensured that this volume ultimately made it to your hands. Thank you to:

Amanda Turen, my youngest daughter, for your never wavering dedication to Jeddah Bride and to me. You have made yourself available, day and night, always generous with your thoughts, skills and knowledge. And you watched this story unfold twice - once in real time, and again as I wrote this book. I could not have accomplished this without you.

Jamie Wilson, my publisher, who was willing to take a chance on me, a first-time author, and saw the importance of letting this story be told. Thank you for your trust.

Jennifer Rynbrandt, my editor, with whom I shared so many painstaking hours of hard work. Your sensitivity showed me how to reach my readers. You brought out everything that needed to be said. Thank you for your acceptance and encouragement.

Keith Korman, my literary agent, the driving force behind this publication and his wife, Maxine, who recognized its value and advocated for it, even when the manuscript was rough.

Mitchell Adelstein, my loving husband, for being proud of the person I am and supporting all my endeavors.

Acknowledgments

Author Bio

When not writing, Patricia Bonis runs her own interior design firm and has designed the homes, offices and embassies of CEOs, ambassadors and international financiers for over thirty years. She has an equally long-standing and passionate career as an equestrian, actively competing in the World Equestrian Festival, the Hampton Classic and numerous other horse shows across America. Patricia splits her time between Wellington, Florida and Millbrook, New York with her husband, Mitchell and their beloved poodle, Harley. Jeddah Bride is her first book.

Printed in the USA
CPSIA information can be obtained
at www.ICGtesting.com
LVHW09082523O824
788905LV00004B/4/J